Between Art and Artifact

Between Art and Artifact

ARCHAEOLOGICAL REPLICAS AND CULTURAL PRODUCTION IN OAXACA, MEXICO

Ronda L. Brulotte

University of Texas Press *Austin*

Printed in the United States of America
First edition, 2012

Requests for permission to reproduce material from this work should be sent to:
Permissions
University of Texas Press
P.O. Box 7819
Austin, TX 78713–7819
utpress.utexas.edu/about/book-permissions

♾ The paper used in this book meets the minimum requirements of ANSI/NISO Z39.48–1992 (R1997) (Permanence of Paper).

LIBRARY OF CONGRESS CATALOGING-IN-PUBLICATION DATA
Brulotte, Ronda L.
Between art and artifact : archaeological replicas and cultural production in Oaxaca, Mexico / Ronda L. Brulotte.
p. cm.
Includes bibliographical references and index.
ISBN 978-0-292-75426-3

1. Indians of Mexico—Mexico—Oaxaca Valley—Material culture. 2. Indian wood-carving—Mexico—Oaxaca Valley. 3. Indian art—Mexico—Oaxaca Valley. 4. Cultural property—Mexico—Oaxaca Valley. 5. Art objects—Mexico—Oaxaca Valley—Reproduction. 6. Antiquities—Mexico—Oaxaca Valley—Reproduction. 7. Oaxaca Valley (Mexico)—Antiquities. I. Title.
F1219.1.O11B78 2012
972′.74—dc23 2012007464

First paperback printing, 2013

Para todos los artesanos de Arrazola

TO ALL OF THE ARTISANS OF ARRAZOLA

Copying is a hermeneutic task, in which the great contending paradigms of hermeneutics are at work, such as understanding, understanding better *than the original, understanding differently, or even demonstrating the impossibility of understanding.*

SÁNDOR RADNÓTI

Contents

Preface

Today in the parking lot at Monte Albán vendors sell junky little vases, like pencil holders, with bat and jaguar effigy faces sometimes molded from original pieces. These may be too simple and common to show up in museum collections 100 years from now, but who knows?

MARCUS WINTER, "ANOTHER FAKE ON GENUINE," 1986:11

WHEN MARCUS WINTER, A PROMINENT ARCHAEologist with the Mexican National Institute of Anthropology and History (known by its Spanish acronym, INAH), penned the above observation more than two decades ago, he gave voice to a concern shared by archaeologists, art historians, and museum professionals alike: that "fake" pre-Hispanic artifacts periodically would slip past experts only to later surface in museum collections around the world. As a professional archaeologist, Winter had spent much of his career working at Monte Albán, a well-known Mesoamerican archaeology site in the southern Mexican state of Oaxaca, where he was apparently troubled by the public circulation of "fake" Oaxacan artifacts.

For instance, he draws the reader's attention to the specific case of a fake Zapotec "Jaguar God" urn that unwittingly appeared in Frank H. Boos's now-classic book, *The Ceramic Sculptures of Ancient Oaxaca* (Boos 1966:290). According to the text, the piece was in the collection of the Leipzig Museum in what was at the time East Germany. The image was disseminated en masse again in 1971, thanks to an East German postage stamp featuring the piece (fig. 0.1). With an archaeologist's trained eye, Winter assessed the stylistic elements of the Jaguar God urns in question (the piece illustrated in both the book and the postage stamp was

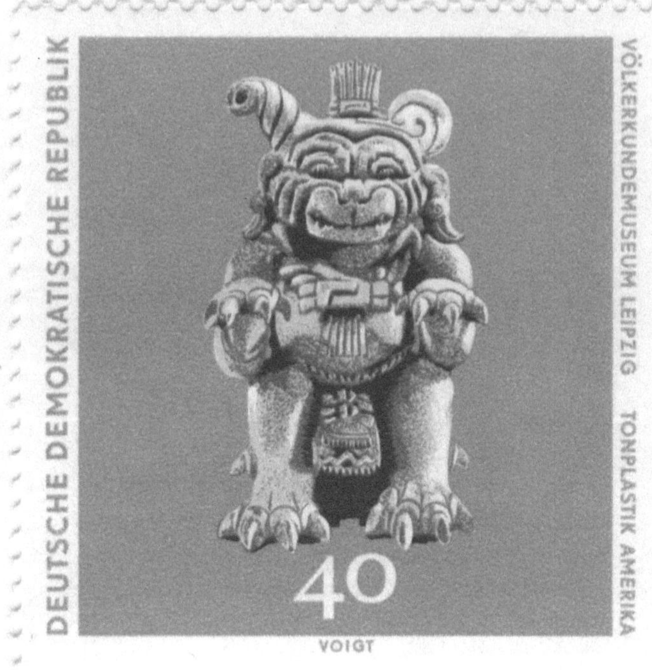

FIGURE 0.1. *The fake "Jaguar God" urn in the Leipzig Museum was featured on a 1971 East German postage stamp. This stamp was purchased by the author on eBay in 2005.*

one of a set of six) and declared that the repetitive "juxtaposition of incongruous and sometimes ridiculous attributes render their authenticity impossible" (Winter 1986:11). He concluded that

> if, in the future, some countries decide to commemorate ancient Oaxacan cultures on stamps, it certainly would be preferable if they selected designs based on pieces from known archeological contexts that had some genuine pre-Hispanic significance. (Winter 1986:12)

For Winter, the recent fabrication (i.e., not in pre-Hispanic antiquity) of these pieces stripped them of the perceived value that once made their image worthy of serialization.

As will become immediately apparent in the text, my concern is far more with the field of archaeology's interest in authenticity and claim to authority than it is with any arbitration of "real" or "fake" artifacts. My intention is to demonstrate that such arguments have effects other than their authors intend and often spin out in fraught and generative ways. I contend that within replicas resides a potent critique of the inner workings of power in the production of cultural and heritage landscapes not only in Oaxaca but throughout Mexico and the world. Replicas demand our attention—better yet, our own self-reflection—as cultural brokers and consumers.

Returning to Winter's cautionary, albeit brief, note concerning the "junky little vases" with bat and jaguar faces sold in the Monte Albán parking lot circa 1986, I suspect that the purveyors of such pieces may have included individuals from the community that is, in large measure, the subject of this book. For over thirty years, residents of San Antonio Arrazola have participated in the archaeological replica trade by making and selling pieces to tourists at Monte Albán. In 1986, before INAH officials enacted tighter restrictions and surveillance at the site, replica sellers moved around the archaeological zone, including the parking lot, in a less restricted fashion than they do today. The objects they sell, whether as authentic pieces to unsuspecting customers or (more commonly) transparently as replicas, are intended to mimic or evoke "genuine" pre-Hispanic artifacts of the type found at the site. Nevertheless, Winter's comment indicates that he judged the replicas of that time as falling short of that goal; the ubiquity of fake objects and their allegedly simple designs seemed to preclude the chance that they would be mistaken for genuine archaeological artifacts. Yet he rhetorically posits that someday the replicas sold to tourists at Monte Albán might, in fact, pass as the real thing, eluding future generations of historical experts.

At the time of my research nearly twenty years later, the sale of unsanctioned copies of archaeological artifacts remained a critical issue for those affiliated with INAH. But despite the prevalence of replica crafts at Monte Albán (and throughout archaeological sites in Mexico), by and large they remain an unexamined form of material culture. This is notable given that Oaxacan handicrafts and archaeological remains have been intensely studied by professional folklorists, cultural anthropologists, and archaeologists since the early twentieth century. Those seeking to document local folk expressions perhaps have found little inspiration in objects that, while handcrafted, lack the supposed authenticity and historical context of the original archaeological objects they mimic. Thus, while a worldwide phenomenon not limited to Oaxaca, replicas are rarely the subject of contemporary cultural analysis.

Similarly, when archaeologists and art historians have written about Oaxacan archaeological replicas, such as the piece by Winter cited above, the objects are "exposed" as fakes and described in relation to corresponding original artifacts—an authoritative move that simultaneously reasserts the authenticity and value of the latter (e.g., Monge 1987, 2000; Sellen 2002, 2004). Nancy Kelker and Karen Bruhns's *Faking Ancient Mesoamerica* (2010) points to the continuity of this discourse of exposure as it operates within both art history and archaeology. Enlisting war as a metaphor, the authors write in the book's introduction:

> Although we are not terribly concerned with the slings, arrows, and curses that might be hurled at us by art aficionados angry about the debunking of their favorite faux works, we see the problem of fakes and forgeries of Pre-columbian art as a serious danger to scholarship, and it is for scholarship that we are willing to strap on our armor, take up shields and swords, and do battle in the name of truth and justice—even if we must, like Joan of Arc, dance in the flames. Forgery is a nasty business and debunking fakes is even nastier, but someone has to do it or all scholastic integrity will be lost. (Kelker and Bruhn 2010:13)

Winter, too, acknowledges the usefulness in studying replicas, but even so, his endorsement contains a warning to would-be investigators. He writes:

> Someday perhaps someone will undertake a careful study of the fakes from Oaxaca. This might be an interesting exercise and expose many of the fakes in museums, but it could also have the negative effect of providing a guide for the careful artisan, instructing him on obvious errors to avoid. (Winter 1986:12)

His observations hint at the possibility that replicas might compete with, and even displace, the rightful objects of archaeological research, a concern well founded within particular scientific and historical epistemologies.

Yet this criticism does not address the broader aesthetic and sociopolitical dimensions of replica crafts. It negates them as legitimate items of material culture that have, to borrow Arjun Appadurai's (1986) oft-used term, a "social life" of their own. These objects circulate alongside other objects of Oaxacan material culture, indexing multiple regimes of social and economic value created on one hand by the tourist art market, and on the other through the practice of archaeological science. In what follows, I take up Winter's challenge of studying contemporary Oaxacan archaeological "fakes," although perhaps not for the reason he had in mind.

In her study of Mayan archaeological sites in Mexico's Yucatán Peninsula, anthropologist Lisa Breglia (2006) cautions against understanding archaeological heritage as a material assemblage whose various meanings and significance are squarely locked in a distant historical past; such a paradigm inherently privileges archaeologists and other technical experts as the rightful interpreters and guardians of cultural materials. Her "heritage-as-practice" approach instead considers archaeological sites and other forms of heritage as "renewable resources" (Breglia 2006:14). That is to say, they are actively (re)produced and reinscribed with social meaning in the present through particular, ongoing social relationships among all kinds of users of heritage.

Taking this as a point of departure, I show that just as archaeological artifacts enshrined in museums provide clues about the social, political, and economic organization of pre-Hispanic Oaxaca, replica pieces illuminate these same issues as they pertain to Oaxaca today. In particular, this book is concerned with what archaeological replicas tell us about Oaxaca's development into a world-class cultural tourism destination and the restructuring of many local Oaxacans' lives that this has entailed. It turns out that replicas, and the people who make and sell them, offer an astute account of this transformation, one perhaps unanticipated by their critics.

Acknowledgments

IT HAS BEEN NO EASY TASK TO CONDUCT THE RESEARCH for and write this book, and I am grateful to the many people and institutions who have offered their assistance in bringing this project to completion.

I owe the biggest thanks to all of my friends and acquaintances in San Antonio Arrazola who generously gave of themselves and their time. I cannot possibly name everyone who contributed to this project, but the following were instrumental in teaching me about the town's history, and specifically the development of its wood-carving and replica trades: Roberto Aguilar, Juan Castellanos, Alejandro Jiménez, Angélico Jiménez, Isaías Jiménez, Manuel Jiménez, Aresenio Morales, Susano Morales, Alberto Ojeda, Agustín Pinos, Carmelo Pinos, Eligio Ramírez, Heriberto Santiago, Mario Santiago and family, and Sabino Santiago. I hope that I have begun to do justice to their community's rich history and creative spirit.

I am truly indebted to my *compadres*, Catarino Carrillo and Leticia Aragón, and their children, Misael and Max, for all the wonderful time we spent together in Oaxaca over the past nine years and for their continuing friendship and support.

For not only opening up their homes to me but for treating me with incredible kindness, I give a special thank-you to Antonio Aragón and his family: Antonio Aragón, Fidencio Aragón, Saúl Aragón, Sergio Aragón, Ramiro Aragón, Alma Arreola, Beatriz Arreola, Adelina Ramírez, and Marta Santiago.

Research in Oaxaca was made possible by numerous grants from the following centers at the University of Texas at Austin: the Teresa Lozano Long Institute for Latin American Studies, the Américo Paredes

Center for Cultural Studies, the Graduate School, and the International Office. Additional funding from the Tinker Foundation allowed me to carry out a pilot study for this project, while a Fulbright-Hays Doctoral Dissertation Research Fellowship, sponsored by CIESAS of Oaxaca, provided generous funding for my 2002–2003 fieldwork in Mexico. Subsequent field research was funded by a Presidential Travel Fellowship from the University of Oklahoma and a Faculty Research Grant from the Latin American and Iberian Institute at the University of New Mexico. I am also grateful to the Welte Institute for Oaxacan Studies and Gudrun Dohrmann for their institutional support of this project in Oaxaca.

Jayne Howell has been a wonderful mentor, colleague, and friend since I first met her in Oaxaca in the summer of 2000. She has seen me through all stages of this project and has been an invaluable sounding board for working through my ideas and approach.

Discussions with scholars working in Oaxaca and in other tourist regions of Mexico have greatly shaped my research questions and theoretical orientation. I have particularly benefited from conversations over the years with Tasha Ahlquist, Shepard Barbash, Bill Beezley, Alanna Cant, Quetzil Castañeda, Michael Chibnik, Jeffrey Cohen, Jack Corbett, Margarita Dalton, Lourdes Gutiérrez Nájera, Michael Kearney, Víctor Martínez, Art Murphy, Kristin Norget, Ramona Pérez, Martha Rees, Laurel Smith, Lois Wasserspring, Joseph Whitecotten, Bill Wood, and Gloria Zafra.

Other friends in Oaxaca who generously offered their assistance include Benito Hernández, Ana Montes, Víctor Ricárdez, and Clemente Rodríguez. Mary Jane Gangier de Mendoza, Víctor Vázquez, and Henry Wangeman provided valuable insight about Oaxaca's art markets based on their own experience as retailers. Nelly Robles García and Eduardo López Calzada were kind enough to speak with me in their official capacities as director of the Monte Albán archaeological zone and director of the INAH-Oaxaca Regional Center, respectively.

At the University of Texas at Austin I was blessed with an amazing group of faculty mentors, and this work has benefited tremendously from their guidance and insights: Richard Flores, Charles Hale, Steven Hoelscher, José Limón, Martha Menchaca, Henry Selby, Suzy Seriff, Joel Sherzer, Katie Stewart, and Pauline Strong. Many other colleagues and friends contributed to this project in some way, including Amy Brandzel, James Brooks, Peter Cahn, Ben Chappell, Catherine Cocks, Nick Copeland, Susie Dorle, Elyssa Faison, Jennifer Goett, Adam Gordon, Neill Hadder, Melinda Harm Benson, Anne Hyde, Christy Johnson, Liz Lilliot, Troy Lovata, Mario Montaño, Ann Moore, Jennifer Nájera, Suzi Nishida, Tey Nunn, Leighton Peterson, John Schaefer, Rebecca Schreiber, Marc Scudamore, Zoe Sherinian, Angela Stuesse, Sarah Tracy, Faedah Totah, Maria Varela, and Catie Wilging.

At the University of New Mexico I am thankful for the support and good humor of my ethnology colleagues, Erin Debenport, David Dinwoodie, Steve Feld, Les Field, Larry Gorbet, Louise Lamphere, Carole Nagengast, Suzanne Oakdale, Sylvia Rodríguez, Beverly Singer, and Marta Weigle, as well as other anthropology colleagues, especially Jennifer George, Michael Graves, Jeff Long, Keith Prufer, and Matt Tuttle.

The University of Texas Press has a long history of publishing excellent ethnographies about Oaxaca and Mesoamerica more generally, and I was very pleased to have the opportunity to work with Theresa May, Victoria Davis, and the rest of the press's excellent editorial staff. Michael Chibnik and Walter Little (both initially anonymous reviewers for the University of Texas Press) deserve a special thanks for generously giving their time and feedback to make this a better text; their own writings about Oaxaca and Antigua, Guatemala, respectively, were critical to the formation of my work. Andrew Canessa and three anonymous reviewers provided critical comments on an earlier version of chapter 6, which was published as "'Yo soy nativo de aquí': The Ambiguities of Race and Indigeneity in Oaxacan Craft Tourism" in the *Journal of Latin American and Caribbean Anthropology* 14(2): 457–482. University of New Mexico geography student Jonathan K. Nelson created the wonderful map of Oaxaca and surroundings featured in chapter 1.

The author's family is usually reserved for the last paragraph, and I now find myself at the end of what has been a very long road, so here it is: a big thank-you to my wonderful family, Judy Brulotte; Ron Brulotte and his wife, Nancy Brulotte; Reggie Brulotte; Robert Brulotte; and my in-laws, G. Eleanor and the late Gregory Trujillo. Finally, I thank Michael Trujillo, who has seen me through this project from the beginning to the end, and has made everything seem possible. Here's to new beginnings and enduring patience and love.

Between Art and Artifact

CHAPTER ONE

Introduction

BETWEEN ART AND ARTIFACT

I DROVE SOUTHWEST FROM THE CITY OF OAXACA toward the artisan village of San Antonio Arrazola, remembering my impressions of the town when I first visited it in the spring of 1995. Much had changed in the intervening years, including the highway itself, which sported freshly paved asphalt. I passed through the outskirts of Santa Cruz Xoxocotlán, a separate town that was increasingly being incorporated into Oaxaca's urban sprawl. I continued along the highway for a few more kilometers before signaling to make the right-hand turn onto the paved but badly rutted road leading to Arrazola. The turnoff had been easy to miss at the time of my first visit, but the Oaxaca state Secretariat of Tourism (SEDETUR) remedied the situation in 2002.[1] In addition to road signs marking the names of select smaller towns, SEDETUR erected a small blue and white sign bearing the image of a stylized ceramic pot, the apparently internationally recognizable symbol for handicrafts. At the turn to the side road a larger, multicolored sign proclaimed, "*ARRAZOLA, CUNA DE LOS ALEBRIJES*" (Arrazola, birthplace of the alebrijes) (fig. 1.1), in reference to the brightly painted, whimsical wood carvings for which the town was famous.[2]

I continued on past a handful of settlements referred to in Spanish as *colonias populares*, some of which had sprouted up only in the past two or three decades to accommodate Oaxaca's growing urban underclass. For tourists, the colonias' dusty façades and overall lack of infrastructure relegated them to scenes from a car or bus window rather than destinations in their own right. Turning my gaze upward, to just above the outline of these settlements, I admired the clearly visible monumental structures of the Monte Albán archaeological zone as I followed

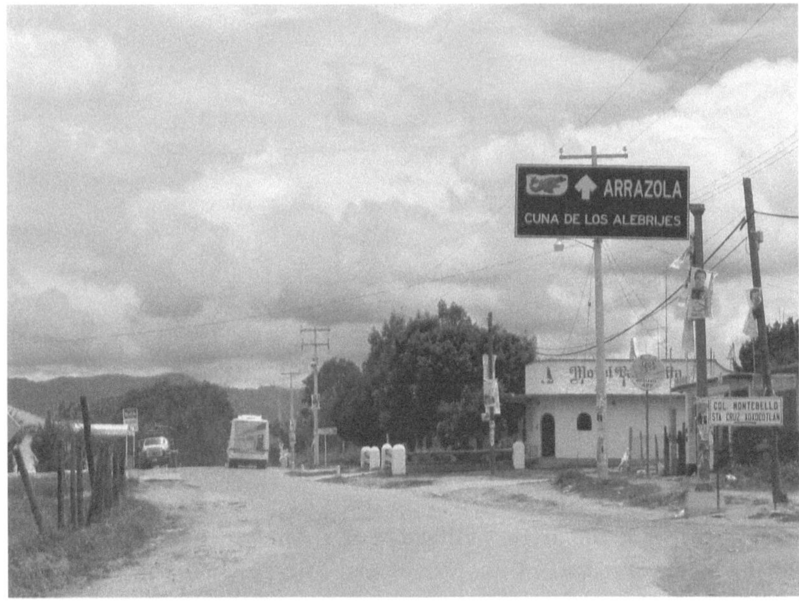

FIGURE 1.1. Arrazola, Cuna de los Alebrijes. *(Photograph by author)*

the road around the base of its southern perimeter. I continued on for about four more kilometers until the urban congestion and grit eventually gave way to more idyllic landscapes composed of green fields growing corn, beans, and the locally prized, extremely fiery *chile de agua*. A final speed bump marked the road's end at the entrance to Arrazola.

Arrazola's mix of amenities and perceived quaintness, both tied in part to the development of the wood-carving trade, makes it a permanent feature on many tourist itineraries. The village's close proximity to the city and Monte Albán makes it a convenient and popular day trip for tourists. Thursdays generally bring the highest volume of tourist traffic, when many package tours include a stop in Arrazola on their way to the weekly market hosted by the nearby town of Zaachila. Wide, paved streets, a well-maintained central plaza outfitted with a wrought-iron kiosk, and neatly trimmed grass and hedges welcome tourist visitors while conveying a sense of relative prosperity and orderliness.

Among the handful of small businesses that flank the entrance to the town are several shops offering wood carvings. A row of three makeshift wooden stalls located adjacent to the main plaza serves as the town's officially designated artisan market until a more permanent structure can be erected. Further into the town, other indicators that Arrazola is a community of artisans, and more specifically wood-carvers, greet the casual visitor. Signs advertising carvings for sale hang or are painted on building façades. Fanciful carved animals in various stages of completion seem to inhabit every patio, and families may even reserve entire rooms in their homes to be used as wood-carving showrooms. Two or three preadolescent boys regularly mill about the plaza area, offering to guide visitors to wood-carving workshops, typically those belonging to a family member or a wood-carver disposed to paying the kids a few pesos for their service. Return visitors or those who consider themselves in-the-know often decline these offers, preferring instead to head directly to the homes of the best-known artisans, whose work they may have previously seen at exhibitions in upscale galleries and stores in the United States. Those striking out on their own sometimes have in their possession one of the colorful maps distributed by the state tourism office, indicating the location of each of Arrazola's more than sixty wood-carving workshops and the name of the family who runs it.

Of course, outward appearances often do not convey the full story. For more than three decades, residents of Arrazola have produced and sold replicas of pre-Hispanic artifacts to tourists at the Monte Albán archaeological zone, one of Oaxaca's premiere tourist attractions and a UNESCO World Heritage site (fig. 1.2). Nevertheless, Arrazola residents' participation in this aspect of the tourism economy has been eclipsed by their fame as artisans who craft brightly colored wood carvings, or alebrijes (fig. 1.3). This book situates Arrazola's internationally famous Oaxacan wood-carving trade in relationship to its lesser-known—and differently valued—economic activity of making and

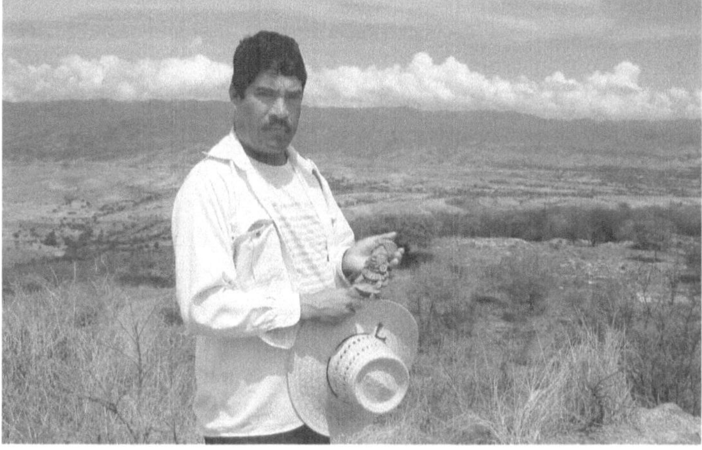

FIGURE 1.2. *Replica seller at Monte Albán. (Photograph by author)*

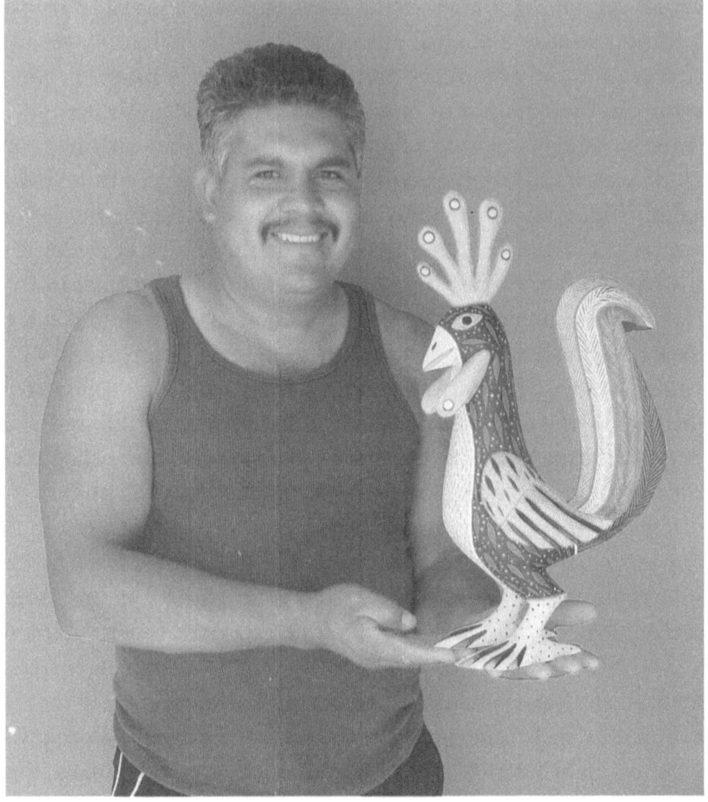

FIGURE 1.3. *Arrazola wood-carver Arsenio Morales. (Photograph by author)*

marketing archaeological crafts. Mention of the latter practice is almost always omitted from official tours and guidebooks but is nonetheless deeply tied to the Oaxacan tourism economy and the idea of cultural patrimony on which it is predicated.

William Roseberry reminds us that "cultural production is not limited to those who control the means of cultural production" (1989:45). And at the heart of this text is a theoretical interrogation of the notion of authentic cultural forms, illustrated by the multiple and often competing ways in which artisans, tourists, and other cultural brokers discursively construct wood carving and archeological replicas. Wood carving is comfortably situated within popular and state discourses of Oaxacan craft production, even though the craft is relatively recent and produced for an outside, predominantly North American market. Replica makers and sellers, in contrast, do not conform to prescribed notions of appropriate and legitimate cultural production as defined by the state, the tourism industry, and even some anthropologists.

When we position replica crafts as creative works in their own right and within the same representational field as other Oaxacan art and material culture, the contradictory ideologies of Oaxaca's art-culture system (Clifford 1988) become apparent. Pierre Bourdieu (1993) theorized the artistic work as emerging within a field of cultural production. He viewed this field not only as a hierarchical but interdependent system of social actors (artists, buyers, art critics, etc.) but also as an arena of "struggles tending to transform or conserve this field of forces" (Bourdieu 1993:30). The account that follows traces one community's efforts to navigate this shifting terrain of cultural and economic values at the nexus of Oaxaca's heritage complex. Following Bourdieu (1993), I approach this "field of cultural production" as a powerful, mutually constituting triangulation of art, archaeology, and cultural tourism through which a selective version of regional "culture" is circumscribed and promoted.

REPLICAS AND ROGUES

In his work with Toba Batak wood-carvers in Sumatra, Indonesia, anthropologist Andrew Causey (2003) observed the making of many "antique" objects: wood carvings made to resemble old religious artifacts traditionally used by the island's indigenous inhabitants that had now come to be prized by tourists and collectors. In this case, artistic intent formed the criteria for the classification of such objects. He found that when recently crafted objects were advertised as copies, they were called reproductions or replicas. However, "when they are offered for sale as actually being old, then they are fakes, and those who make or sell them are spoken of with scorn as frauds, cheats, and swindlers" (Causey 2003:150).

I too encountered such judgments and categorical distinctions; as a result, I struggled over the terminology to be used to describe the material culture that is the book's subject. Throughout the text I refer to modern objects that stylistically mimic pre-Hispanic artifacts as "archaeological replicas" because this phrase follows from the Spanish word *réplicas*, the term, along with *artesanías* (handicrafts or folk art), most often used by replica creators and purveyors themselves.[3] I am not wholly comfortable with this designation, mainly because, as I describe in chapter 4, replica objects mimic but do not fully duplicate their original archaeological referent. That is to say, replica artisans are engaged in their own creative acts of interpreting the pre-Hispanic past—acts that reproduce and at the same time transcend the aesthetic limits of ancient Mesoamerican sculptural forms. Nevertheless, I find the term "replica" preferable to the more contemptuous language of "fakes," "forgeries," "frauds," and "dupes" that pepper certain archaeological and art historical discourses (such as Kelker and Bruhns 2009). The tourists I encountered in my fieldwork described replicas using some of the above terms, and alternately as "tchotchkes" and "knick-knacks," or their Spanish equivalent, "*chucherrías*." All of these descriptors ("replicas" included) are value-laden and indicative of the multiple, fraught relationships between differently positioned subjects and replica objects.

Few would have trouble identifying a Mesoamerican artifact or Oaxacan folk art piece as such; yet archaeological replicas resist naming in such a straightforward way, as evidenced by the wide-ranging terminology applied to them. Instead, replicas represent a unique, hard-to-classify type of material culture, and this, I suggest, is precisely where their power as cultural forms resides. They inhabit a gray area of materiality within the Mexican nationalist tradition of folk art and archaeological remains described in the next section. I say "gray area" because replicas are generally denied the social legitimacy of these two other forms of material culture.

Indeed, as I demonstrate throughout the book, replicas are subject to ongoing discursive moves that seek to dislodge them from the realm of so-called authentic cultural goods—the very material culture that underlies the Mexican national origin story and is the bedrock of the contemporary tourism economy. Neither legitimate folk art (according to some) nor "original" archaeological artifacts, replicas nevertheless reference the aesthetic codes and production techniques of both of these categories. They are, for the most part, handmade by self-taught artisans out of locally sourced materials, not unlike other Oaxacan handicrafts. More critically, replicas, to varying degrees, mimic the stylistic elements and appearance of the original artifacts prized by archaeologists, art historians, and others concerned with historical authenticity (fig. 1.4).

Theorizing the work of forgery in the fine arts, philosopher Sandór Radnóti (1999) likens the art "forger" to the rogue or rascal (*pícaro*) character of the Spanish and Latin American picaresque literary tradition, which flourished in the seventeenth and eighteenth centuries. This genre of prose fiction features the exploits of a lower-class, roguish hero who manages to live by his or her wits in a corrupt, hypocrit-

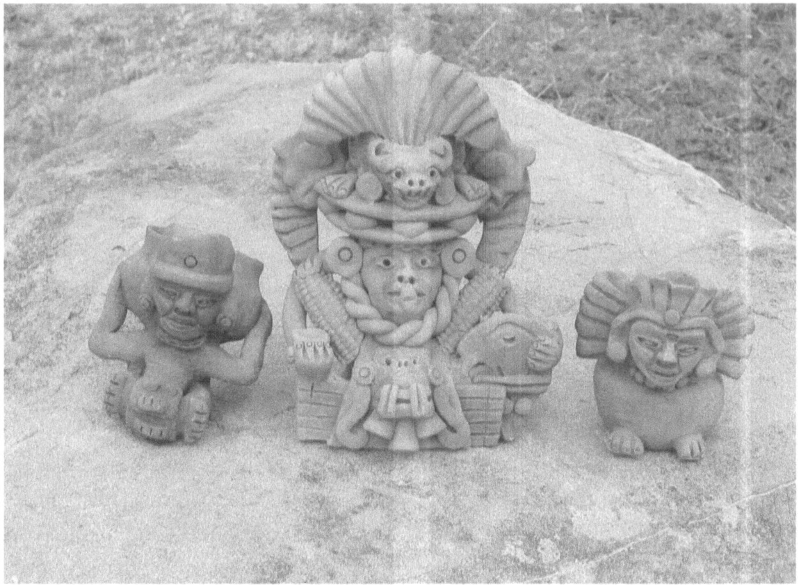

FIGURE 1.4. *A trio of archaeological replicas for sale at Monte Albán. (Photograph by author)*

ical society.[4] The appeal of the rogue is his or her playful subversions of society's dominant moral and juridical codes (e.g., the vagabond who, through verbal erudition, tricks a wealthy aristocrat out of a sum of money). The rogue's transgressions are humorous but nevertheless draw attention to the relations of power and authority operating at a given moment as well as their cumulative effects.

In the case of the art forger, what is being critiqued, according to Radnóti, is the art establishment's unchallenged authority to determine all that is beautiful and historically original—and therefore valuable. Through his actions and the replicated form itself, the forger mocks the fetish character of the original work of art by creating copies that may exist in different historical times from the original and populate multiple geographic spaces. In other words, the "aura" of the original, as famously theorized by Walter Benjamin (1968) in his essay "The Work of Art in the Age of Mechanical Reproduction," is undermined by the presence of the "fake" artwork. In this subversion Radnóti locates a productive critique of Enlightenment claims to historicity and authenticity, which are central to the modern system of art since the Renaissance.

I propose Radnóti's art forger as a frame for thinking through the practice of making and selling archaeological replicas. Rather than simply denouncing replicas and their makers (a much-deployed strategy documented throughout this text), I invite the reader to consider the following: What is the social "work" of the archaeological replica? Their very existence as in-between, modern artifacts—neither "real" art nor "original" archaeological piece—threatens to rupture a representational system that fuses together select landscapes, expressive forms, and ethnically/racially marked bodies into an otherwise seamless "heritage-scape" (Di Giovine 2009). Like the picaresque literary rogue or Radnóti's art forger, I suggest that through their material and discursive practices replica purveyors draw our attention to the systems of power that collectively work to produce Monte Albán, and Oaxaca more generally, as a site of safe, consumable heritage.

In his ground-breaking study of Chichén Itzá as a modern-day artifact of state-sponsored archaeology and tourism, anthropologist Quetzil Castañeda (1996) questions the uncontested logic of heritage-making that selectively authenticates historical or cultural ideals through material forms like archaeological ruins. He notes that "the imposition of a social convention that would differentiate a given moment as the authentic, original, fully present phase of a society, building, art style, civilization, institution, or city is an inherently contested act of power in the register of knowledge" (Castañeda 1996:105). Castañeda's reading of Chichén Itzá as a Foucauldian terrain of power and knowledge production (Foucault 1972, 1980) presents clear affinities with the situation at Monte Albán; a similar confluence of modern archaeological science, a fervent postrevolutionary nationalism, and tourism-based development have formed a discursive matrix for delineating and disseminating a particular version of Oaxacan history and culture.

Archaeological replicas and those who make them signal a type of refusal of this system (even when they reproduce certain of its logics) or, at the very least, make us aware of its latent contradictions. It is their destabilization of and semiotic play with taken-for-granted categories of Oaxacan "culture" (not only archaeological remains but also folk arts) that give replicas their inherent capacity for social critique.

ARTESANÍAS AND ARTIFACTS IN POSTREVOLUTIONARY MEXICO

Anthropologist and material culture scholar Fred Myers notes that "very commonly, objects—in the form of cultural property, heritage, and art—are subsumed in projects of nationalism, in which indigenous cultural production and identities are engaged with the state's ideological dynamics" (Myers 2001:55). Anthropologist Shelly Errington further contends that the conceptualization of time as a linear progression, the discipline of archaeology, and the notion of art/folk art all "had their modern origins in the late eighteenth century and developed into something like their modern forms in Europe and the Americas during the nineteenth" (Errington 1998:161). The parceling of material culture into today's recognizable social categories of folk art and archaeological heritage is therefore a historical process tied to the emergence of the modern nation-state and national identities. As part of nationalists' discovery of folk art and folklore described by Roger Abrahams (1993), material culture represented the tangible expression of a shared national history and sentiment.[5]

In Mexico, the special preoccupation with the country's folk heritage and pre-Hispanic antiquities began to take shape in the period immediately following its independence from Spain in 1821, and was later fomented with the establishment of a national museum system in 1831. Despite this development, throughout much of the turbulent nineteenth century the Mexican government frequently found itself more concerned with fighting wars than with forging national identity. The tide began to shift, however, under the dictatorial rule of President Porfirio Díaz (1876–1880 and 1884–1911), who implemented a wide-scale modernization program that had as one of its goals improving Mexico's national image abroad.[6] The centralization of political rule in Mexico that began during the *porfiriato* accelerated under the postrevolutionary state.[7]

But even as the regime dismantled regional configurations of power and consolidated political and economic resources, it still faced the difficult task of unifying disparate, predominately rural populations that had never before imagined themselves as integrated national subjects. To that end, the state appropriated specific cultural forms in a strategic effort to produce and foment a sense of *mexicanidad*, or Mexicanness. This process continued well after the revolution and to this today informs conceptions of Mexicanness both within and outside of Mexico, as documented by numerous scholars (Delpar 1992; García Canclini 1995; López 2010; Joseph and Nugent 1994; Novelo 1976; Vaughn and Lewis 2006).

State-sponsored museums and archaeological monuments in particular served as vehicles for the staging of an emergent Mexican nationalism through material culture (Bartra 2000; Coffey 2010; Errington

1998; García Canclini 1995, 1997; Kaplan 1993). Such displays prominently featured two potent symbols of the modern Mexican nation: (1) pre-Hispanic archaeological remains, and (2) *artesanías* produced by present-day indigenous or mestizo (mixed European and indigenous ancestry) "peasants." These cultural forms became equated in the Mexican national story as past and present manifestations of the nation, "because the people who produced these crafts were regarded as the living descendants of the people who had built the great temple complexes excavated by archaeologists" (Errington 1998:161–162). But as Roger Bartra (1987) and other scholars have suggested, the construction of "*lo mexicano*" represented an essentialized version of national culture and history, the product of revolutionary intelligentsia discourse rather than the reflection of an a priori popular conscience.[8] The very people identified and celebrated by the state as producers of cultural patrimony in reality were often relegated to the margins of Mexico's national project of socioeconomic advancement, which early on included the development of a tourism industry (Berger 2006; Saragoza 2001).

Claudio Lomnitz (2001) observes that Mexico developed one of the world's earliest and most deep-rooted national anthropologies, which seamlessly fused with the racial politics of *indigenismo*. Following historian Alan Knight (1990), *indigenismo* is best described as a discourse about indigenous peoples by largely nonindigenous postrevolutionary state officials, policymakers, and educators. *Indigenistas* advocating for the recognition of Mexico's indigenous heritage at the same time sought to incorporate indigenous populations into the national mestizo body. Two of the key architects of *indigenista* government policy were well-known anthropologists, Manuel Gamio and Alfonso Caso. Trained in the United States under cultural anthropologist Franz Boas, Gamio was a prolific writer and intellectual whose works included the 1916 pronationalist tract *Forjando patria* and essays that addressed the so-called Indian problem in Mexico.[9] He also served as the first director of the Interamerican Indigenista Institute. Alfonso Caso was the head of various state-run institutions, including the National Museum, the National Institute of Anthropology and History, and the National University (Knight 1990:102).

Archaeology was central to the imagining of the Mexican nation, and his list of impressive high-level appointments notwithstanding, Caso's legacy as a national hero still derives primarily from archaeological work that he carried out in Oaxaca at Monte Albán during the 1930s and 1940s. His ability to present Monte Albán as a site of national cultural heritage on par with the great civilizations of the world, including the Greeks and Romans, was critical to both the developing positivist science of archaeology and Mexico's nationalist project. Anthony Smith (2001) posits a mutually constituting relationship between national identity and the disciplinary methods and assumptions of history and archaeology in the late nineteenth and early twentieth centuries. Archaeological concepts of antiquity, relative chronology, and stratification were easily mapped onto nationalism's project of locating the authentic nation in the distant past and within a distinct geographic territory (see also Díaz-Andreu 2008).

In Mexico, the material remains of pre-Hispanic settlements allowed proponents of *indigenismo* to trace a singular line of human cultural development from the pre-Hispanic past to the geographically and culturally bounded Mexican nation-state. Establishing direct links to grandiose ancient civilizations was critical to internally fomenting Mexican identity while at the same time dispelling foreign (especially U.S.) beliefs about the country's inherent social and economic backwardness (Pike 1992; Bartra 1987).[10] Interestingly, while much attention has been paid to the postrevolutionary period of Mexican nation-building, in fact Caso was continuing a prior tradition of utilizing archaeology to serve nationalist aspirations. As historian Christina Bueno points out, Mexico's first official archaeological site, Teotihuacán, was reconstructed during the presidency of Porfirio Díaz for the centennial celebration of Mexican independence in 1910; underlying this archaeological spectacle was the desire to showcase Mexico "as a unified and modern nation with ancient and prestigious roots" (Bueno 2010:54). Archaeological motifs and artifacts not only figured predominantly at in-country locations and events, but also represented Mexico's grandiose legacy abroad at multiple world's fairs throughout the late nineteenth century—for example, the Aztec palace at the 1889 World's Fair in Paris (Bueno 2010; Tenorio-Trillo 1996).

If archaeology is a modern enterprise that may be situated within the context of modern nation-building, so too is the "discovery" of Mexican handicrafts that also occurred during this period. As part of the fascination with the peasantry and folklore that emerged in late eighteenth- and early nineteenth-century Europe, the concept of folk art enabled the literate elite of stratified societies in Europe and its former colonies to distinguish and label the arts and crafts production of the lower classes (Graburn 1976). By the turn of the twentieth century, indigenous handicrafts and "peasant" handicrafts had attracted the attention of the Mexican intelligentsia, who thought them to represent the untainted spirit of a country recovering from violent social upheaval and struggling to implement left-leaning policies and reforms. Furthermore, Mexican textiles, pottery, wood carvings, and other handmade crafts satisfied a modernist nostalgia for an imagined preindustrial past, in which pure, native artistic expression existed independently of capitalist modernity. From a purely economic standpoint, the promotion of handicrafts was part of a state strategy for curbing postrevolutionary peasant migration to urban areas, whose inadequate infrastructure was unable to absorb the massive, largely unskilled labor force (Novelo 1976). Today artisanry is promoted in some rural Mexican communities as an alternative to an out-migration that has become transnational in its scope.

In the 1920s and the 1930s, the economic and symbolic value of *artesanías* was evidenced by the fervor with which certain members of the Mexican intelligentsia began to commission, collect, and display them. Yet as historian Rick López argues, the embrace of Mexican popular art did not signal a widespread nativist movement, as much of the Mexican elite still harbored ambivalent feelings about the Indianized Mexican nationality that these crafts symbolized (2010:95). Rather, López identifies the struggle to elevate the status of Mexican crafts to national patrimony as a transnational one, waged as much by left-leaning U.S. political tourists, writers, and artists as by a select group of Mexican artists and cultural elite (see also Delpar 1992; Errington 1998; Lomnitz-Adler 1992; Wood 2000). The rise of primitive art in early twentieth-century Europe, exemplified by Picasso and Léger (Clifford 1988; Price 1989), also warrants mention here. The art establishment's fascination with so-called primitive forms, particularly from Africa, undoubtedly served to legitimate Mexican crafts as authentic, native expressions (Bartra 2000). The lack of formal training and technology that made primitive art so appealing to European audiences was also a quality that piqued the interests of early twentieth-century collectors of Mexican folk art, including Mexican artists Diego Rivera and Frida Kahlo.[11]

Yet in this seeming glorification of Indian and other rural artisans resided both paternalism and racism. Producers of cultural patrimony may have symbolically represented the spirit of the Mexican nation, but, as anthropologist and *indigenista* intellectual Manuel Gamio expressed, as individuals they were considered to be languishing in the "backward cultural stages" of human development (Gamio 1925:6). The isolated and impoverished conditions out of which many popular and folkloric cultural forms emerged simultaneously represented an impediment to the modernizing Mexican state. For instance, the 1925 inaugural edition of the bilingual journal *Mexican Folkways* featured an introductory essay in which Gamio advocated understanding folklore as a means to "civilize" its primitive producers (Gamio 1925).[12] His comments reveal a hegemonic political project informed by anthropological approaches to folklore:

> As it would be impossible to make that Indian-mestizo majority abandon their folkloric ideas all at once in order to incorporate itself with the minority of advanced civilization, it is indispensable to analyze and to know their diverse and peculiar modes of thinking, in order to formulate later educational means that may make progress easy for the gradual forming of the Indian mentality until it is molded into the ways of modern thought. (Gamio 1925:7)

Néstor García Canclini (1993) has argued against the construction of crafts as premodern cultural forms by demonstrating their integral position in the struggle for hegemony within Mexico's modern capitalist economy. His analysis focuses on the period from the late 1970s and early 1980s. However, he shows the production and promotion of folk arts to be inseparable from the national political discourse and economic strategies of the early twentieth century. In order to integrate the popular classes into the process of capitalist development, dominant classes reorganized the cultural products of subaltern groups into a unified system of symbolic and economic production (García Canclini 1993: viii). Folk art may be cast as a precapitalist survival or part of a separate, parallel peasant economy, but handicrafts persist in Mexico precisely because they are fully articulated with modern capitalist production. Anthropologist Scott Cook corroborates that crafts "satisfy a special social demand that . . . cannot be satisfied through machinofacture or capital-intensive production processes" (Cook 1993:77). In her ethnographic study of miniature palm crafts produced in the state of Puebla, Katrin Flechsig (2004) asserts that the idea of historical continuity is central to the craft's commercial appeal. "Accordingly, people in Mexico make miniatures not just because they are a pre-Hispanic tradition but because consumers believe they are a pre-Hispanic tradition and have promoted them as a coveted national legacy" (Flechsig 2004:174).

Craftwork takes on added political significance as a way of concretizing "Mexicanness" in the face of the perceived homogenizing effects of neoliberal market forces. Under what circumstances artisans themselves recognize and strategically engage (or not) the politics of difference has been an important site of analysis for recent anthropological discussions of craftwork not only in Mexico but throughout Latin America (e.g., Field 1999; Castañeda 2004a; Little 2004a; Meisch 2002; Nash 1993; Stephen 1993; Wood 2008; Zorn 2004).

OAXACA, ARRAZOLA, AND CULTURAL TOURISM

Named by Lonely Planet as one of the top ten world destinations for 2010, Oaxaca state's popularity among tourists has steadily grown since the late 1960s, when the first wave of *jipis* (hippies) and *mochileros* (backpackers) arrived, looking for an alternative to the mass tourism of Mexico's coastal resorts, including the often-derided "gringolandia" of Cancún (Torres and Momsen 2004), and the far wealthier, manicured colonial cities of the central interior.

For some, Oaxaca's status as a countercultural destination was embodied by pilgrimages to the Sierra Mazateca, specifically the town of Huautla de Jiménez, to partake in the ritual consumption of hallucinogenic mushrooms, a practice associated with the popular figure of local healer María Sabina (Feinberg 2003). Today, even as Mexican and international tourists arrive in droves, Oaxaca is still imagined as a place off the beaten path, where indigenous culture reigns supreme, unencumbered by strip malls, fast-food chains, and gated communities of aging North American expatriates. Its coast attracts surfers and sunseekers, but the capital city of Oaxaca de Juárez, with the surrounding *Valles Centrales* (Central Valleys) that radiate out from it, is the real attraction for many tourists. These travelers parallel the "ethnic tourists" in neighboring Chiapas—described by sociologist Pierre Van den Berghe—who want "unspoiled natives, not bilingual waiters and beachboys" (Van den Berghe 1994:9).

Oaxaca, as the city is more simply known, is 475 kilometers southwest of Mexico City and serves as the geographic and bureaucratic center of the state (see map 1.1). It is nestled in a Y-shaped valley formed by the intersecting Sierra Madre Occidental, Sierra Madre del Sur, and Sierra de Oaxaca mountain ranges. Prized for its colonial architecture, unique regional cuisine, and nearby Mesoamerican archaeological sites, the area also boasts a number of artisan villages dedicated to the specialized production of folk arts and crafts, notably wood carvings, textiles, and ceramics. Mexican nationals still constitute the majority of visitors, but Oaxaca increasingly hosts tourists from the United States, Canada, Europe, and Japan who have heard about both its dynamic contemporary art scene and its well-preserved folkloric traditions.

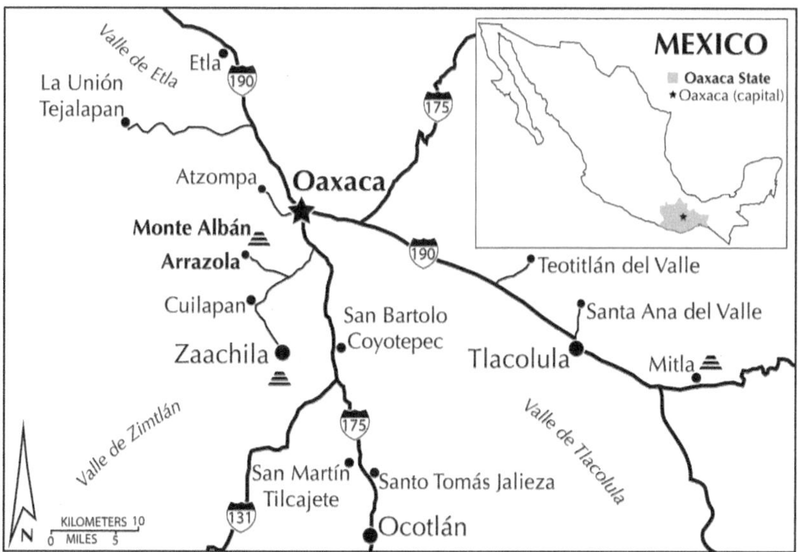

MAP 1.1. *The state of Oaxaca* (inset) *and the Central Valleys. (Map by Jonathan K. Nelson)*

Despite the growth of the tourism sector, Oaxaca, along with neighboring Chiapas, remains one of the poorest states in Mexico. The same rugged geography that provides the dramatic natural setting so cherished by visitors has been a key factor in historically isolating the region from the large-scale industrial development and commerce networks found in central Mexico and parts of northern Mexico. In their 1991 work on social inequality in Oaxaca, Arthur Murphy and Alex Stepick paint a portrait of the region that sharply contrasts with its idyllic image as a center of art and culture:

> Aggregate economic statistics reveal that the state's per capita production ranks next to last and it produces only one percent of the nation's total industrial goods. The statewide illiteracy rate is more than 40 percent, and indicators of malnutrition, infant mortality, and disease point to a generally poor, underprivileged population. In short, the state of Oaxaca is among the least developed in Mexico. (Murphy and Stepick 1991:79)

Murphy and Stepick (1991) further argue that the authenticity so prized by visitors to Oaxaca is in large measure a by-product of the region's underdevelopment. Even as indigenous and other poor Oaxacans work to acquire the material goods and amenities associated with a middle-class, urban lifestyle, outsiders pour into the region seeking bucolic scenery and culture unblemished by industry and new technologies.

Twenty years later, while there have been improvements in local living conditions, Oaxaca continues to lag behind the rest of the country in terms of the indicators mentioned by Murphy and Stepick above. Tourism and remittances sent by migrants working in the United States are two of the state's most important sources of revenue, both of which were negatively affected by the 2009 economic downturn in the U.S. Fears about the H1N1 virus in Mexico furthered the decline in tourism that year, with the Oaxaca state tourism office reporting a 15 percent decrease in foreign visitors from the previous year.

Oaxaca also has a long history of social unrest and violence brought about by intracommunity disputes over land, ethnic and political struggles, and the general impoverishment of its citizenry (e.g., Campbell et al. 1993; Dennis 1987; Greenberg 1989; Stephen 2002). Conflict and civil unrest in recent years have propelled Oaxaca into the international spotlight, much to the dismay of locals whose livelihoods are directly tied to the tourism industry. Even today, Oaxacan tourism has yet to fully recover from a well-publicized teachers' strike in 2006 and the political instability that ensued. Led by members of Section 22 of the National Union of Teachers (SNTE), the strike grew into a violent movement to oust an unpopular state governor, Ulises Ruiz Ortiz, a member of Mexico's PRI political party.[13] The strike precipitated the formation of the Popular Assembly of the Peoples of Oaxaca (APPO), a broader coalition of representatives from Oaxaca's state regions and municipalities, NGOs, unions, and other grassroots organizations. Ruiz Ortiz is no longer in office, following a historic PRI defeat in the summer of 2010 in a state that has historically been a PRI party stronghold, but the APPO continues to stage demonstrations and protests around other social justice issues. The widespread, violent confrontations of 2006 (which resulted in the death of an American journalist) may have subsided, but the national and international media attention that they received, along with increasing drug-related violence not only in Oaxaca but all over Mexico, have managed to deter many would-be visitors.

Oaxaca is not only one of Mexico's poorest states, it is also one of the most ethnically diverse, with at least fifteen different indigenous languages spoken. Ethno-racial identity in Oaxaca, like elsewhere, is a complex matter and may not be reduced simply to quantifiable markers such as native-language retention (a topic I take up in chapter 6). Yet it may be said that most modern Oaxacans are considered to be the indigenous or mestizo descendants of pre-Hispanic Mesoamerican peoples that historically populated the region. The Central Valleys have a strong Zapotec and Mixtec presence, whose history has been extensively interpreted and documented through the archaeological remains of important urban and ceremonial centers such as Monte Albán, Mitla, Zaachila, and Yagul (e.g., Blanton 1978; Caso and Bernal 1962; Flannery and Marcus 1983; Paddock 1966; Whitecotten 1977; Winter 2002). Central Oaxaca's pre-Hispanic population centers and their interconnected marketing systems are also cited as the historical antecedent for the pattern of village handicraft specialization presently found in the region (Cook and Diskin 1976). Today, Mesoamerican archaeology and handicrafts, respectively cast as the material culture of pre-Hispanic and contemporary indigenous peoples, represent the twin pillars of Oaxaca's modern tourism economy.

Located about twelve kilometers from Oaxaca, San Antonio Arrazola (more commonly referred to as Arrazola) is a semi-rural town adjacent to the southern perimeter of the Monte Albán archaeological zone (see map 1.1). With a population that hovers around one thousand people (INEGI 2000), it is a high-profile artisan community nationally and internationally famous for the production of fanciful wood carvings. In addition to Arrazola, two other central Oaxacan communities have developed into centers for wood carving since the 1980s: San Martín Tilcajete and La Unión Tejalapan. Although each of these towns has developed its own style and client base, Arrazola is generally marketed as the place where Oaxacan wood carving, as practiced today, first emerged.

As I explore in detail in the first two chapters, however, state and popular discourses that render Oaxacan artisans as bearers of ancient, indigenous tradition make for an imprecise fit with the community's actual history. The town itself is a former sugarcane hacienda, and residents are the descendants of laborers who migrated from various parts of Oaxaca to work on the estate prior to the 1910 Mexican Revolution. Moreover, even though the town is widely known for its wood-carving craft, community members engage in a range of economic activities. In addition to making replicas and selling them at Monte Albán, residents also farm; attend local universities; serve as military and police officers; and work as electronic technicians, small business owners, and mechanics. When I lived in the community in 2002–2003, Arrazola's mayor was a general manager at a Ford dealership in the city. In other words, the town is far from being what Eric Wolf (1957) and other scholars of the Mesoamerican "peasantry" once characterized as a "closed corporate community" (Kearney 1996). Residents are thoroughly integrated in the transnational tourism and art market, but also actively participate in urban Oaxaca's nontourist economy, providing a wide variety of goods and services for local consumption. Migrant work in the United States and other parts of Mexico (discussed in chapter 2) has also significantly contributed to household incomes since World War II, a trend that continues into the present.

RESEARCH IN AN ANTHROPOLOGICAL LOCATION

So many anthropologists (not only Mexican but also U.S. American in particular) choose Oaxaca as a fieldsite that they have earned their own title of "*oaxacólogos*," a play on the Spanish term for anthropologists (*antropólogos*). Cosmology, sociopolitical organization, gender roles, handicraft production, agricultural practices, indigenous languages—virtually no aspect of local life has gone unstudied. Indeed, a long-running joke asks, "What one thing do all indigenous households in Oaxaca have in common?" The answer: an anthropologist. Among anthropologists and scholars working in related disciplines, these commentaries on our ubiquity are humorous if somewhat disconcerting, since they remind us of Oaxaca's ongoing colonization by outsiders, however well informed or well meaning.

From early explorers and colonial European travelers to early twentieth-century artists and present-day tourists, Oaxaca has long indulged outsiders' desires for cultural otherness. Anthropologists, too, have made Oaxaca their object throughout much of the discipline's modern history, mining rich data from the region's extensive archaeological record and distinctive indigenous communities. This legacy is reflected by the fact that many Oaxacans, from taxi drivers to store clerks, are not the least bit surprised (and occasionally annoyed) to learn that someone is an anthropologist.

This was the case in Arrazola, where I was not the first outsider to arrive and start asking questions. Over the past thirty years the town had welcomed not only anthropologists, but also legions of tourists, folk art dealers, journalists, photographers, and film crews intent on observing or documenting aspects of its wood-carving craft. The community received significant international publicity from a book published in 1993 by American journalist Shepard Barbash and his wife, photographer Vicki Ragan. *Oaxacan Woodcarving: The Magic in the Trees* reached a broad audience of folk art collectors and tourists, and its enduring appeal is evidenced by the fact that it is still widely sold by local businesses catering to this clientele seventeen years later. The duo published a follow-up volume in 2007, *Changing Dreams: A Generation of Oaxaca's Woodcarvers*, a more somber exposé featuring then-and-now, black-and-white photographs of select Arrazola carvers and others from the community (as well as wood artisans from other nearby Oaxacan towns). Wood carving in Arrazola has provided subject matter for three anthropology master's theses (Ahlquist 2005; Brulotte 1999; Serrie 1964) and a book published in 2003 by University of Iowa anthropologist Michael Chibnik. On the nonacademic side, there are at least two children's books inspired by Arrazola wood-carvers (Cohn and Cordova 2002; Weill 2007).

In contrast, the town's involvement in the archaeological replica trade at Monte Albán has received scant attention from the media or anthropologists. Chibnik (2003) briefly describes it in his account of Arrazola's economic history before the wood-carving boom of the mid-1980s. Nelly Robles García, a prominent Oaxacan archaeologist, a former director at Monte Albán (1997–2010), and the director of the INAH-Oaxaca Regional Center since 2010, gives the issue cursory treatment in her 1996 Ph.D. dissertation at the University of Georgia on the management of archaeological resources.[14] Her work, which focuses on the Oaxacan sites of Monte Albán and Mitla, mentions Arrazola replica sellers as only one of multiple social groups who utilize heritage resources in ways that are frequently at odds with Mexico's state-sponsored archaeology.

I admit that I too was initially drawn to Arrazola because of its wood carving and not its archaeological replicas. My original plan was to investigate shifting perceptions of identity among wood-carvers, more specifically, if there was an emergent, politicized identity tied to artisan production, as documented for producers of folkloric culture in other Oaxacan communities (e.g., Stephen 1991; Whitecotton 1996) as well as other regions of Latin America (e.g., de la Cadena 2000; Field 1999; Guss 2000). But as I learned more about Arrazola residents' longstanding relationship to Monte Albán, first as laborers on early archaeological excavations, and later as purveyors of pre-Hispanic replicas, the elision of this history from anthropological, state, and touristic accounts begged further inquiry.

Arrazola seemed to occupy a contradictory position within the social economy of tourism. Its wood-carving inhabitants were nationally and internationally celebrated as bearers of a rich artistic heritage that supposedly stretched back to pre-Hispanic times. At the same time other residents were perceived by some as a threat to Oaxaca's cultural patrimony through their vending activities at the nearby archaeological zone. Cultural theorist Raymond Williams defined a selective tradition as "an intentionally selective version of a shaping past and a pre-shaped present, which is then powerfully operative in the process of social and cultural definition and identification" (Williams 1977:115).

If, following Williams, that which is marked as tradition in practice is an expression of hegemonic forces, we then must ask: What social, economic, or political conditions have permitted such divergent discourses about the same community to flourish? Both wood carving and archaeological replicas are forms of material culture, but how is it that they have come to be so differently positioned—as objects of aesthetic, economic, and cultural value—within a terrain of local/global heritage that includes not only artisans, but tourists, guides, gallery owners, and anthropologists, among others? Notably, in a location that has been a center of anthropological research for nearly a century, neither cultural anthropologists nor archaeologists had ever deemed the replica trade a topic worthy of study, even though Mexican archaeologists working in Oaxaca during the Porfirian era, prior to the 1910 Revolution, noted such activity taking place (Batres 1909).[15]

Although I had spent varying periods of time in Oaxaca since 1995 for other professional and academic endeavors, the research for this project was carried out in 2002–2003 and on subsequent trips in 2006, 2007, and 2009. Interviews with the numerous government agencies involved in promoting handicrafts, local archaeological attractions, and other forms of cultural heritage were indispensable to understanding the sociopolitical milieu in which Oaxacan material culture is constituted. These included the National Institute of Anthropology and History (INAH); SEDETUR, the state Secretariat of Tourism; FONART and ARIPO, federal and state-run crafts stores, respectively; CONACULTA, the Oaxaca branch office of the National Council on Culture and the Arts; the Oaxaca Municipal Tourism Office; and the Oaxaca office for the Secretariat of Indigenous Affairs. I also interviewed employees and owners from a number of well-established, privately owned craft stores and art galleries and spoke with numerous craft vendors in the *zócalo*, the main downtown plaza; the Benito Juárez and Abastos markets, both located in the city; and at markets in the nearby communities of Ocotlán, Mitla, and Zaachila. All of these retailers sold some variety of wood carvings, but none carried archaeological copies of the type sold by Arrazola vendors at Monte Albán.

Participant observation in the town of Arrazola was critical to understanding local peoples' subjectivities, which were in great measure constituted through participation in the community's dual-craft economy. During my extended residence in Arrazola (as well as subsequent visits), I lived in a household consisting of a wood-carver and his wife, both in their mid-thirties, and their two preadolescent sons. The carver maintained a workshop on his parents' property in another part of the town, and the couple spent a good part of their days there making wood carvings and receiving any tourists or other buyers that happened to stop in. Members of their extended family participated in both the wood-carving and replica trades. Thus I was introduced to a large social network of extended family and town residents engaged in one way or another in the town's two craft industries.

As a new researcher in the community, I found all the previous attention lavished on Arrazola to be a mixed blessing. On one hand, Arrazola residents were used to fielding questions from and having their photographs taken by outsiders, although few of these individuals had remained in the community for extended stays. On the other hand, certain residents stated that they were not always happy with the way that their community had been represented. During my first week there I was warned by one townsperson that people might not want to talk to me for fear that I would portray Arrazola in a negative manner. She told me that a few resented that author Shepard Barbash had portrayed the town and its residents as "*muy humildes*," or very humble, in his popular Oaxacan wood-carving book (the Spanish term is a euphemism for poor or impoverished).[16] A Mexican cultural anthropologist at INAH alternately informed me that replica makers and sellers would likely refuse to talk to me because they would think I was a spy sent by INAH or another federal office to monitor them, with the end goal of getting them removed from the site once and for all. The tense relationship between artisans and vendors and state/federal authorities that I observed is not unique to this particular location. Anthropologists Quetzil Castañeda (1996) and Walter Little (2004a) encountered similar allegations and suspicions about their recurring presence in local market spaces in their respective fieldsites of the Chichén Itzá archaeological ruins in the Yucatán Peninsula and the market zones of Antigua, Guatemala.

Neither of these predictions turned out to be accurate in my case, and I was fortunate to spend a great deal of time talking to community members in a variety of contexts. I interviewed people who represented a diversity of wood-carving and replica-vending experiences; because the vast majority of wood-carvers and replica makers and sellers are men, they are heavily represented throughout the text. However, in terms of my participant observation in the community, I also spent a great deal of time in the company of Arrazola women as they attended to various household and artisan tasks related to both wood carving and replica making. From them I learned about the daily life and concerns of Arrazola residents, information that has informed and shaped this work in countless ways.

Following the lead of W. Warner Wood (2008), a fellow anthropologist who carried out extensive research on textile craft tourism in Oaxaca, I actively participated in multiple commercial tours led by Oaxaca-based operators. Significantly, on these tours I learned how craft communities were presented to tourists and observed how visitors experienced Oaxaca's cultural heritage through sightseeing. Trips geared to English-speaking Europeans and North Americans and Spanish-speaking nationals almost always featured visits to the Monte Albán or Mitla archaeological zones, along with local markets and craft villages. I always made it a point to identify myself and my project to both the guides and the other people on the tour. However, I found that once our trip was underway, the boundaries between tourist and researcher often fell away as we spent the better part of a day squeezed together in a passenger van. I frequently found myself enjoying an easygoing camaraderie forged with strangers as we explored tourist sites, snapped photos of each other, and shared our impressions of Oaxaca over lunch or sodas. On their part, tourists saw me as a sort of unofficial guide, someone who seemed fairly well versed in the area and could answer questions if the guide was unavailable. Nearly everyone I met expressed interest in my project and voluntarily offered accounts of their experiences with Oaxacan attractions and local people. The guides for these trips, all of whom were Mexican, did not seem to mind my presence and even offered very candid comments about their personal experiences as employees in the tourism industry.

Some of the richest data were those gathered through my many days spent at Monte Albán. Sometimes I went with the intention of just observing how tourists interacted with each other, the ruins, and of course, the replica sellers. While I never acted the formal part of tour guide, as had anthropologist Edward Bruner (2004), my ethnographic descriptions attest to the many occasions on which I took part in or facilitated unstructured tourist activities. I took countless photos for tourists as they posed in front of interesting structures and helped those who did not speak Spanish haggle over and ask questions about replicas being offered for sale. Tourists are notoriously difficult to interview, as the last thing that their frequently packed agendas allow is spending precious time talking to a researcher whom they will most likely never see again. Apart from participating in commercial tours, I developed a strategy for speaking with tourists by positioning myself at the top of one of Monte Albán's large pyramid mounds; visitors were usually so tired and out-of-breath by the time that they reached the top of the enormous stone staircase that I was able to engage them in rather lengthy conversations before they moved on to the rest of the site. When vendors took breaks from selling, we had informal conversations as well as more structured interviews when time allowed. Finally, I conducted interviews with Monte Albán guides and INAH personnel at the archaeological zone as well as other locations in the city.

OVERVIEW OF CHAPTERS

This book looks at members of one Oaxacan community who are doubly positioned as cultural producers within a tourism economy that is both national and international in scope. The ethnographic focus is on the making and marketing of pre-Hispanic replicas, but these activities are necessarily defined in relation to Arrazola's wood-carving craft and the particular place it occupies within tourist discourses and practices. My intent is to capture the dialectical tension that exists between the two crafts, working from the proposition that archaeological replicas may be viewed as a type of shadow industry against which "legitimate" Oaxacan material culture is defined. Thus, replicas represent the antithesis of both folk art and archaeological artifacts; replicas continuously reaffirm these other objects' value—economic, cultural, historical, and otherwise—precisely by being what they are not: cultural copies or "fakes."

The juxtaposition of replica making and wood carving is one strategy for critically reflecting on cultural production in Oaxaca, and particularly its insertion into a global art and heritage tourism market. Throughout my fieldwork I encountered situations tangentially related to wood carving or the making and selling of replicas, but which directly spoke to Arrazola's wider participation in a tourist economy. Consequently, the reader will find several separate but related ethnographic vignettes throughout the book; they should be seen as snapshots in which the multiple inflections of discourses about Oaxacan identity, culture, and history are experienced by tourists, local Oaxacans, and anthropologists, all of whom participate in their making.

I have necessarily changed the names of individuals involved in the making and selling of replicas, unless the individual specifically consented to being identified. The fact that it was wholly appropriate, and even expected, that I use the real names of individual wood-carvers (a situation also encountered by anthropologist Michael Chibnik when researching the craft) contrasted sharply with the need to maintain the privacy of those involved in the replica trade. This in itself is telling, as it illustrates how one craft industry is lauded and publicized as the locus of community identity while the other forcibly remains in the shadows.

The next chapter traces the history of Arrazola, from its beginnings as a sugarcane hacienda in the period prior to the 1910 Mexican Revolution to its international rise to fame as a wood-carving artisan village beginning in the 1980s. The aim of this chapter is to present the historical and economic conditions that set the stage for the emergence of its wood-carving craft, and, as discussed in the subsequent chapter, a parallel pre-Hispanic replica craft industry. I demonstrate how wood carving has become the public face of the community, not only through the manufacture and sale of material objects but also through the various media representations that accompany it.

In chapter 3 I track the historical development of Arrazola's lesser-known cottage-craft industry in pre-Hispanic replicas. The community's location adjacent to Monte Albán tied residents' livelihoods to the archaeological site throughout much of the twentieth century. Working as hired laborers at the site, residents eventually took to selling original artifacts and, later, replicas to visitors as Monte Albán was transformed into Oaxaca's most important site of heritage tourism. I discuss the conflict-ridden relationship between the vendors and INAH, the federal agency that manages archaeological work and tourism at Monte Albán. This ongoing struggle highlights what Breglia (2006) has identified as the intense and ambivalent politics around the making of heritage, particularly in instances when the authority of the state and the archaeological apparatus that it maintains is called into question through alternative practices. It also touches on the question of who "owns," or at the least can claim rights to utilize, heritage resources, a topic of central concern to studies of cultural property (see Brown 2003), and within the emerging field of scholarship best characterized as the ethnography of archaeology (e.g., Abu El-Haj 2002; Breglia 2006; Castañeda and Matthews 2008; Edgeworth 2006, Hamilakis and Duke 2007; Meskell 2009). Mortensen and Hollowell contend that "the dilemmas and interplays of power and meaning infused in archaeological sites, objects, and interpretations require a deeper and more nuanced investigation of these 'archaeologies' within broad and social contexts" (Mortensen and Hollowell 2009:9).

Chapter 4 shows how Arrazola residents went from selling replicas made solely by outside artisans to developing craft production within their own community. Here I address the various types of replica crafts and the creative and physical labor that go into their making, including artisans' strategies and motivations for creating certain pieces. This chapter also describes the organizational structure that facilitates the craft's production and distribution at Monte Albán. As Chibnik (2003) has demonstrated for wood carving, the replica trade involves a network of artisans, middlemen, and sellers that is more complex than is first apparent.

In chapter 5 I explore the discourses of cultural patrimony that imbue replica objects with particular social values and meanings. These crafts are unique in that they mimic the aesthetic codes of two other material forms that are critical to national and tourist imaginings of Oaxaca: folk arts and archaeological artifacts. They are handmade by (mostly) local people with no formal training. At the same time, replicas have the look and feel of original archaeological artifacts even when they deviate in their designs. I examine various perceptions of replica crafts, including those of tourists and the replica makers and sellers. Replicas both reveal and at the same time partially reproduce hegemonic discourses of cultural patrimony espoused by state institutions and the modern tourism industry. Yet I argue that the mimetic mode opens up a space where new forms of representing and comprehending the past become possible.

The sixth chapter looks at how state and popular discourses of race and ethnicity shape perceptions of vendor identity at Monte Albán. Even though indigenous ethno-racial identities are often assigned to Arrazola and other Oaxacan artisan communities, I suggest that the replicas' status as an institutionally unsanctioned craft may prevent their makers and sellers from claiming indigenous heritage. Just as the authenticity of replica crafts is called into question, so too is the authenticity of vendor identity. I further argue that the indigenous/mestizo model that has dominated ethno-racial classification since the postrevolutionary period is inadequate for understanding the complex, ambivalent notions of identity evidenced by replica makers and sellers today.

The conclusion offers final thoughts on Arrazola's position within the social economy of tourism. I suggest that the community's participation in two different craft industries provides a unique vantage point from which to examine the broader phenomenon of Oaxaca's development and marketing as a site for cultural tourism. In many ways it brings us full circle, back to the sign that welcomes visitors to "*ARRAZOLA, CUNA DE LOS ALEBRIJES*."

THE SKULL OF BENITO JUÁREZ

SITTING ON THE TOP STEP OF THE SOUTHern Platform, one of Monte Albán's impressive pyramid mounds, I scribbled the final notes from my morning observations and then glanced down at my watch. It was still early afternoon, just about 2:30 p.m. However, by that time the crowds that had earlier converged upon the archaeological zone had dwindled down to a few stray tourists who, I imagined, lingered to take advantage of the unobstructed photo opportunities. The blazing sun and thoughts of lunch waiting for me back in Arrazola cut short my mental musings, and I carefully began my descent down the steep steps of the monumental structure to the plaza floor. As I made my way toward the site entrance, I noticed a group of three replica vendors, all from Arrazola, hanging out near Building J, an arrowhead-shaped structure whose original function still eluded archaeologists.

Not wanting to appear rude, I approached the group. After we exchanged greetings, their conversation returned to the day's sales, or more precisely, the lack thereof. It was late November; the tourist traffic generated by the Day of the Dead had subsided, and the Christmas holiday, another peak period for tourism, was still a month away. Yet I had seen all three men speak with tourists that morning, even if they had not succeeded in selling any merchandise. A few more minutes of small talk passed before I cautiously asked if anyone had approached them about buying original artifacts that day. This was a potentially touchy subject, but the vendors knew that I was aware of such tourist indiscretions. One man, who seemed slightly amused by my fascination with the interplay between archaeological pieces and replicas, declined to answer the question, instead asking me if I wanted to hear a joke. He narrated the following parable—not exactly a joke—to me and the other men gathered around him:

> A gringo was traveling through the Sierra Norte and happened to pass through the town where Benito Juárez was born.[1] He noticed that some of the Indian townspeople had set up a stand on the side of the road where they were selling souvenirs. The gringo stopped at the stand and asked if they had anything besides the usual tourist junk, and one of them pulled a human skull out of a basket. The local said that it was the skull of Benito Juárez. The tourist, excited about the possibility of owning the real skull of Mexico's first indigenous president, quickly paid the man and went on his way.
>
> However, just a little further down the road the traveler encountered another stand on the side of the road where a local offered him what he, too, claimed was Benito Juárez's skull. The gringo was stunned. How could this be? He had already purchased the real skull from another seller. Surely this man was mistaken. Besides, this skull was clearly much smaller, a fact he pointed out to the vendor. Unfazed by the doubting tourist, the local replied, "Yes, Señor, but don't you see? This is the skull of Benito Juárez when he was a child."

CHAPTER TWO

A Wood-Carving Community

A beefy, friendly man who is proud of his craft and his heritage, Ojeda is one of the village's most prosperous and talented wood-carvers. The village is Arrazola, and the state is Oaxaca, where Zapotec and other Mexican Indians still reign when it comes to culture.

FROM THE *AUSTIN AMERICAN-STATESMAN* TRAVEL SECTION (FERRISS 1998)

AS TWO POPULAR ENGLISH-LANGUAGE BUYING guides attest (Hancock Sandoval 1998; Rothstein and Rothstein 2007), the opportunity to purchase unique, locally produced crafts is one of central Oaxaca's biggest draws. Crafts abound not only in Arrazola, but also in the city's numerous shops and other nearby towns.

A pattern of village craft specialization with roots that scholars have traced to pre-Hispanic market systems (Cook and Diskin 1976) has afforded certain Oaxacan communities a measure of fame and economic stability as craft producers. Notable are Teotitlán del Valle and Santa María Atzompa, famous for their woolen textiles and green pottery respectively, which have histories of artisan production spanning hundreds if not thousands of years (see Fischgrund Stanton 1999, Stephen 1991, and Wood 2008 on Teotitlán; similarly, see Thieme 2007 and Wasserspring 2000 on Atzompa). Such histories have served these artisan communities well. Being able to establish links to colonial and pre-Conquest craft traditions has helped local artisans promote their wares in the highly selective niche market for ethnic arts. Nelson Graburn's (1976) seminal work on ethnic and tourist arts suggests that the marketing of the producers' primordial ties to place and their indigenous heritage heightens the cultural cache of artisan objects for consumers.

Despite its current public identity as an artisan community, the village of Arrazola, unlike Teotitlán or Atzompa, was not historically recognized as a center of craft production. As Michael Chibnik (2003) has documented, the town only recently joined the ranks of these other long-standing craft-producing communities in the 1980s, when numerous residents took up wood carving in the style typically credited to its famous founder, Manuel Jiménez. Not only is wood carving a relatively recent craft in Arrazola, but it has always been produced for an outside market. In contrast with local ceramic goods and textiles, which were once produced for use in the community or for exchange with other villages, the target consumers of Arrazola wood carvings almost from the beginning were mainly foreign tourists and folk art collectors, particularly from the United States. In other words, by some measures that dictate what are authentic or traditional handicrafts, wood carvings from Arrazola may fall short because they are of recent origin and were never produced for local consumption (García Canclini 1993).[1]

This chapter explores the historical and economic conditions that led to Arrazola's emergence as one of the leading producers of Oaxacan handicrafts. It provides an account of the community's history, from its beginnings as a sugarcane estate in the colonial period through its transformation into an independent community in the wake of Mexico's postrevolutionary land reforms. I address how Arrazola's paltry agricultural land base and general lack of economic opportunities spurred residents to pursue income-generating activities outside of the community throughout much of the twentieth century. Yet Arrazola's long history of participation in interregional, national, and transnational networks of economic and cultural production and exchange fit uncomfortably within a master narrative of Oaxacan artisans that fixes them in a "traditional," unchanging indigenous present. The final section of this chapter takes up this issue by examining popular and media representations of Arrazola's wood-carving craft and looking at how they work to contain the town's history of artisan production within a particular discourse about Oaxacan artisans. Importantly, all of these processes must be considered as the mutually constituting terrain of the archaeological replica trade as well.

HISTORICAL ANTECEDENTS

Outsiders may be surprised to learn that just as wood carving is a product of the twentieth century, so too is the town of Arrazola, which was officially recognized as an independent community only in 1937. According to an 1883 source documenting eighteenth-century landholdings in Oaxaca, Arrazola Beita was the surname of the individual who in 1780 handled the legal sale and transfer of the lands that encompassed the present-day village (Martínez Gracida 1883:44). The scant records do not indicate if this person purchased the property or was a close family member who assumed the legal duties associated with the sale of the estate. The original founding date of the *finca* (the Spanish term for the small, landed estates of the period),[2] which eventually came to be known by the family name of Arrazola, is listed as unknown. Also unclear is the specific nature of land use under the ownership of the Arrazola family and the total size of their holdings.

The *finca* was later purchased in the late nineteenth century by the Larrañaga Calvo family, who had immigrated to Mexico from Spain's Basque country. They added the Arrazola *finca* to their extensive network of holdings, which included large tracts of land within what is now the federally protected archaeological zone of Monte Albán as well as other parcels scattered in and around the city of Oaxaca. Under their proprietorship, the estate produced a variety of agricultural crops, including native plants such as corn, squash, beans, and chiles, which continue to be an important part of the diet in Arrazola. The cultivation and processing of sugarcane, however, was the estate's primary economic activity. The structure that once served as the landowner's residence still sits today at the entrance to Arrazola, where it houses the deteriorated remains of the original farm equipment: the *trapiche* (press) used to process sugarcane into two of its most common local forms, *panela* (an unrefined sugar) and *aguardiente*, a strong, distilled cane liquor.

The labor force of the Larrañaga estate comprised workers who had migrated from surrounding communities in the Central Valleys of Oaxaca as well as from the coastal and northern mountain regions of the state. Those originating from indigenous communities spoke native languages such as Zapotec, Mixtec, and Chatino. However, Spanish served as the lingua franca of the *finca*, and, as Chibnik notes, by 1900 most of the approximately two hundred residents were monolingual Spanish speakers (Chibnik 2003:66–67). Workers' lives were predominantly organized around the social and economic structure of the estate. They resided in simple homes on the property that they constructed themselves from a combination of thatched palm, *carrizo* (a native plant resembling bamboo), and adobe. A small chapel inside the landowner's home served the religious needs of the community and was the center for annual gatherings based on the Catholic calendar of feast days and celebrations.

Although Arrazola workers did not endure the forced labor conditions that had characterized the *encomienda* system of the early colonial period, life on the nineteenth-century estate was one of poverty and hardship.[3] Most residents functioned as low-paid agricultural workers, while a few were sharecroppers, obligated to give the Larrañaga family half of whatever they sowed in turn for the privilege of using the land. At that time there were no paved roads connecting the estate to the city of Oaxaca, only a series of single-lane dirt paths that traversed the slopes of nearby Monte Albán or, in longer fashion, circumvented it. A trip to the city to attend the weekly market was a time-consuming affair that could take two days round-trip with a heavy load. The exhausting work schedules of the Arrazola workers prevented them from making the trip on a regular basis and obliged them to purchase much of their outside-produced food and other items at the *tienda de raya*, the estate-owned store, which offered goods at extremely inflated prices.[4] Rations of estate-produced *aguardiente* were also distributed from here, with devastating effects for many workers previously unaccustomed to regular alcohol consumption. A present-day Arrazola resident, whose grandfather migrated to Arrazola in the early 1920s from his hometown of Ixtlán de Juárez in the Sierra Norte region, remarked on the history of debt peonage, connecting it to the alcoholism with which some in the community struggled:

> Life here, well, it was a simulated slavery. Even though they weren't beaten, they were always under the control of the *patrón* [master]. And there was something else, something you can see all over Mexico, in the poorest families in the rural areas, we're very addicted to alcohol. . . . Because the *hacendados* [hacienda owners] also left us this legacy. They made the alcohol from the sugarcane, the *aguardiente*. If the campesino came to them on Saturday, the day when they handed out things from the company store, they always included a little bottle of *aguardiente*.

Arrazola, under the authority of Pedro Larrañaga Calvo, along with his wife, Zenaida, was one of nineteen estates operating in the center district of Oaxaca at the onset of the Mexican Revolution (Velasco Rodríguez and Aguilar Sánchez 2000).[5] However, the status quo of life on the Arrazola *finca* remained intact despite the violent upheavals throughout much of the rest of the country. Rural Oaxacans' relative lack of participation in the revolutionary movement is generally explained in terms of the unique history of the region's colonization. Historian William Taylor (1972) describes the revolution elsewhere in Mexico as a struggle for land and economic independence, not for political freedom. Indigenous communities in the Central Valleys of Oaxaca were able to retain control over much of their pre-Conquest landholdings, remaining agriculturally self-sufficient. Thus the revolutionary movement never gained the momentum there that it did in other parts of Mexico, where land-ownership was consolidated in the hands of the elite.

Still, this does not fully explain why Arrazola workers were not moved to insurrection; nearly all had migrated to the estate from communities in other regions of Oaxaca, while the lands on which they lived and worked were not ancestral lands, but belonged to a member of the Spanish landowning class. In this regard, the status of Arrazola workers resembled that of the peasantry in other parts of Mexico where the revolution took hold. It might be surmised that workers did not participate in the historical struggle out of fear of forfeiting what meager wages they did earn if the estate were forced out of business or due to the general lack of momentum of the revolutionary cause in Oaxaca.

Despite the relative stability of the Larrañaga estate throughout the elsewhere-turbulent revolutionary period and the decade following it, it did not survive the subsequent large-scale agrarian reforms implemented by President Lázaro Cárdenas (1934–1940). The 177 hectares that made up the Arrazola estate at the turn of the twentieth century were ultimately broken up, and in 1937 became the independent community known as San Antonio Arrazola. While the Larrañaga family retained a small parcel of land, including the piece on which the family home was located, the majority of the holdings were designated as *ejido* lands and redistributed among the residents of Arrazola.[6] Small portions were also allocated to the adjacent communities of San Pedro Ixtlahuaca, Santa María Atzompa, and Cuilapan de Guerrero. Arrazola did not have the long-standing legal status as an independent community that the other towns did, having only recently been granted the official designation as an *agencia* under the jurisdiction of the nearby municipality of Xoxocotlán.[7] In comparison with the other *ejido* endowments, the land originally allocated to Arrazola was small; by the time I carried out my fieldwork, the town possessed just 144 hectares of *ejido* land, according to the head of the local *ejido* commission.[8]

Despite poor working and living conditions on the estate, its patronage system fostered a sense of loyalty among certain Arrazola residents toward Pedro Larrañaga, a man described by one elderly Arrazola woman as being extremely "bad-tempered." Oral histories conducted with her and another of the town's oldest residents, whose family worked on the estate prior to its dissolution, revealed that some workers sided with the landowner during the legal proceedings by which the property was redistributed, causing a degree of strife among families. After the breakup of his estate, Larrañaga decided to leave Oaxaca and resettle his family in the state of Veracruz, where he went on to become a wealthy naval officer (Serrie 1964). The family rarely returned to Oaxaca, and the large home that had once served as the headquarters of their sugarcane-processing operation fell into disrepair.

Even after Arrazola became an independent town, the overall standard of living remained relatively unchanged, despite the minor improvements ushered in by postrevolutionary policies and programs. The community received its first permanent schoolteacher in 1942, the result of a national push to educate Mexico's largely nonliterate (often indigenous) rural population, but still lacked electricity, sewage and drainage systems, paved roads, and a clean water supply.[9] Male residents supported themselves and their families primarily through subsistence agriculture and by working as hired laborers in and around Oaxaca. Some worked for just over a peso per day at the nearby Monte Albán archaeological site, where archaeologist Alfonso Caso had initiated an extensive excavation project in 1931 (see chapter 2).[10] Employment options for Arrazola women were far more limited. The lack of transportation between the village and the city prevented them from vending in the weekly local markets, which would have been a socially acceptable form of economic participation outside of the home for rural women at the time. Most instead devoted their time to caring for their homes and children in addition to helping with agricultural production on the small plots of *ejido* land.

The United States' entry into World War II presented another income-generating opportunity for Arrazola men. A depleted American labor force, coupled with a wartime demand for manufactured goods, led to a mutual agreement between the U.S. and Mexico (under presidents Franklin D. Roosevelt and Manuel Avila Camacho, respectively) to allow Mexican migrants to enter the U.S. as a temporary workforce. Legislation for the Emergency Farm Labor program, also known as the

Bracero Program ("bracero" meaning laborer in Spanish), was enacted in 1942. Although it was initially designed to supply agricultural workers to parts of the American Southwest, U.S. lawmakers expanded the program soon after, in 1943, to also include nonagricultural labor. At the termination of the program in 1964, the U.S. was host to at least 300,000 Mexicans working in twenty-five different states (Meyer and Sherman 1995). In Arrazola, as similarly noted for other central Oaxacan craft-producing communities (Cohen 1999; Stephen 1991), participation in the Bracero Program was a major factor in the large-scale penetration of commercial capital into the local economy.[11] It also set in motion a pattern of international out-migration to the U.S. that continues at an accelerated rate today, though a large percentage of present-day Arrazola transnational migrants are undocumented.

The nostalgia with which many Arrazola men today recount their stories of going to the U.S. as braceros is also tinged with memories of backbreaking work, low wages, and substandard living conditions in the work camps. The social climate of the pre–civil rights era was far from welcoming to these racially marked workers, few of whom spoke any English. One seventy-year-old former bracero recalled the humiliating physical examination he received upon arriving at a Texas inspection station. He and other men in his group were ordered to line up against a wall and then, without explanation, were required to strip off their clothing so that they could be liberally doused with insecticide powder from head to toe.

Equally disturbing were the financial abuses suffered by the braceros. The terms of the program required that a 10 percent deduction be taken from workers' earnings and deposited in a savings fund set up with a Mexican bank, in most cases without the workers' knowledge. However, the funds were never paid back to the workers, and by the time they found out about the 10 percent deduction they were unable to claim their money, since the bank that had originally managed the funds no longer existed.[12] Neither government was able to account for the lost money, to which should be added the interest accrued over the past forty years. Today in Arrazola twenty-six former braceros are active participants in a bi-national movement called the *Alianza BraceroProa* (BraceroProa Alliance) that seeks to recuperate the lost wages through organized political protest as well as class-action lawsuits; they are regular fixtures at bracero rallies in Oaxaca and other Mexican cities (fig. 2.1). In 2003 a former bracero from Arrazola served as the general secretary on the advisory committee of the Oaxacan division of BraceroProa, responsible for organizing the twenty-one central Oaxacan communities that originally sent guest workers to the U.S.

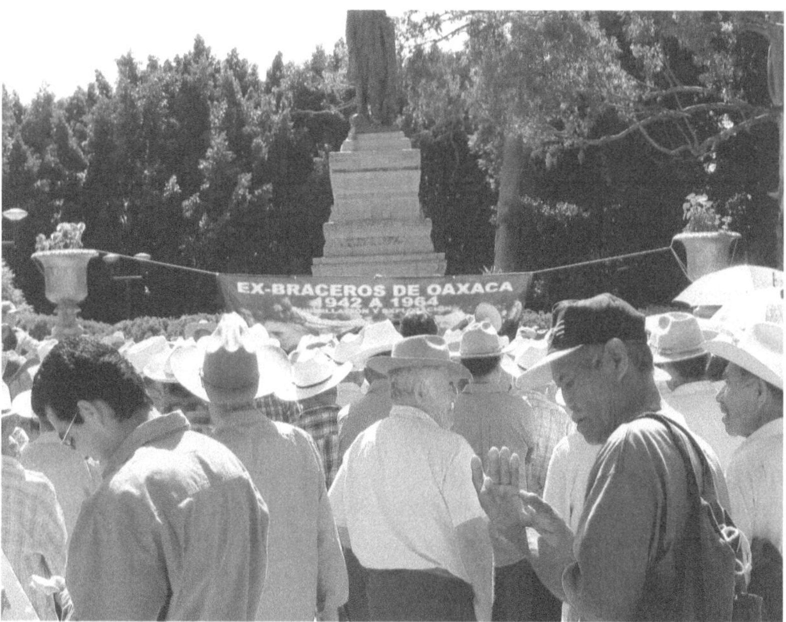

FIGURE 2.1. *Former braceros from Arrazola and other communities attend a rally in Oaxaca as part of the movement of former U.S. guest workers to reclaim their garnished wages. (Photograph by author)*

The Bracero Program provided only a temporary economic stimulus for Arrazola, a town with far too little land to support its growing population, which by the early 1960s had reached nearly four hundred people (Chibnik 2003:67).[13] Work contracts were short (usually 8–12 months), and although returning workers could reapply for contracts, they recognized the limits of wartime employment. With the termination of the guest worker program in 1964, some residents resumed work as wage laborers on construction jobs in the city in order to supplement the small harvests yielded by their *ejido* land. Other enterprising individuals had begun selling archaeological fragments to tourists at Monte Albán, a trade that eventually gave way to the organized sale of replica crafts (see chapter 3).

Economic transformations notwithstanding, Arrazola remained one of the poorest communities in the municipality. The situation improved somewhat when a dirt road to Oaxaca was completed in the early 1960s and automobile traffic could finally reach the town. Regular, twice-weekly bus service presented greater possibilities for work and commerce in the city. This was especially true for Arrazola women, who could now buy and sell goods in the city's bustling Abastos market, relocated in 1972 from its downtown location to its present site on the city's south side. The paving of the road in 1976 further facilitated travel to and from Arrazola, but even through the mid-1980s bus and taxi service was still intermittent and unreliable.

BECOMING A VILLAGE OF ARTISANS

The lives of Arrazola residents changed rapidly and dramatically—most would say for the better—when the town emerged in the mid-1980s as one of the principal producers of Oaxacan wood carvings. Wood carving not only precipitated widespread economic development, but also established the town's reputation as a community of innovative and talented artisans. According to one source, by 1998 the wood carvings had become the "bestselling Mexican folk art in the U.S." (Hancock Sandoval 1998:123), and today the village's public image is tightly bound to the production of wooden figurines. Even as sales of wood carvings began to taper off in the late 1990s and many talented carvers left the village to work in the United States, Arrazola maintained its national and international fame as a community of woodcarving artisans.

The creation of the wood-carving genre familiar to today's consumers—fantastical carved animals adorned with acrylic paints—is often attributed to Manuel Jiménez, who continued to live and work in Arrazola at the time of my fieldwork, but later passed away, in the fall of 2005, at the age of eighty-six. As Chibnik (2003) notes in his extensive study of Oaxacan wood carving, Jiménez was not the first individual in the village to try his hand at carving. In fact, several Arrazola carvers achieved considerable local recognition in the 1930s for the masks they made for All Saints' Day celebrations. But it was Jiménez who initiated the transformation of wood carving from a local tradition, albeit one with a limited outside market, to a fully commercialized folk art genre that would eventually attract the attention of collectors from all over the world.

Jiménez's personal history was truly a rags-to-riches story, one which he enthusiastically recounted to inquiring journalists, tourists, children's book authors, and anthropologists alike, but which was also confirmed by other Arrazola residents. Born on the Arrazola estate in 1919, Jiménez always maintained special ties with the Larrañaga family despite the impoverished conditions in which he and his family lived on their estate. As the godson of the landowner, a relationship established through the fictive kinship system of *compadrazgo*, Jiménez enjoyed certain privileges that other laborers on the *finca* did not, including serving as the sacristan at the estate's small chapel.[14] His allegiance to his patrons was unwavering even during the postrevolutionary land reforms, when Jiménez refused to claim any share of the lands divested from the estate. With no land and no other means of supporting himself, he left Arrazola for the neighboring state of Veracruz, where he worked for approximately three years cutting sugarcane (Serrie 1964). When Jiménez returned to Arrazola in 1940, job opportunities were nearly as limited as when he had left. He worked as both an agricultural laborer and an adobe mason in order to support his wife, whom he married in 1941, and their growing family. According to Jiménez and others in the village, his household was one of the poorest in Arrazola.

Jiménez later joined the work crews at the nearby Monte Albán archaeological zone, where he was hired as a guard and worked various excavation seasons throughout the 1940s and into the early 1950s. Like other men from Arrazola, Jiménez recalled tourists occasionally approaching him at the site and asking if he had unearthed any figurines he would be willing to sell. While he admittedly sold the occasional ceramic fragment, his employment at Monte Albán opened up the possibility of a more lucrative venture. According to Jiménez, as a young boy he had always enjoyed whittling, mainly because it helped him pass the long hours he often spent away from home while tending the Larrañaga family's livestock. His fondness for woodworking and an admiration for the masks traditionally crafted for village celebrations led to his carving during the long and mostly uneventful hours that he was on guard duty at Monte Albán.

Jiménez's early pieces were primarily masks of stylized human forms, but also included experimental carvings such as fanciful owls with moveable parts. He sold his work to both locals in the Oaxaca market and interested tourists whom he met up at the archaeological site. His network of clients expanded as word of his talent spread. In 1957 two Oaxaca-based folk art dealers, Arthur Train and Enrique de la Lanza, offered him a contract for the unlimited production of wood carvings (Chibnik 2003:25). By the late 1950s, Jiménez had abandoned other job pursuits in order to devote himself to carving full-time, and for the duration of his life he produced pieces for an almost exclusively foreign clientele.

Even with the success of Manuel Jiménez, the rest of Arrazola was slow to embrace wood carving. Through the end of the 1960s, Jiménez remained the only resident to earn a significant income from wood-carving production. Chibnik (2003) attributes the slow development of wood carving to a variety of reasons, notably the incipient market for the wood-carving craft as well as Jiménez's policy of keeping his techniques and materials a well-kept secret from other villagers. To this I would add that wood carving first emerged in Arrazola during a period in which many male residents were going to the United States as *braceros*. As noted above, these contracts were short but perhaps regarded as less financially risky than wood carving, a craft whose profit margin was still undetermined. Additionally, the late 1960s and early 1970s witnessed a surge in the number of men selling archaeological fragments and, increasingly, replica crafts at Monte Albán (the topic of chapter 3). According to vendors who worked at Monte Albán during this time, sales of pre-Hispanic pieces (both originals and replicas) were high. Tourism at the site was still something of a novelty, and many tourists reportedly believed they were buying original artifacts when in fact they were purchasing replicas. The relative success attained by some Arrazola vendors at the archaeological zone delayed their entry into the wood-carving trade or prevented it altogether.

Manuel Jiménez's monopoly on wood carving was temporary. The 1970s and 1980s witnessed an increase in the number, albeit small, of Arrazola families involved in the part-time production of wood carvings. Chibnik (2003) cites two factors contributing to the village's economic transformation. First, Train and de la Lanza grew tired of dealing solely with Jiménez, who has been described elsewhere as nothing less than "a difficult artist" (Barbash 1993:19). The two began to seek out and encourage new talent, not only in Arrazola but also in La Unión Tejalapan, a smaller village located to the northwest of Oaxaca. Second, the Mexican government launched a number of initiatives and programs, particularly during the presidency of Luis Echeverría (1970–1976), aimed at stimulating artisan production throughout the nation. Despite these developments, wood carving remained a supplemental rather than a primary economic activity for most Arrazola residents up through the mid-1980s (the exception being the Jiménez family and a few of their close relatives). The bulk of household income was still generated from vending at Monte Albán, agriculture, wage work such as construction, and remittances sent by family members working in the United States.

Things began to change in 1986 as the market for Oaxacan wood carvings saw a tremendous increase in demand fueled by clients from the United States. Over the next five years, a period identified as "the woodcarving boom," nearly every household in Arrazola began to participate in the production of wood carvings (Chibnik 2003:39). Demand for the pieces was high, especially among middle- and upper-class American collectors. Families found themselves working around the clock in order to fill the orders placed by the wholesalers and retailers who now frequently visited the village. The household division of labor usually meant that men carved, while women, and some children, painted and sanded.[15] During the boom years, it seemed that any Arrazola man who could wield a machete and the arsenal of razor-sharp knives tried his hand at carving.[16]

Among those eager to achieve economic stability through wood carving, a promising and socially encouraged occupation, were a number of young men who regularly sold replicas at Monte Albán. At least five of them, all in their late teens and early twenties at the time, decided to abandon replica vending in favor of full-time carving, achieving varying degrees of success. Others combined their vending at Monte Albán with intermittent activities associated with wood carving, from making pieces to painting or merely reselling the work of others in the community. The emerging craft trade appeared so promising relative to other occupations available to Arrazola families that it is estimated that by 1990 roughly 70 percent of village households included an individual who derived part of his or her income from wood carving (Chibnik 2003:46).

It is difficult to overstate the role of the wood-carving trade in the socioeconomic transformation of Arrazola. Not only did wood carving become one of the town's primary sources of income (along with remittances sent by residents working in the United States), but it also became its principal marker of identity in the competitive tourism market that is the bedrock of the Oaxacan economy (fig. 2.2).[17] Despite a significant downturn in sales since 2000, particularly during the periods immediately following the 9/11 attacks in the United States and the 2006 teachers' strike, the alebrijes remained, in the words of an Oaxacan Secretariat of Tourism official, "perhaps the craft most representative of Oaxaca, maybe even more popular than black pottery."[18] At the time of my fieldwork, Arrazola residents conceptualized themselves as primarily a community of wood-carving artisans, even though not everyone was directly involved with wood carving; outsiders, tourists, and local Oaxacans alike generally shared this perception.

Arrazola has enjoyed relative prosperity in comparison with surrounding settlements, and tourists today are welcomed by a town much changed from twenty, and even ten, years earlier. The manicured plaza, mostly paved roads, a regular taxi service running every fifteen minutes,

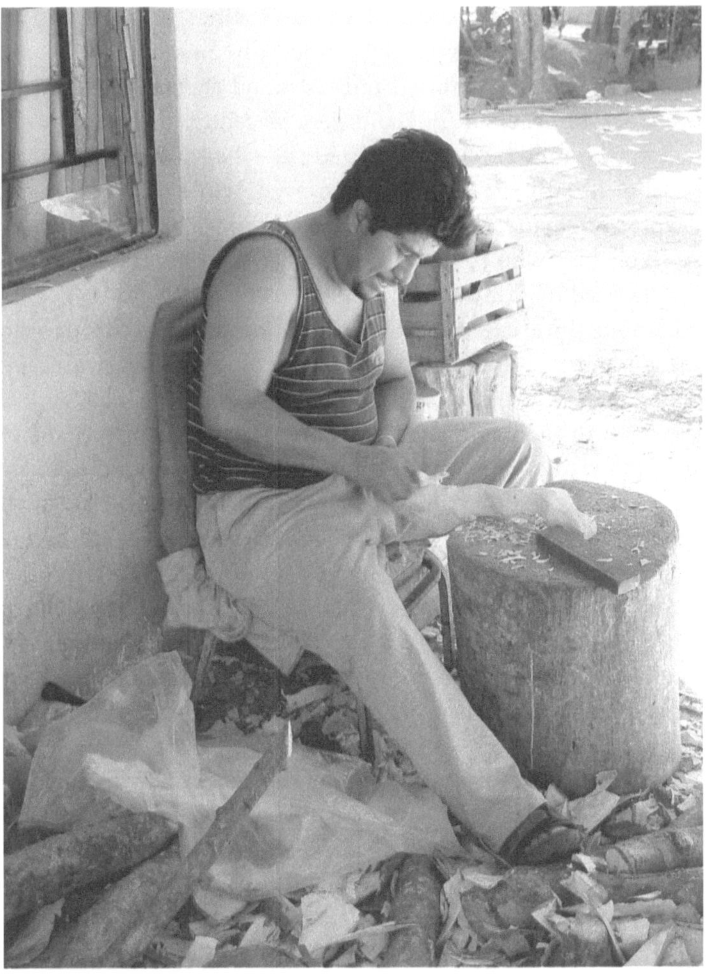

FIGURE 2.2. *Catarino Carrillo carving in front of his workshop. (Photograph by author)*

and cement-block homes—some wired for telephone service and sporting digital television dishes—are physical testaments to the economic transformation of the village, particularly during the last decade. As of 1997, the town benefits from a weekly garbage collection service and a regularly staffed government health clinic, both of which have improved the overall health of residents. With the addition of elementary and secondary schools, people no longer have to travel to nearby Xoxocotlán or Oaxaca in order to access basic healthcare and educational facilities. To be sure, all residents have not benefited equally from Arrazola's entrance into the highly competitive world of Oaxacan folk art, and the discrepancies in the material standards of living of its wealthiest and poorest families are tangible. Many households are now able to purchase cars and benefit from time-saving appliances such as washing machines.[19] Meanwhile others still live in adobe-walled homes and cook family meals on wood-burning stoves. Nevertheless, the growing numbers of residents with cell phones, DVD players, iPods, and cars make Arrazola feel increasingly like a suburb of Oaxaca, rather than the rural community it was fifty years ago.

Even the old estate, whose crumbling, vine-covered walls sat undisturbed at the village entrance for nearly half a century, is receiving a makeover (fig. 2.3). In addition to holding title to 25 hectares of Arrazola land, the original landowner's grandson, Arturo Larrañaga, a successful medical doctor and businessman who owns several pharmacies in and outside of Oaxaca, retains control over the large estate home in which his ancestors once resided. In limited consultation with Arrazola's town council members, he had started to restore the property to its original condition. Once it was completed, he hoped to open a luxury hotel and restaurant that would capitalize on Arrazola's convenient

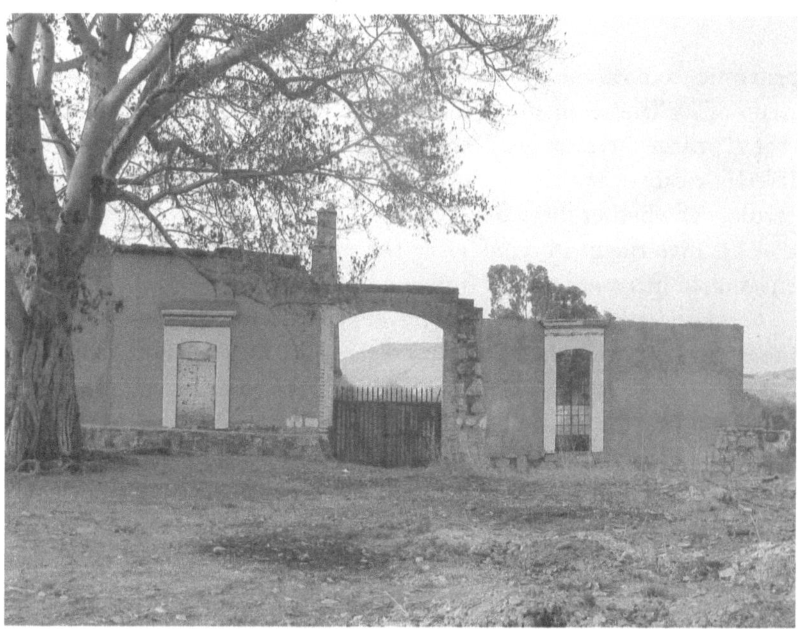

FIGURE 2.3. *The outside façade of the original Arrazola estate home, located at the entrance to the town. (Photograph by author)*

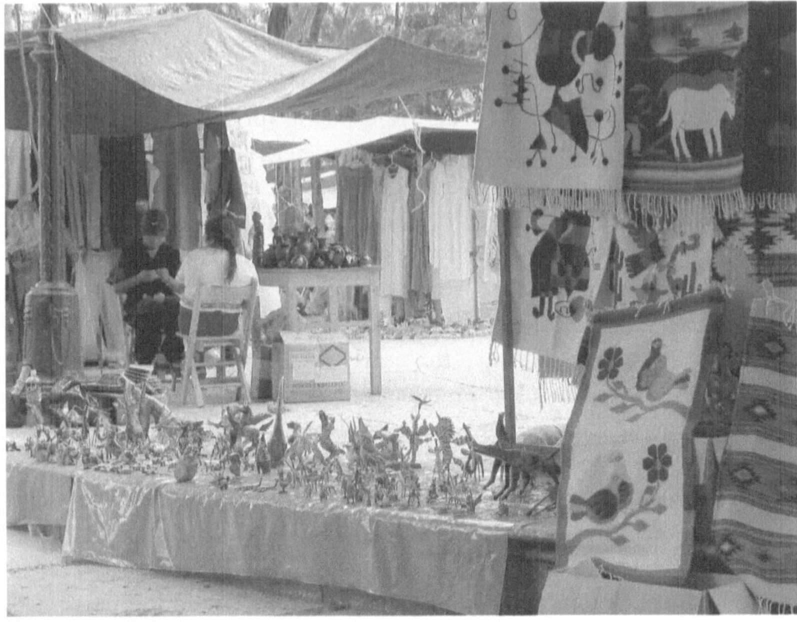

FIGURE 2.4. *Wood carvings paired with woven rugs at an Ocotlán market stall. (Photograph by author)*

proximity to both the city of Oaxaca and Monte Albán—and the popularity of its handicrafts. According to Larrañaga, there was speculation that a private investor was looking to build (pending approval from INAH) a cable car that would connect Monte Albán to Arrazola. Regardless of whether the cable car project materialized, he was confident that his investment in remodeling the property would pay off, and he envisioned increased tourist traffic to the town.

Mexican and foreign folk art buyers and dealers also profited from the explosive popularity of the wood carvings. Folk art stores throughout the city of Oaxaca added wood carvings to their inventories, from well-established, upscale galleries such as Mano Mágica (owned by a Canadian expatriate and her Oaxacan husband), to smaller stores carrying less expensive regional crafts. At least two stores in the city of Oaxaca specialized exclusively in wood carvings. Wood-carving vendors became permanent fixtures in the city markets and the *zócalo*, the epicenter of tourist traffic. Temporary craft stalls are erected during a number of festivals and major holidays, including Christmas and Holy Week, when thousands of Mexican and international tourists descend upon the city to partake of its festive atmosphere. When Arrazola and

San Martín Tilcajete became regular stops on organized commercial tours, visitors increasingly purchased carvings directly from the artisans themselves. Wood-carving sales have spilled over to other nearby towns such as Ocotlán, which does not produce wood carving but hosts a large weekly market frequented by tourists (fig. 2.4).

Oaxacan wood carving became ubiquitous among foreign folk art dealers' inventories. By the end of the 1990s, Oaxacan wood carvings were carried by nearly all U.S. stores dealing in Mexican folk art, as well as by Canadian, European, and Japanese retailers. Many of these retailers maintained online catalogues of their products, making the pieces easily obtainable over the Internet for would-be buyers unable to shop at the stores' physical locations (Brulotte 1999; Chibnik 2003). Other wood-carving retailers depended solely on the Internet to market their products; eBay.com, a popular web-based auction site, also promoted and sold Oaxacan woodcarvings to a virtual audience of folk art consumers.

POPULAR AND MEDIA REPRESENTATIONS OF OAXACAN WOOD CARVING

Arrazola artisans' rise to fame in the tourist art market was accompanied by a host of narrative and visual representations about their work. Community members suddenly found themselves and their carvings featured in tourist brochures, magazines, Internet websites, and newspaper articles, which also highlighted the two central Oaxacan towns that produced wood carvings, San Martín Tilcajete and La Unión Tejalapan.

Another great boon to Arrazola's woodcraft industry was the writing of Shepard Barbash, an American journalist and long-time collector of Oaxacan wood carvings. Working in conjunction with his wife, photographer Vicki Ragan, Barbash first covered the Oaxacan carvers in an article he wrote for a 1991 edition of *Smithsonian* magazine.[20] He subsequently published an entire book on the subject, *Oaxacan Woodcarving: The Magic in the Trees* (Barbash 1993), whose colorful, coffee-table format appealed to both folk art collectors and Oaxaca aficionados alike. More recently, Arrazola wood-carvers were prominently featured in the book *Mexican Folk Art from Oaxacan Artist Families* (Rothstein and Rothstein 2007). They were also the inspiration for a children's book entitled *Dream Carver* (Cohn and Córdova 2002), a story that, according to its authors, is based on the life of Arrazola carver Manuel Jiménez.

Portrayals of Arrazola and its woodcraft at times veer into fanciful speculation, such as descriptions of carvers ingesting hallucinogenic mushrooms to find inspiration for the psychedelic designs of some of the wood carvings.[21] This claim notwithstanding, most narratives of Arrazola wood-carvers, like those of other Oaxacan artisans, stress their hardworking character, humble origins, and deep-rooted ties to nature and the land, a relationship that has supposedly been cultivated through their prior history as peasant farmers. Ample discussions of the rustic tools and techniques employed by carvers, as well as the uniqueness of each individual piece, are intended to evoke the handmade quality of the wood carvings and set them apart from mass-produced commodities; these are the attributes the carvers themselves identify as central to the creative process and key to stimulating consumer demand.

Perhaps more importantly, representations of Oaxacan wood carving frequently assert a link between the craft and the indigenous heritage of its producers (Brulotte 1999). A fascination with the material culture of indigenous Oaxacans has been noted by other scholars (Cohen 1999; López 2010; Stephen 1993; Wood 2008), and in the case of wood carving, indigeneity is a value-added component in their marketing to a foreign, overwhelmingly North American audience (Chibnik 2003). Ethnicity in Arrazola (as elsewhere in central Oaxaca) is an issue with deep historical roots—one whose very complexity defies the simple indigenous/mestizo dichotomy to which it is frequently reduced. As I discuss at length in chapter 6, the process by which Arrazola residents are racialized as indigenous is never complete, as community members both identify and dis-identify with such classifications.

That many modern Mesoamerican arts and craftwork reflect in their very form a dynamic, creative interaction with the emerging demands of tourists and other cultural brokers has not been lost on anthropologists. For instance, Jeff Kowalski's 2009 volume on contemporary wood sculptures from the Puuc Region of Yucatán, Mexico (also designed as an exhibit catalogue), explores how its makers reclaim and retask the cultural imagery of Mayan archaeology to produce an innovative modern art genre. Contributors to the volume critically distinguish the creative play of aesthetic form and content of traditional Mesoamerican iconography from some deeply accumulated local traditions or knowledge. Rather than being perceived as inward-looking cultural survivalists, carvers are depicted as cosmopolitan social actors who engage with broad transnational forces that include international museum worlds, archaeological practice, and heritage tourism.

This critique finds its opposition in popular media that insist upon casting Oaxacan craft production, including wood carving, as a linear continuation of pre-Hispanic social and material life. The tendency is implicit in the popular travel guide *Oaxaca Handbook*, which opens with a section entitled "Arts and Crafts" with the following passage:

> Many [craft] traditions reach back thousands of years, to the beginnings of Mesoamerican civilization. The accumulated knowledge of manifold generations of artisans has, in many instances, resulted in finery so prized that whole villages devote themselves to the manufacture of a certain class of goods. (Whipperman 2000:74)

Elsewhere, wood carvings are attributed ceremonial or religious functions in concordance with a folk Catholicism tinged with remnants of pre-Hispanic superstitions and beliefs, such as this description by an Internet retailer:

> Steeped into traditional folktales and beliefs, the Oaxacan wood carvers borrow and improvise themes and motifs from the region's diverse Indian tribes. Folkways have intermingled alongside Spanish ideologies as the populations overlapped, while still uniquely remaining intact. (http://oaxacanwoodcarving.com/mythnatr.html, accessed Feb. 19, 2010)

When the newness of Arrazola wood carving is acknowledged, this detail is often qualified with additional commentary about how rural Oaxacans have been carving wooden toys and religious figures for centuries. Wood carvings, then, are slotted into readily recognizable and consumable tropes of cultural syncretism or continuity in which archaeological and anthropological notions of "culture" are refracted through a popular lens.

Noticeably less sentimental, and meriting attention here, is Shepard Barbash's previously mentioned book, *Oaxacan Woodcarving*, perhaps the single most widely read work on the subject. It is sold in many of the same stores that carry Oaxacan wood carvings (and incidentally, at the Monte Albán gift shop) and is often referenced on Internet websites that market the pieces. A small, compact book, it features eye-catching color photographs. These photographs of individual wood carvings perhaps take center stage, but the text itself is equally compelling. What is interesting about Barbash's writing is that it makes explicit use of the standard tropes employed by journalists and other cultural brokers, including some anthropologists, to capture the everyday rhythm of life in the wood-carving villages. Chibnik in fact describes Barbash as a "quasi-anthropologist," noting that his research for the book relied heavily on participant observation in the wood-carving communities (Chibnik 2003:176). Thus Barbash's work addresses not only the aesthetic aspects of wood carving, but also the social and economic contexts of its production, giving it the feel of ethnography rather than a simple catalogue of promising artisans' work.

Like anthropology of an earlier era, Barbash's text focuses on woodcarvers' inherent fatalism, love of fiestas, and superstitious beliefs. Notably, these perceptions owe much to older—now thoroughly problematized—anthropological representations.[22] This is demonstrated, for example, by the structure of the book; it is organized into four thematic chapters, each of which addresses a cultural component or trait that apparently provides the artistic template for individual creations. While the author's chosen categories—fiestas, nature, death, and superstition—are important concepts that are both structured by and give meaning to artisans' experiences, they are certainly not the only ones that do so. Factors such as ongoing transnational migration (even during the years when wood-carving sales were at their peak) and residents' increasing access to and implementation of new media technologies also form part of the cultural milieu in which new wood-carving styles emerge. Barbash mentions these phenomena in passing as anecdotes from carvers' personal biographies, but in this volume the more traditional aspects of village social life are given primacy as a source of artistic inspiration.

A subsequent book by Barbash and his wife, *Changing Dreams: A Generation of Oaxaca's Woodcarvers* (2007), revisits many of the artisans featured in the first book, tracking the changes in their lives since the start of the wood-carving boom; it is visually and textually darker in tone, featuring Ragan's black-and-white photographs alongside prose detailing the travails experienced by individual wood-carvers and their families. Still, the appeal of the original story is undeniable, and as one folk art dealer in Santa Fe, New Mexico, stressed to me, "Shep [Barbash] singlehandedly created a market for wood carving. He did more to help those guys than anyone else."

WOOD CARVING ON DISPLAY

Many of the discourses identified in the marketing of Oaxacan wood carvings and other craft forms are reproduced through the everyday interactions of tourists, guides, and the artisans themselves. W. Warner Wood (2008), for example, describes a textile workshop tour in the Oaxacan town of Teotitlán del Valle (also an easy day trip from Oaxaca City), where cultural authenticity and continuity with the pre-Hispanic past are asserted through the medium of cochineal, a traditional, native red dye obtained from the insect of the same name. During colonial times, before the production of synthetic dyes, Oaxaca was a major supplier of red dye to the rest of the world. Today, woolen textiles colored with natural dyes like cochineal and indigo command higher prices from discerning buyers. Wood observes that a textile's symbolic and market value is enhanced through widely circulating ideas about cochineal, mobilized in the space of the workshop encounter. He writes:

> Mexican tourists who come to Oaxaca and take guided tours to Teotitlán already know about the famous cochineal. [One Teotitlán weaver] strongly suggests to them that Zapotec textiles (and especially Zapotec textiles dyed with cochineal) are valuable because they embody secret knowledge passed down to Zapotec weavers as the living descendants of those who built the great pre-Hispanic settlements of ancient Mexico. Through their experience of the tour and weaving demonstration, Mexican tourists create for themselves their own version of why a Zapotec textile is worth owning, and correspondingly, why cochineal is famous. (Wood 2008:72)

Wood's experiences in the weaving workshops of Teotitlán echo my own in Arrazola wood-carving workshops, where I found tourists eager to get to the "back stage" (MacCannell 1999) area of the wood-carving process—the region where authentic, nontourist activity allegedly takes place (fig. 2.5). Yet as other tourism scholars (e.g., Bruner 2004; Kirshenblatt-Gimblett 1998) have emphasized, reaching the "back stage" is an ever more elusive goal as tourism penetrates more deeply into the social fabric of the communities being toured. In this case, the performance of daily life for tourists centers on the wood-carving workshop, which, given their central locations within home spaces, are often simultaneously public and private domains.

In the fall of 2002 I visited the home of one well-known Arrazola wood-carver as part of a day tour organized by a downtown Oaxaca hotel. Standing above the carver as he worked in a kneeling position on a bare cement floor, our Mexican guide drew our attention to the "rustic

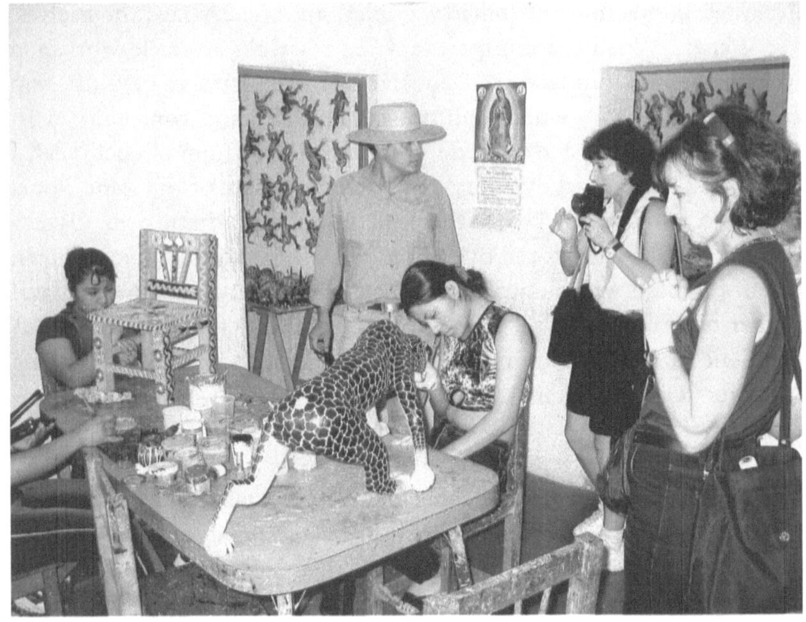

FIGURE 2.5. *A tour group from Mexico City and an Oaxacan guide look on as young women paint wood carvings in an Arrazola workshop. (Photograph by author)*

tools" used by the artisan and the uniqueness of each handcrafted piece. He added that "the Indian people of Oaxaca have a love for bright colors," his explanation for the vivid, and sometimes psychedelic, designs found on finished pieces. As we stood transfixed by the fluid motions of the carver at work, a woman in our group from Mexico City (who incidentally did not buy any wood carvings) turned and commented to no one in particular, "These people are truly artists." The awe in her voice was unmistakable, yet the wood-carver, a young man in his early twenties most likely accustomed to such reactions, acknowledged neither the woman's praise nor the guide's comment. Instead, he continued to focus all of his attention on the details of the iguana tail taking shape under his knife.

After giving us sufficient time to admire the young artisan at work, our guide led us to another workshop just down the street. Having already spent time in Arrazola, I knew that this workshop was the town's largest wood-carving operation and that it utilized an assembly line form of production to create the hundreds of wood carvings that decorated its expansive showroom walls. On a previous visit, I had entered a separate room off to one side of the compound that housed some electric tools, including a table saw. Not surprisingly, this room was mainly off-limits to tourists. (I should add that this particular workshop was not representative of the majority of Arrazola workshops, which neither relied on power tools nor employed artisans from outside of the community.) The tour guide drew our attention to the individual craftsmanship that went into the pieces. "All of them made by hand," he proclaimed. He also introduced us to the woman in charge, whom I recognized as the wife of the workshop's owner. The guide explained to our group that this was a family operation as the woman nodded in agreement. Just in case we were not convinced, she added, "We're all from the same family." I resisted the urge to correct the guide by pointing out the fact that two of the five wood-carvers that were chipping away at pieces of copal wood were from a small settlement nearby, locally referred to as a *ranchería*, something I had learned on a previous visit to the workshop.[23]

Another incident just two weeks later further underscored how Arrazola and its most famous craft, both products of the twentieth century, have been cast as vestiges of a premodern past. While in the city on some errands, I met an Italian photographer who had just returned to Oaxaca after shooting the Day of the Dead celebration in Arrazola, which included a colorful procession known locally as a *calenda*. He intended to display his work as part of a photography exhibit on traditional village life at a downtown Oaxaca art gallery. When I explained to him that I was living and conducting research in the community, he expressed approval of my choice of an anthropological fieldsite, noting that the town's wood-carving tradition would make a fascinating research topic. His concluding remark to me was that "Arrazola is a beautiful and artistic town, and the villagers there aren't yet too spoiled by the outside." The photographer, like most tourists I met, seemed unfamiliar with Arrazola's participation in the Monte Albán replica trade, a topic to which I turn in chapter 3.

FAMILY PHOTO

Convincing his sister to let him borrow the photo would not be easy, warned Antonio Aragón,[1] a longtime replica seller at Monte Albán. When his father passed away some years ago, Antonio's sister appointed herself caretaker of all of the important documents and the few family heirlooms that he left behind. She kept the photo under lock and key at her home, guarding the valuable family possession, somewhat jealously it seemed, from the other siblings. Yes, he stressed, it would be difficult to convince her to loan him the photo, even if only for a day or two. But he had been promising to show me the photograph for over a month, and Antonio was a man true to his word; he gently but unrelentingly reminded his sister that he needed to borrow the photo until she finally gave in.

Antonio was well aware of my interest in the early archaeological excavations at Monte Albán, particularly the role of Arrazola residents in those early projects. He was a consummate storyteller who loved to recount the stories that his grandfather had told him about the pre-Hispanic artifacts and architecture he had seen while working at Monte Albán in the 1930s. In one of our many interview sessions, Antonio told me the story of how his grandfather had been part of the work crew that discovered the famous Tomb 7, considered to be among the richest finds in Mesoamerican archaeology.

The photo turned out to be much smaller than I expected, not quite the dimensions of an index card. At some point it had been run through a laminating machine and now re-

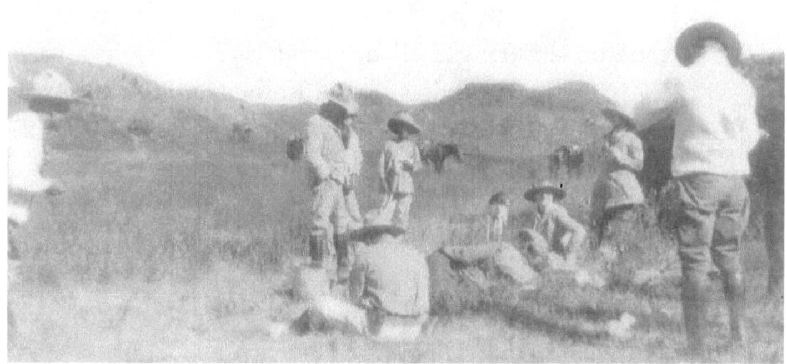

FIGURE 3.0. *Photograph of an early expedition to Monte Albán, ca. 1920s or 1930s. (Photo courtesy of the Antonio Aragón Hernández family)*

sembled a black-and-white trading card. The plastic coating was beginning to split open at the bottom right-hand corner, threatening to expose the delicate paper underneath. A few gray speckles dotted the bottom of the photo near the spot where the laminated material had started to split open—mildew, I would later find out, from having been carried in his brother-in-law's pocket as he sold replicas through many an afternoon rainstorm at Monte Albán. The image itself had the hazy quality of many early twentieth-century photographs. Although no one knew for certain the exact year in which the snapshot had been taken, Antonio guessed that it was around 1920, and certainly before 1932, the year in which Alfonso Caso discovered Tomb 7.

The scene was one of small group of men and women taking a break (fig. 3.0), maybe stopping for a drink or perhaps lunch, after making their way to the flat, open space at the top of Monte Albán that would later be identified by archaeologists as the main plaza. The party consisted of at least nine individuals (including the photographer), the horses that likely carried them up the steep slopes, and a dog who, given its close proximity to the elegantly attired woman, may have been the pet of one of the group's members. Although I hardly considered myself to be a photography expert, I could tell that the image was not technically well composed. Most of the subjects had their backs turned away from the camera or were only partially facing it, suggesting a candid shot rather than a planned portrait. In fact, the only person who appeared to be making eye contact with the camera was a small-framed man, his face virtually hidden by the shadow of his large hat, who stood on the fringes of the gathering.

My eyes squinted as I tried to focus more closely on this man who seemed at once present yet strangely distant. He clutched something close to his chest that I could not make out. With his gaze fixed straight ahead, he did not seem to share in the casual conversation and company of the others. Unlike the others in the photo, who wore ensembles consisting of fitted jackets, vests, belts, and riding boots, the seemingly dark-skinned man donned none of these items, which at that time would have been requisite for a well-outfitted ride or expedition to the countryside. The man wore a loose shirt and pants, and, although I could not see his shoes, I imagined a pair of leather huaraches encasing his hidden feet. I would still need Antonio's help in identifying the other individuals depicted in the photo, but there was little doubt in my mind as to the identity of the man whose gaze now met mine through the photographic image. It was his grandfather. According to Antonio, on this day he had been hired to escort Alfonso Caso and his party up the then-unexcavated slopes of Monte Albán.

Dusk was giving way to nighttime as I stood there with Antonio in the outside courtyard of his home in Arrazola studying the photo, my eyes straining to see in the rapidly fading light. I heard an unidentifiable shout from the interior space of one of the rooms, and suddenly the single lightbulb strung on a wire overhead lit up. Antonio's brother-in-law, husband to the sister who served as the photo's guardian, and his daughter Leticia, with whom I lived, also happened to be at the house. The four of us stood in a huddle under the light of the bare bulb and stared at the photo.

Leticia had never seen the picture before that evening, but the two men had obviously studied it closely on other occasions, and they regarded it with the same familiarity normally reserved for a cherished family album. As if to confirm my suspicions, Antonio pointed to the man in the middle, whose wide-brimmed hat obscured all but the contours of his face. "Look. That's him, that's my grandfather," he exclaimed with pride. He keenly noted that his grandfather, dressed in homemade peasant clothes, stood apart from the finely dressed group of men and women and that he appeared to be much darker—in his words, "more Indian [*más indio*]"—than the others. "Look at how the people used to dress back then. That's when people still wore clothes they made themselves out of *manta* [homespun cotton cloth]." Leticia and I were silent as we stared at the man in the photo, the great-grandfather she was too young to remember. The brother-in-law eagerly interjected, "And see how he's got his tortilla in his hand? They must have stopped to eat. You can tell because of the basket that's on the ground there in the middle."

Antonio's attention shifted to the animals. "They had to go up Monte Albán by horse back then. There weren't any roads like there are now. No, the roads are recent. It used to be much more difficult to get to the top. See, they're letting the horses graze in the background while they take a break. They even brought their dog with them." He paused for a moment, and then continued, "Remember how I was telling you a few weeks ago that people from Arrazola used to farm the land around Monte Albán?" His finger traced the outline of what appeared to be tall grass and weeds filling the main plaza. "People would plant their *milpas* right here![2] You can't really tell from the photo, but even through the sixties and seventies you could still find corn and beans growing in patches all over Monte Albán. We used to graze our animals there too, our goats."

I was fascinated by these details—both the ones contained in the photo and those added by my companions. Nevertheless, a critical question still remained. "Well, which one of these men is Alfonso Caso?" I asked, anxious to place the name of Mexico's most revered archaeologist with one of the black-and-white faces that appeared in the photo. Perhaps the man with his gaze turned downward, standing to the left of Antonio's grandfather?

"That's him standing right there," he answered, pointing to the image of the man closest to the photographer. The man in the photograph had his back turned completely away from the camera. I was perplexed. "But you can't even see his face. So how can you tell it's Caso?" I pressed.

Antonio turned his head to look at me, and his eyes scolded my impertinence. "Because the gringo, I think he was German, the gringo who gave me the photo at Monte Albán showed me which one he was. He also told me that he thought that the other guy there, next to my grandfather, was an archaeologist too, but he couldn't remember his name. But he was pretty sure that it was one of the archaeologists who worked directly under Caso. My guess is that it's Martín Bazán, or maybe Manuel Valenzuela. I know both of them worked on the excavations, and according to my grandfather both were there when Tomb 7 was discovered."

A loud knock sounded on the metal door to the compound and the huddle around the photograph broke. The brother-in-law announced that he should be heading home, but the fact that he lingered about was his signal to us that he was not going to leave without the photo. Antonio, aware of the potential spousal wrath facing his brother-in-law should he return empty-handed, assured him that he would talk to his sister and let her know that we would be keeping the photo for a couple of days. The brother-in-law accepted his word and slipped out the door without protest. I cannot be sure that the man turned away from the camera was indeed Caso, but the shine in the man's eyes as he spoke left no room for doubt as to the personal connection he felt with Monte Albán's history. I carefully placed the photograph in a folder and took my leave.

CHAPTER THREE

Arrazola's Other Craft

As THE OFFICIAL "BIRTHPLACE OF THE ALEBRIJES," Arrazola is much touted by guidebooks and other media promoting the art and culture of Oaxaca. But complicating Arrazola's image as a traditional wood-carving village is a group of men who dedicate themselves to the production and sale of replicas of pre-Hispanic artifacts at Monte Albán, the largest, most visited archaeological zone in Oaxaca. Unlike wood carving, with its associations of artistic genius and rags-to-riches success stories, the history of the archaeological replica trade and Arrazola's participation in it is little known outside the community except within INAH archaeology circles. In fact, the only publicity it receives is generated by the vendors themselves, who unflaggingly market their wares to tourist visitors at the site (fig. 3.1).

This chapter presents an alternative narrative of Arrazola's historical development, one that focuses on the community's participation in the Monte Albán replica trade. As with wood carving, the production and sale of replicas must be contextualized within Oaxaca's development as a site of cultural tourism for both national and international publics. Archaeologists, state officials, local landholders, and other entrepreneurs have long recognized the import of Monte Albán as a historical, cultural, and tourist resource, and have utilized the site to various ends (Robles García 1996). Arrazola's limited employment opportunities, inadequate land base, and geographic proximity to the ruins were all factors that shaped residents' range of economic activity at Monte Albán. Yet it is the history and nature of replica selling that has been subject to scrutiny and condemnation by INAH archaeologists.

Anthropologist Kees van der Spek (2008) discusses Egyptian artisans from the village of al-Qurna in the Theban Necropolis on Lux-

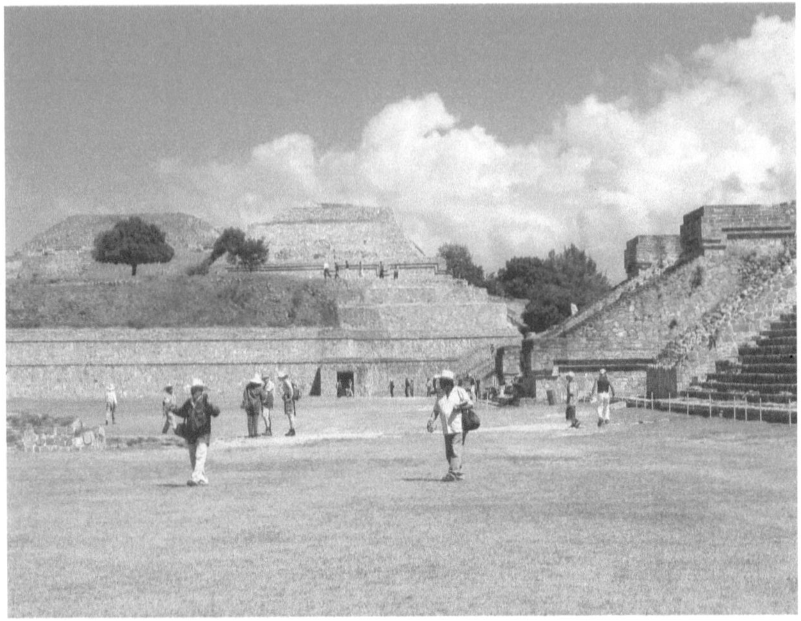

FIGURE 3.1. *Replica vendors positioned to sell in Monte Albán's main plaza. (Photograph by author)*

or's West Bank, which also bears the UNESCO World Heritage designation. Qurnawi villagers have a history of provisioning pharaonic artifacts for foreign interests that goes back to the second half of the eighteenth century, but have more recently turned to making "faked *antikas*" for the tourist trade. I cite van der Spek's work not only because he provides one of the few sustained ethnographic accounts of the production and marketing of modern "ancient" artifacts, but because the relationships and tensions he describes between local craftspeople, tourists, and archaeologists bear a striking resemblance to those I observed at Monte Albán. Indeed, he remarks that "the dynamics that exist between local villagers and international visitors at archaeological sites are obviously not unique to the Luxor west bank" (van der Spek 2008:164). By the same token, he acknowledges archaeology's active role in shaping tourist and other popular representations of al-Qurna and its artisanal output. Noting that local villagers have worked as laborers on foreign archaeological excavations for nearly two hundred years, he found that

> most references about al-Qurna and the reputation of its inhabitants mainly come from, and are coloured by, the professional re-

> ports and popularized accounts which result from archaeological fieldwork practice and from the popular fiction it has inspired. Damage to the archaeological monuments, theft of antiquities, or the illicit excavation and trade in antiquities feature in all these literary forms, but they are inspired by archaeological motivations and concerns rather than by anthropological considerations about how people live and make a living in this archaeological landscape. (van der Spek 2008:165)

A close examination of how Arrazola was historically drawn into the material and social regimes of Monte Albán's production reveals similar forces at play. It was residents' labor that enabled Monte Albán to become a sphere of archaeological knowledge and practice (and tourism) at the same time that it exposed them to a range of physical and discursive disciplinary techniques emanating from within archaeology itself. Today the replica trade manifests a set of self-policing dispositions conditioned by archaeological discourses about vendors' apparent "disregard" for the material relics of history. But these containments, however effective, are never complete, and, as Lena Mortensen and Julie Hollowell remind us, "the subjects and objects traditionally claimed by the discipline of archaeology do not remain 'disciplined' by it but have other, nonarchaeological lives" (2009:11).

In short, Arrazola residents' historical relationship to Monte Albán has been characterized by both cooperation and conflict with state-sponsored archaeology. I present this history as a means to begin disentangling cultural heritage's "layers of morality and politics that undergird various discourses and silences" (Mortensen and Hollowell 2009:11), which shape Monte Albán as both patrimony and spectacle.

LOCATING MONTE ALBÁN

The Monte Albán archaeological site is situated approximately nine kilometers to the southwest of Oaxaca City. Perched on a hilltop artificially leveled by its builders, it is considered by many to be one of the most spectacular archaeological remains of the great Mesoamerican civilizations that once flourished in parts of Mexico and Central America (fig. 3.2). Archaeological evidence suggests that it was an important Zapotec urban center with an occupation period of more than twelve hundred fifty years, from approximately 500 B.C. to A.D. 750 (Winter 2002 [1989]:111).

Archaeologist Richard Blanton characterized Monte Albán as an

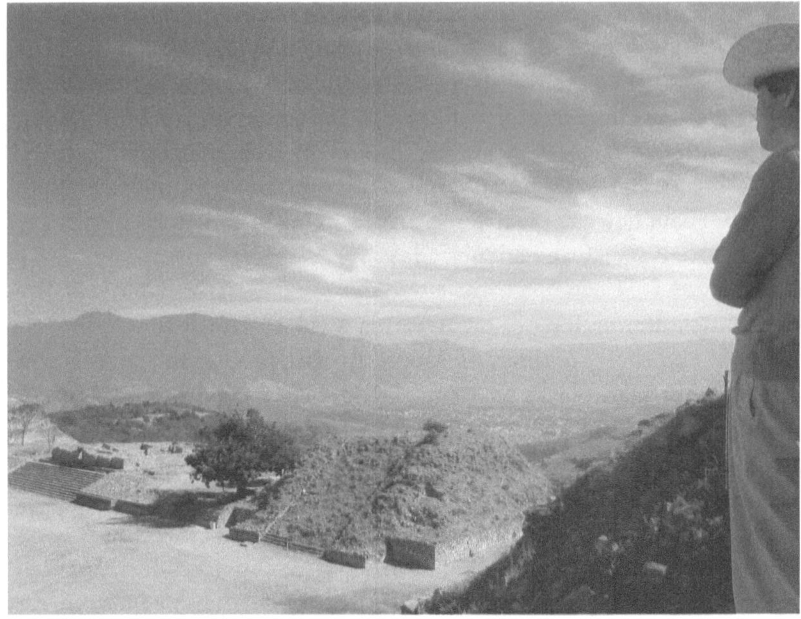

FIGURE 3.2. *A tourist takes in the view from Monte Albán's South Platform. (Photograph by author)*

urban-ceremonial complex dispersed over a series of hilltops, identified as Atzompa, El Gallo, Little Monte Albán, Mogollito, and the Main Plaza, the part of the site that most tourists visit (Blanton 1978). At its apex, the city covered approximately ten square kilometers and was home to approximately 25,000–30,000 inhabitants, making it far and away the largest and most important urban center in ancient Oaxaca in terms of both area and population (Robles García 1993:10). By A.D. 800 Monte Albán was in decline and by A.D. 1000 it had been abandoned; archaeologists are not fully in agreement about whether this was due to epidemic disease, revolt, drought, or some other natural catastrophe. Mixtec populations from the region later made use of the site for religious ceremonies and burials, enhancing the city's legacy as a ritual and political center (Robles García 1993). Most notable were elite burials accompanied by finely worked objects of gold as well as precious stones, obsidian, ceramics, and other goods that marked the interred individuals' high status. When one such burial, the now-famous Tomb 7, was discovered at Monte Albán on January 9, 1932, the preeminent Mexican archaeologist Alfonso Caso appraised its contents as the "richest archaeological find in America" (Caso 1932).[1]

Modern explorations at Monte Albán first commenced in the nineteenth century, and well-known archaeologists Guillermo Dupaix and Adolph Bandelier both contributed early descriptions of the site. A more thorough investigation was later conducted in 1902 by Mexican archaeologist Leopoldo Batres, at the time General Inspector of Monuments under the dictatorial regime of President Porfirio Díaz (see Batres 1902). Nevertheless, it is Alfonso Caso—also the founder and first director of INAH—who is uniformly commemorated as the "discoverer" of Monte Albán, as most of the extensive excavation and reconstruction work was carried out under his direction over the course of eighteen field seasons between 1930 and 1958 (fig. 3.3) (Robles García 1996:42).

The postrevolutionary Mexican government declared Monte Albán a federally protected zone in 1931. Upon its formation in 1939, INAH was charged with the care and preservation of not only Monte Albán but all of the federally declared monument zones throughout the country.[2] Monte Albán was transformed over the next seventy-five years from barely discernible, foliage-covered mounds into the prominent structures that today dominate the landscape. While ostensi-

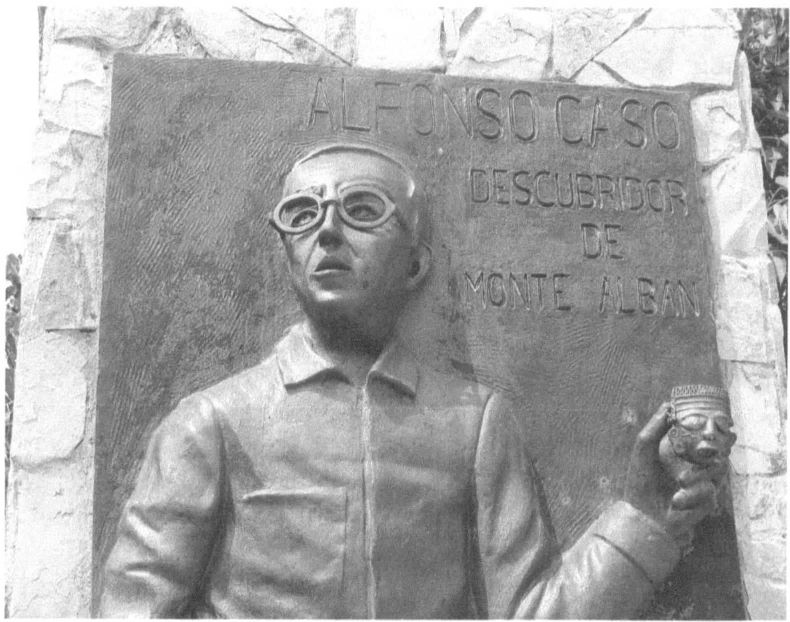

FIGURE 3.3. *A bronze relief sculpture at the entrance to the site commemorates Alfonso Caso as the "Discoverer of Monte Albán." In his hand is the likeness of a gold mask found at the site. (Photograph by author)*

bly advancing scientific knowledge of Mexico's pre-Hispanic past (see Vázquez León 1996), the massive reconstruction and interpretation efforts spearheaded by Caso and his team simultaneously created the conditions for another modern enterprise, the development of Monte Albán as the region's premiere tourist attraction.

Monte Albán was not conceived of and promoted as a site of national or international tourism early on in the same way that Teotihuacán was in central Mexico, where the two-thousand-year-old city was almost entirely rebuilt for the centennial celebration of Mexican Independence in 1910 (Bueno 2010). But this is not to say that the Porfirian government neglected to recognize the tourism potential of archaeological sites in Oaxaca. In 1910 Leopoldo Batres, the key architect of the Teotihuacán restoration, also published the Spanish-language *Guía para visitar los monumentos arqueológicos situados entre Puebla y Mitla, Oaxaca* (Guide for visiting archeological monuments located between Puebla and Mitla, Oaxaca). This suggests a nascent plan for the development of an archaeological corridor catering to national visitors, which no doubt was halted by the start of the Mexican Revolution that same year.

When archaeological work resumed at Monte Albán after the revolution under Alfonso Caso, the site still did not have a systematic plan for monitoring and fostering tourism; admission fees were not charged, and systematic records of tourist activity were not kept in this period. One scholar familiar with the history of the site estimated that through the 1950s it received only a trickle of daily visitors (Jack Corbett, personal communication, 2003). The number of tourists continued to increase throughout the 1960s, but it was not until the 1970s, with the creation of a regional branch of INAH in Oaxaca City in 1972, that the on-site regulation of tourism at Monte Albán began. The number of tourist visitors has steadily grown since that time, and today Monte Albán consistently ranks among the top five most-visited archaeological sites in Mexico, receiving over 500,000 visitors annually, according to its now former director, Nelly Robles García. Its designation in 1987 as a UNESCO World Heritage site had the dual effect of channeling national and international monies into more recent reconstruction and preservation projects while further bolstering Monte Albán's image as a world-class tourist spectacle.

Much to the consternation of INAH archaeologists, the progressive development of Monte Albán into a high-traffic tourist zone generated a host of problems, including the obvious risk of physical damage to the site as visitors scaled the ancient stone structures, traversed terrain still holding artifacts, and left other undesirable marks such as graffiti and trash. But the increase in the number of tourists was only one issue confronting INAH employees. The same visitors sought souvenirs of the site; some simply took photographs while others chipped off pieces of rock from the various stone structures around the site. Still others sought ceramic artifacts, anything from relatively intact ceramic figurines to the ubiquitous potsherds, and, perhaps not surprisingly, an informal network of artisans and vendors formed in response to this demand.

MONTE ALBÁN "*MONEROS*"

No official records were kept that specify when vending began at Monte Albán. However, interviews with present-day vendors indicate that the practice likely originated in the 1930s with the excavation field crews, whose ranks largely comprised men from nearby villages.[3] Elderly men from Arrazola recalled grandfathers, fathers, and uncles working under Alfonso Caso and other Mexican archaeologists, specifically Martín Bazán and Juan Valenzuela. These workers interacted with tourists visiting the site, offering them potsherds and other small archaeological pieces that they uncovered in exchange for a few pesos. As word spread that there was an incipient market for *ídolos* (idols), the term used by workers to refer to figural artifacts, more and more men began to devote themselves to the full- or part-time sale of archaeological pieces. As time went on, increased surveillance at the site and the ongoing removal of artifacts by archaeologists prompted several enterprising individuals in the 1960s to begin to make replicas of the original artifacts, which were then sold as authentic pieces to unsuspecting tourists. The early sale of pre-Hispanic artifacts has today almost wholly given way to a prolific trade in ceramic and stone copies.

From the beginning, the town of Arrazola has been tied to archaeological tourism at Monte Albán and its attendant market for souvenirs. The dissolution of the Larrañaga estate during the postrevolutionary land reforms and the subsequent founding of Arrazola as an independent community in 1937 coincided with Alfonso Caso's extensive explorations and excavations at the site. The formation of archaeological work crews came at an opportune moment for residents who faced an uncertain economic future after the demise of the estate's sugarcane operation. The Monte Albán jobs were seasonal and paid poorly but were more lucrative than employment confined to agricultural work alone. Regular wages along with rewards such as cartons of cigarettes for those who discovered new caches of artifacts were attractive incentives that lured workers to the site through repeated field seasons. At times the work also proved exciting. An Arrazola man, Fidencio Aragón, was part of the work crew that discovered Tomb 7 in 1931 (Zárate Aquino 1995). Aragón's role in the making of modern Mexican history has remained a great source of pride for his descendants, and his grandson and his family never tire of recounting the story of how he helped unearth one of the world's greatest archaeological treasures.

An unintended consequence of employing an economically disadvantaged labor force from Arrazola and other nearby communities such as Xoxocotlán and San Pedro Ixtlahuaca was that some individuals took to selling bits and pieces of the material culture they had been hired to excavate. To what extent such activities occurred is difficult to estimate. Tourism in Oaxaca in the 1930s was certainly limited. Monte Albán, for example, reportedly received a mere 304 visitors in 1931 (Robles García 1996:51). The expansion of the Pan-American Highway in the 1940s gradually opened up the region to foreign and national visitors, in particular, tourists from Mexico City and other parts of central Mexico. An Arrazola resident who worked on the Monte Albán excavations in the late 1940s and early 1950s estimated that he was approached on the average two or three times per week by both Mexican nationals and American tourists looking to purchase archaeological pieces. He recalled complying with their requests, but maintained that he rarely sold anything larger or more valuable than ceramic *caritas*, the fragments of facial images he found scattered throughout the site. He noted that INAH archaeologists tended to turn the other cheek as long as the workers were not trading off bigger, more intact pieces that could be earmarked for private or public collections. At that time, there were no international accords guarding against the sale and transfer of pre-Hispanic artifacts from Mexico, although an earlier piece of national legislation passed in 1938, the *Ley Orgánica del Instituto Nacional de Antropología e Historia*, stipulated that objects from monuments and museums could not be sold, loaned, or alienated from the custodianship of INAH (Breglia 2006:46).

Inquiries by American travelers about purchasing archaeological pieces may also be attributed to shifting trends in the U.S. art market. The general vogue of Mexican art and culture among elite American collectors in the 1920s and 1930s included a new aesthetic sensibility premised upon ancient Mesoamerican expressive forms (Delpar 1992). Art historian Holly Barnet-Sanchez specifically identifies the period from 1933 to 1945 as a time when pre-Hispanic artifacts were collected and displayed as works of art for the first time in the United States (Barnet-Sanchez 1993:177). This signaled an unprecedented shift in the meaning ascribed to archaeological artifacts, with pre-Hispanic pieces for the first time taking on an aesthetic dimension in addition to their value as objects of scientific study. For an American public of art connoisseurs whose appetite for the exotic and unusual was whetted by the art establishment's earlier primitivist movement, pre-Hispanic art represented an unexplored genre of human expression that was at once primal (i.e., closer to nature) and aesthetically distinct (Hill Boone 1993; see also Price 1989, 2007). Furthermore, in this period of flourishing cultural relations between the U.S. and Mexico, the trends and tastes of American connoisseurs greatly influenced those of the Mexican elite (López 2010). U.S. audiences' preoccupation with Mesoamerican forms and styles served to legitimize them back in Mexico, in effect shaping an emerging aesthetic sensibility via transnational circulation.

The dictates of the fine art market and its newfound appreciation of pre-Hispanic artifacts stimulated the demand for archaeological pieces not only in Oaxaca but throughout Mexico. An extended network of buyers and distributors formed to facilitate their purchase. As has been documented for archaeological zones in the Mexican state of Nayarit, antiquities dealers—and the middlemen who supplied them—for years relied on local people for locating and procuring artifacts, typically men who lived and farmed in close proximity to archaeological zones (García Moreno 2000). Van der Spek (2008) traces a similar development in Egypt. No study exists indicating the degree of involvement of Arrazola or other nearby communities in the early organized artifact trade at Monte Albán, but residents likely established contact with interested parties while working as laborers at the site. Robles García (1996) suggests that Arrazola residents' longtime practice of farming and grazing livestock on Monte Albán's western slope provided opportunities to locate and loot tombs. A thorough knowledge of the terrain aided by contacts developed over years working on excavation crews may have facilitated certain Arrazola men's early participation in the antiquities market.

As Caso's final project drew to a close in 1958, sales of artifacts and, increasingly, replica pieces had become commonplace. The handful of vendors present at the site in the 1950s steadily grew in number throughout the 1960s. By the early 1970s the "*moneros*," the name given to the vendors by INAH guards because they sold *monos*, or doll-like figurines, numbered at least sixty, if not more.[4] Men from Arrazola were the dominant force behind on-site vending, but were eventually joined by men and women from other communities, particularly the nearby Colonia Monte Albán.[5] One older Arrazola vendor, who still worked at the site in 2010, remembered the 1970s as "a time when almost everybody, all of the men from Arrazola, went to Monte Albán to sell! There was no other way to earn a living back then." A confluence of factors precipitated the sharp increase in informal vending during this period. The dwindling seasonal work opportunities at Monte Albán as well as the termination of the Bracero Program in 1964 significantly diminished Arrazola men's wage-earning potential. The development of the wood-carving trade and the relative prosperity it would eventually bring were still over a decade away. Some from the community took assorted odd jobs in Oaxaca City, such as working on construction crews, but wages were low and limited transportation networks made for a long commute each day.

Tourism in Oaxaca, in contrast, was on the upswing. The completion of the Mexican portion of the Pan-American Highway in 1950 opened up a new era of tourism for the country, and by the 1970s Oaxaca had become part of the so-called Gringo Trail, a string of Latin American destinations frequented by the North American and European backpacker set. Nevertheless, "*los jipis*" (hippies), as these travelers were known, were not received with open arms; local Oaxacans "tended to view this class of tourists with suspicion and even active dislike, as the values of the two groups frequently clashed" (Murphy and Stepick 1991:84). Indeed, a big part of Oaxaca's draw for this group was the opportunity to partake of inexpensive, high-quality marijuana as well as the hallucinogenic mushrooms made famous by the indigenous healer María Sabina, who lived in Huautla de Jiménez, an indigenous community in the Sierra Mazateca (Feinberg 2003). Not only did "hippies" engage in public behavior deemed offensive by Oaxacans, who tended to be more socially conservative, but they were usually traveling on a limited budget and did not pump as much money into the local economy as Oaxacan entrepreneurs would have liked.

After the countercultural invasion of the late 1960s and 1970s, Oaxaca developed into a choice vacation spot for Mexicans from more affluent areas of the country, such as Mexico City and the industrial states of central and northern Mexico. Short on modern infrastructure but perceived to be rich in folkloric culture, Oaxaca had always occupied a special place in the national imaginary as a location where the pre-Hispanic past and its living incarnation—rural indigenous people—were to be found. Foreign cultural tourists, especially from the United States and Western Europe—soon followed, but even into the new millennium Mexican nationals accounted for nearly 70 percent of Oaxaca's tourist visitors (SEDETUR 2001). On the surface, folk art stores, bed-and-breakfasts, and certain restaurants may appear eager to attract a "gringo" clientele, but a small but growing Mexican middle class and upper-class Mexicans are considered by many who work in tourism in Oaxaca to be the industry's lifeblood.

The founding of the INAH-Oaxaca Regional Center in 1972 significantly paved the way for the touristic development of Oaxaca's archaeological and cultural attractions—and provided for their systematic surveillance. Although its mission as a federal agency was primarily anthropological and historical documentation, these functions were inseparable from the state government's vision that tourism just might be the region's economic panacea. At Monte Albán, INAH worked to create new infrastructure that would facilitate visitation to the site. Construction of a visitor center began in 1973, and the Oaxaca state tourism office provided funding for expanding the facility in 1976. The site complex grew to include a small exhibit area, restaurant, three concession spaces, public restrooms, storage space, and lobby (Robles García 1996). Even with these new additions, INAH struggled to accommodate the growing demands of tourism.

CONFLICT AND CONTESTATION

The surge in tourism at the site inevitably stimulated the activities of the Monte Albán vendors, who by this time were making daily appearances at the monument zone. As their numbers swelled and they became more persistent in their selling efforts, the INAH administration increasingly viewed the vendors as a threat to the integrity of the site. In 1972 Mexico passed its Federal Law on Monuments and Archaeological, Artistic, and Historic Zones in response to the Convention Concerning the Protection of the World Cultural and National Heritage, adopted by the General Conference of UNESCO in that same year.[6] This provided INAH with the legal pretext it needed to mount an offensive against the vendors. Under Article 27 of the new legislation, all archaeological remnants, immoveable structures, and transportable artifacts were declared the inalienable property of the Mexican nation. An individual caught removing or tampering with archaeological evidence was henceforth in direct violation of Mexican federal law.

The escalation of tension between the vendors and INAH is documented in a series of written reports submitted by Monte Albán guards in the period 1975–1985, archived in the Archaeology Division of the INAH-Oaxaca Regional Center in the city of Oaxaca. A recurring complaint concerned the grazing of goats and other livestock by Arrazola residents within the officially designated limits of the archaeological zone. Although some of the individuals cited in the reports did not work as vendors, others were men who combined their pastoral duties with vending activities at Monte Albán. Other reports describe the confiscation of original artifacts, which often entailed protracted cat-and-mouse chases and rock-throwing. On at least one occasion, in August 1981, an Arrazola man fell and sustained a head wound after being chased by a guard at the site. A letter issued on January 11, 1982, by the center's director, Rogelio González, requested police assistance in forcibly removing vendors from the premises.

Arrazola men also remembered this period as one filled with daily confrontations that occasionally turned violent. According to them, the INAH guards regularly carried firearms that they used to scare off not only wild animals but vendors as well, firing shots into the air or close to men's bodies as they attempted to flee. Police raids at Monte Albán reportedly employed similar tactics. An Arrazola man, whose inherent ability to outwit and avoid entrapment by INAH guards earned him the nickname "the Rat" from his fellow vendors, recalled what it was like when he first started going to the site in 1976 at the age of eleven.

> They treated us like animals, you know? We just wanted to sell our figurines, but they always tried to catch us. If the guards grabbed you, they would take all your pieces and smash them on the ground right in front of you. Others would keep your idols and then later sell them and keep the money for themselves. . . . Sometimes I would be on top of the pyramid and they would chase me down by throwing rocks or firing their pistols. Every day you went up there scared that something was going to happen to you—that you could be arrested or hurt.

For nearly twelve years the man made daily afternoon trips to Monte Albán to earn money for school expenses. He eventually abandoned vending in favor of a career in wood carving—a craft with which he had began experimenting in 1987—and today is a prominent woodcarver whose work commands hundreds of dollars and is sold throughout the United States and Canada.

Most significantly, what is revealed by the man's comments, and corroborated by two INAH reports from 1980, is that by the late 1970s Monte Albán vendors were no longer engaged in the exclusive sale of archaeological pieces.[7] Rather, faced with increasing pressure from INAH and the state police, as well as a dwindling supply of artifacts, the vendors had begun to offer tourists stone and clay replicas of original pieces found at the archaeological site. Indeed, the idols that INAH guards readily confiscated and destroyed as the vendors looked on were frequently copies. During our interview the one-time replica seller touched on this issue:

> Well, during the time that I went to Monte Albán, that type of thing wasn't going on as much, because it was no longer necessary to sell the old pieces. It was a lot easier to go and buy the replicas already made, treat them [to look old], and then sell them as originals, and in the case that they caught you or something, they couldn't punish you because they were only copies. Nothing more than the crime of having tricked the tourist, right?

This is not to say that vendors had given up selling artifacts entirely. Another vendor estimated that his sales from the late 1970s through the early 1980s comprised "perhaps 10 percent original pieces, mostly *caritas*, you know, little broken pieces, and maybe 90 percent replicas," all of which he admittedly sold to tourists as authentic pieces.

A memorandum dated November 25, 1980, from INAH archaeologist Marcus Winter to the administrator of the INAH center in Oaxaca identifies a practice apparently adopted by some vendors of offering a mixed selection of real and imitation artifacts. After inspecting a group of confiscated pieces, Winter concluded the following:

> There are five pieces, of which four are stone masks of various colors, green, brown, blue, etc. They were recently made, and therefore they are not pre-Hispanic. The other piece is a fragment of a gray clay figure, from Monte Albán Period I or II, dating from approximately 200 B.C. to 250 A.D. It is a portion of the figure's face, but is already eroded. This figure is Pre-Hispanic.

Van der Spek observed a similar strategy among "antika" vendors at the Theban Necropolis, noting that

> even if all items displayed during such transactions were fakes, the incidental presence of some genuine pieces would be essential to serve the mystification which blurs the distinction between real and false categories taking place in this environment of uncertainty. (van der Spek 2008:168)

The strategically inserted original artifact served to confirm the veracity of sellers' stories and heighten the uncertainty of prospective buyers, some of whom will be always be "'left wondering' if they decline to commit to the purchase of an object which may well have been genuine" (van der Spek 2008:168).

Throughout the 1980s friction mounted between the vendors and the INAH staff, even as the number of vendors began to stabilize. This situation mirrors the conflicts between state and local authorities and unauthorized vendors that are well documented for other sites of Latin American cultural tourism—not coincidentally, where we find the tourist trifecta of indigenous peoples, *artesanías*, and architectural heritage, be it pre-Hispanic or colonial (Castañeda 1996, 2009a; Little 2004b, 2009; Meisch 2002, 2009; Steel 2009). Vendors are pegged as "invaders" when their physical movements, types of wares, sales tactics, and revenue streams cannot be effectively managed through official decree or other coercive means (Castañeda 1996).

The precarious work environment created at Monte Albán led some to abandon vending altogether while most of those who remained switched to selling replicas instead of original pieces. From the perspective of some within INAH, the fact remained that the vendors had no authorization to engage in commercial activities within the legally defined boundaries of the archaeological zone, regardless of the merchandise being offered, and officials proclaimed that the vendors' presence at the very least created a bad image for Monte Albán. They reasoned that visitors would be put off by the sight of the roaming vendors and their presumably unwanted advances. There was constant concern that the situation would spiral out of control, effectively turning the site's open spaces into one big *tianguis*, a Mexican term for open-air markets.

This moment marks a recasting of the vendors' supposed criminality—no longer simply just "looters," they were now effectively constructed as purveyors of bad taste. Castañeda (1996 and 2001) describes an almost identical response—down to employing some of the same disparaging adjectives—by officials from the INAH administration in Yucatán to unauthorized artisan vending at Chichén Itzá. "The massive intrusion of *vendedores* who converted the site into an open-air handicraft market gave tourists a 'bad' *image* of Yucatán and Mexico: the aggressive sales tactics were said to be unappealing, typically rude, deceitful, tacky, and so on. In short, it was all but explicitly stated that it was aesthetically polluting because it was definitively too Third World" (Castañeda 1996:87). At Chichén Itzá, CULTUR (Yucatán's state tourism bureau) finally intervened in 1987 to put a stop to a problem that not even previous police or military efforts on behalf of INAH had been able to resolve; it provided the resources to build a new handicrafts market outside of the ruins for the purposes of relocating itinerant vendors. Nevertheless, CULTUR's strategy was only partially effective, as some vendors rejected the new location in favor of vending (illegally) on the outskirts of the site and the streets of the nearby town of Pisté (Castañeda 1996:87).

Rather than constructing a separate *artesanía* market, INAH took a different tack at Monte Albán. In 1985 the administration drew up a contract to be distributed to and signed by each vendor, acknowledging that it was prohibited to sell replicas at Monte Albán. The contract stipulated that if individuals were ever found in violation their wares would be subject to confiscation by INAH officials. Not surprisingly, few vendors were willing to sign the document, and the ones who did paid it little notice and carried on with their regular activities despite INAH personnel's ongoing warnings and threats. Although the vendors had always recognized the precariousness of their situation, their fear of being permanently dislodged from the site was heightened when Monte Albán was declared a UNESCO World Heritage site on December 10, 1987. With this prestigious designation, Monte Albán secured its place among the world's premiere cultural sites, attracting increased tourism in addition to financial resources from abroad. The vendors worried that the more international attention the archaeological zone received, the more energy and resources INAH would invest in keeping them out.

In 1988, tired of the constant run-ins with the INAH guards and other staff members, and uncertain about what the future held for them as the site was developed into UNESCO "world cultural patrimony," the vendors sought outside counsel regarding their situation. They turned to Víctor Carmona Castillo, a lawyer in Oaxaca City, who had taught law courses at a local university during his career and had a history of providing legal advice and representation to a number of left-leaning organizations and unions, including the *Sindicato 3 de Mayo*, the city street cleaners' union.[8] A few of the men had met Carmona years before in 1976, when they contracted his services in handling a land dispute between community residents and the descendant shareholders of the former Arrazola estate. The lawyer agreed to advise the vendors and eventually helped them secure an appointment to meet with a high-level representative from the state governor's office to discuss the problem.

Carmona effectively defended the actions of the vendors under Mexican constitutional law, which guarantees all citizens the right to work and to elect the occupation that is best suited to their individual circumstance. He argued that since INAH's stated mission was to care for, preserve, and improve the archaeological zone, then as long as the vendors did not interfere with those goals (by selling no artifacts but only replicas) it was legally difficult to keep them out of the monument zone. After hearing the case, the government official called the director of the Oaxaca police and requested that the order to use police force to remove the vendors from Monte Albán be suspended indefinitely. Despite this significant victory, Carmona recommended that the vendors organize themselves as a legally recognized civil association of artisans and craft vendors in order to avert future conflicts with INAH officials and the police. With his assistance, the vendors selected the six individuals who would serve as the association's elected officers and drafted a formal constitution stating the group's bylaws and procedures; the list of its forty-nine founding members included eight women. On November 14, 1988, the *Unión de Expendedores y Fabricantes de Artesanías Monte Albán, A.C.* formed as a civil association in accordance with Mexican federal law.[9]

The group also decided at this time to implement a policy of only permitting male vendors access to the interior portion of the monument zone; female vendors would remain in the parking areas outside the entrance.[10] It was agreed that the women would sell primarily bead and stone jewelry and other items such as key chains or straw hats, but would not offer replica crafts of the type sold by the men inside Monte Albán. Group members reasoned that this would cut down on competition between vendors. Since tourists were more likely to buy items either when first arriving or as they were leaving, individuals working in the site entrance or parking lot typically had a better chance at moving merchandise. With replica pieces only being offered in the interior of the site, tourists interested in that particular type of souvenir would have no choice but to conduct business with the vendors inside. All agreed that it would be easier for a female to sell jewelry since these purchases were most often made by women.

I later discovered competing explanations for this gendered division of labor. An interview with one of the group's founding male members in 2003 revealed the perception that women were generally "more confrontational" than men in dealing with the INAH staff—in other words, they were more likely to argue and talk back. He claimed that in the past some of the women developed intimate relationships with guards and custodians in order to gain special favors and treatment. He added that the men were better able stand up for themselves and to tolerate the occasional physical dangers and verbal abuse inflicted by the INAH guards. When I later asked the wife of one of the Arrazola vendors about the spatial arrangement, she described situations in which several of the male vendors had developed relationships with female vendors, and concluded that "it was a temptation for everyone." This led to infighting and in the case of the married vendors, domestic discord. She herself claimed to have suffered through a period of spousal infidelity when her husband maintained a less-than-discreet relationship with a fellow vendor. Whatever the underlying motives, the arrangement appears to have largely eradicated the romantic liaisons that once plagued the group, and to this day the policy of permitting only male vendors access to interior portions of the archaeological site has been maintained by everyone in the group.[11]

The legal protection afforded by the group's status as a civil association ultimately proved to be not nearly as important to the vendors' day-to-day survival as did the informal agreement established with INAH archaeologists, particularly Arturo Oliveros, Monte Albán's acting director at the time. In exchange for permission to sell their replicas on the grounds, vendors agreed to perform small maintenance duties, including picking up trash and using machetes to cut down weeds, and to keep a watch out for acts of vandalism and petty theft by site visitors. On his part, Oliveros made it clear that this agreement was not an official invitation from INAH encouraging the vendors to permanently remain at Monte Albán or to expand their existing numbers. He also warned the vendors that the sale of original artifacts would not be tolerated and those caught engaging in such activity not only would jeopardize their individual rights to be at the site, but could subject the entire group to legal action. Vendors increasingly policed themselves and others in the group, anxious to retain access to the space.

The formation of the vendors' association and the informal truce called between the vendors and the INAH administration broke the established pattern of physical conflict that had characterized relations at Monte Albán throughout much of the 1970s and early 1980s. Oliveros was able to mitigate most disputes involving the vendors, earning him a reputation among them as a fair and honest individual, as well as criticism from other INAH employees who felt that he was not strict enough in dealing with them. The only notable incident to arise during the rest of Oliveros's tenure as director occurred in 1993. He, along with INAH archaeologist Marcus Winter, helped oversee the Monte

Albán Special Project, a two-year endeavor (1992–1994) that received both state and federal support during the Salinas de Gortari presidential administration. The project enlisted the services of more than three hundred archaeologists and workers to further the exploration and conservation of the zone, and culminated in the opening of an on-site museum. The extensive construction and remodeling efforts required that certain portions of the site be closed off at various times to the general public, including the vendors.

In 1993, as Monte Albán was receiving its makeover, the INAH-Oaxaca Regional Center was appointed a new director, cultural anthropologist Eduardo López Calzada. While López Calzada demonstrated no immediate plans to dislodge the replica sellers from the site, they feared that the major renovations already underway would provide the necessary pretext for others within the administration to push for their relocation or complete removal. Encouraged by the response to their earlier meetings with government officials in 1988, vendors again took their concerns to the secretary general's office. They also prepared a public statement about their plight, which they read on a local radio program.

López Calzada was both sympathetic to the vendors' position and eager to avoid negative press for himself as the new INAH director. In a letter to the union's officers dated March 23, 1994, he offered written assurance that neither INAH nor the state authorities had any plans to remove the group from the site, stating that the temporary measure to constrain vending activities was actually in the interest of protecting the vendors' "physical integrity":

> Due to the nature of the project being completed at the site, it will be advisable to protect the physical integrity of the sellers who occupy this area, and as such it is necessary that they occupy some place where they may sell their products for the duration of this work. . . . With regard to the presumed order to displace the vendors by this authority, under no circumstances do we intend to impede or hinder their freedom to sell their products, and much less dislodge them completely.[12]

At the time of my initial fieldwork in 2002, the vendors remained an active presence at the site and the *Unión de Expendedores y Fabricantes de Artesanías Monte Albán, A.C.* counted sixty members.[13] Forty-one men, all but eight from Arrazola, sold ceramic and stone replicas based on pre-Hispanic designs in the interior portion of the site, while the other nineteen vendors, now a mix of men and women, offered jewelry to tourists in the parking lot and on the steps leading up to the site entrance. Nevertheless, the replica vendors were still marginalized figures whose tenuous existence at Monte Albán hinged as much on the good graces of INAH officials as on the vagaries of the tourism market.

"Everything went downhill with the Twin Towers," remarked one vendor, who noted that his sales dropped precipitously after the 9/11 terrorist attacks in the United States. Adding to the competition for sales, another group of vendors going by the name of *Dani Di'paa* had formed and now sold jewelry and small souvenir items on the steps of Monte Albán's entrance.[14] The vendors took another hit in sales in 2006, when an Oaxaca teacher's strike became the impetus for a broader display of civil unrest (see chapter 1); tourism was effectively shut down in the city and nearby tourist zones, including Monte Albán. More recently, the U.S. economic recession of 2007, whose impacts are still being felt in and outside of Mexico, and the 2009 global outbreak of the H1N1 influenza virus (with much-publicized origins in Mexico) have prevented a return to pre-2006 levels of tourist visitation.

In 1997 Monte Albán received a new director, Nelly Robles García, who proved less tolerant of unauthorized entrepreneurial efforts taking place at the site. Robles García was already well known for her work at Mitla, a Zapotec archaeological site approximately fifty kilometers east of Oaxaca, and had experience as a researcher and conservator at Monte Albán. Work at both of these sites formed the basis for her 1996 doctoral dissertation at the University of Georgia on the management of cultural resources in Oaxaca, which was published in English as an online document in 2000 by the Society for American Archaeology.[15] This document addresses the complex social dynamics characterizing contemporary archaeological management efforts by outlining the multiple social actors at both Mitla and Monte Albán and demonstrating how each group seeks to utilize archaeological resources to various ends. From her perspective, *ejido* landholders, state tourism officials, vendors, and city planners are largely motivated by short-term economic gain rather than a genuine concern for archaeological knowledge or heritage preservation. She concludes that tourism, real estate development, commerce, and agriculture have undermined the core philosophical values of conservation and restoration.

She finds these values to be exemplified by Alfonso Caso's work at Monte Albán from 1930 until 1958, during the "Golden Age" of Mexican archaeology (Robles García 1996:306). Her admiration for Caso and the general scientific rigor of this period of archaeology is evident in her text, as demonstrated by the following passage:

> This period is known for the careful weighing of archaeological data collected in a systematic manner, a practice which permitted Caso to propose a fine chronology for Monte Albán which continues to be used to this day. . . . At the level of restoration the practice of monumental reconstruction continued, but now with a socialist vision that implied returning the pre-Columbian past to the community for its educational benefit. (Robles García 1996:42–43)

This assessment of Golden Age archaeology as a force for the democratization of Mexican cultural history nevertheless sidesteps other discussions that more critically implicate archaeology and anthropology more generally in the nationalist politics of assimilation (Breglia 2006; Bueno 2010; Castañeda 1996; Lomnitz 2001; Vázquez León 2003).

On the topic of the Monte Albán vendors, she states that replica sales may have been a front for the clandestine sale of legitimate artifacts (Robles García 1996:286). She maintains that although they rarely sell original artifacts at the site, some vendors strategically offer replicas to tourists and then, once contact has been established, invite them to their homes to see original artifacts. (In the year that I lived in Arrazola, which included frequent trips to Monte Albán, I never witnessed activities of this kind.)

Distrust appeared to characterize the relationship on both sides. On the vendors' side, some assumed (incorrectly) that Robles García was not from Oaxaca, since she demonstrated little public sympathy to their economic plight. "She doesn't even give us the time of day," one man complained, noting that she largely ignored the vendors on occasions when she was at the site. The vendors found that she was unwilling, for the most part, to engage in the patronage politics of her predecessor. She permanently relieved them of the maintenance duties that they had previously performed, so that they could no longer use their unpaid labor at the site as a leverage tool. She also drew up a list of all the members who officially belonged to the association and informed the group that no others could be added. This permanently capped the number of vendors permitted inside the site at any given time, which benefited the vendors to a certain extent because it helped stabilize competition for sales. Robles García reasoned that, as neither archaeologists nor INAH employees, the vendors should not be granted rights not enjoyed by other visitors at the site. For example, tourists were prohibited from entering with large backpacks and luggage, and yet some vendors reportedly used to carry their wares in enormous duffel bags or suitcases; this practice came to a halt, and most vendors now used small duffel bags or backpacks. Vendors were also to refrain from eating inside the ruins and from setting their wares down on the ground to display.

One rule that INAH personnel were unable to enforce, however, was the collection of an admission fee from vendors as they entered the ruins.[16] The vendors refused to pay a daily sum to enter what they considered to be their place of work, and since there existed no physical barrier surrounding the ruins' main structures, it was difficult to monitor their entry and exit from the site. At the time of this writing, negotiation between the two parties has resulted in a stalemate.

When I met with Robles Garciá in the spring of 2003, she reiterated her position on the vendors, even as she made it clear that she understood the economic constraints (namely the paucity of arable land) that were the impetus for informal commerce. In this spirit, she said that for years INAH had encouraged the vendors to form themselves into a legitimate business enterprise within the site. However, she said they declined offers by the administration to designate a space that would serve as an official artisan market, such as the one that was approved by INAH in Mitla in 1976, which was designed to limit vendor traffic inside the archaeological zone (see also Robles García 1996:269–270).

She believed that the vendors' adamant refusal stemmed from the fact that many had developed elaborate sales strategies for convincing tourists that their homemade replicas were pre-Hispanic archaeological artifacts. It followed that if the vendors were all grouped together in a clearly defined market space, the elaborate stories used to convince tourists that their wares were authentic would not be as effective. When asked why they resisted INAH's relocation efforts, the vendors, too, acknowledged that their wares would be less likely to sell if they were all sitting in permanent market stalls, the men and their merchandise, literally and figuratively, piled on top of one another (*amontonados*). No one articulated Robles García's explicit concern, but one man hinted at the power of the ruins as performative space when he stated, "An artisan market? They're everywhere you look in Oaxaca. For the tourist, it's nothing special [*no tiene chiste*]. Here inside the ruins [the tourist] feels the history." Suggestive selling was enabled precisely through tourists' emotional responses and expectations within the heritage landscape. Van der Spek describes an analogous logic among vendors at the Theban Necropolis. "Rather than to protect a livelihood based on illicit excavation and trade in illegal antiquities, as it is often assumed, it is for [the sake of maintaining the illusion of authenticity]—combining economic pragmatism with the art of storytelling—that many Qurnawi have long been opposed to leaving the Necropolis" (van der Spek 2008:168).

Robles García also noted that, while perhaps not as physically destructive as trafficking in original archaeological pieces, the practice of attempting to sell replicas as originals was itself dishonest and created "a bad image" for Monte Albán. In her opinion, the quality of the vendors' wares had also diminished over time. She referred to the proliferation of low-quality, repetitive designs as the "Mitla effect," and added that she believed that the rustic, one-of-a-kind pieces vendors used to make and sell had largely given way to serially produced replicas that perhaps were not even made in Oaxaca. She said that the same crafts had started to appear at all of the archaeological sites in Oaxaca and throughout Mexico, although she admitted that she did not really know if and how many vendors made their own crafts.

In making her case against the vendors, Robles García cited an incident that occurred in March 2002, in which a local television crew looking to air a sensationalist story entered the site armed with hidden cameras and microphones. They proceeded to approach vendors and ask if they had any original artifacts to sell. While most responded that they only sold replicas, three of the vendors offered pieces that they claimed to be originals. One man brazenly claimed that he looted tombs and that INAH did not stop him. Later tests conducted by archaeologists proved the pieces to be of recent origin, meaning that no crime had technically been committed. However, the negative publicity generated when the segment aired on a local news program, *Zona Crítica*, was a serious blow to both INAH officials and the vendors, including those who were up-front about the origins of their crafts.

Fearing that their position at Monte Albán had been jeopardized by the actions of a few, the vendors took matters into their own hands and voted to expel the three men from the group. Yet the internal disciplinary measures taken by the association did little to sway the opinions of the upper-level site administration. For them, replica vendors remained an undesirable presence at the archaeological zone, one that they would begrudgingly tolerate for the time being until a more permanent solution could be implemented. The idea of relocating the vendors to a more easily monitored artisan market is still on the table, but as of this writing the vendors continue to market their wares directly to tourists within the main structures of the ruins.

While INAH officials and other outsiders may view vendors as contaminants and, worse yet, looters of Monte Albán and the national heritage it represents, vendors in contrast view themselves as legitimate artisans and entrepreneurial stakeholders in the archaeological site (see also Castañeda 1996 on vendors at Chichén Itzá and Little 2004b on Mayan vendors in Antigua, Guatemala). García Canclini strongly cautions against such black-and-white assertions of culpability and the assertion of heritage's so-called pure value. He reminds us that

> if we consider the uses of patrimony from the perspective of studies on cultural reproduction and social inequality, we find that the goods gathered in history by each society do not really belong to everyone, although they formally appear to belong to everyone and to be available for everyone's use. (García Canclini 1995:135)

The ongoing tension between the replica vendors and INAH employees discussed here demonstrates the contested, even contradictory nature of archaeological as well as other forms of cultural heritage in Oaxaca. As Lisa Breglia insists, the "preeminent 'site' of monumental ambivalence is located not within the ruins themselves (as material icons) but rather in the historical interplay between the territorial assertions of the nation over its patrimonial resources and the interventions of private interests seeking to benefit from those same resources" (Breglia 2006:7). It follows that institutional definitions of cultural patrimony are often at odds with the way in which local people envision and ultimately make use of the material resources at hand.

Archaeological practice at Monte Albán has accommodated and benefited from local labor throughout the twentieth century. It first created a system of wage work and subsequently utilized unpaid maintenance work at the site, which, ironically, included monitoring the activity of tourists. At the same time, some vendor activities at Monte Albán threaten to undermine the taken-for-granted authority vested in INAH as a federal institution charged with constructing, managing, and policing Monte Albán as a site of not only national but also world patrimony. More critically, as the chapter's opening vignette suggests, financial motivations may be construed as being at the heart of heritage claims, but they are frequently suffused with personal or collective sentiment that may not simply be reduced to economic rationale.

TO THE TOP OF MONTE ALBÁN

I GLANCED DOWN AT MY WATCH: 9:25 A.M., only five more minutes until we were scheduled to leave. My gaze settled on the hot pink wall in front of me, where someone had painted a giant multicolored map of the state of Oaxaca. A connect-the-dots pattern informed tourists of the principal places of interest, namely colonial churches, craft villages, and archaeological sites. In a selective rendering of local geography, towns lacking these attractions were mostly absent from the map. Arrazola's location was indicated on the mural by a brightly colored armadillo, its mark of wood-carving fame. I patiently sat in the lobby of the Hotel Rivera del Angel, waiting to be called to the small green bus parked in the inner courtyard of the hotel that would transport me to the top of Monte Albán. For more than a decade, this hotel at the southern edge of the city had run a regular bus service to and from Monte Albán that was utilized by tourists and locals alike.

My friend Josefina sat next to me, her eyes heavy from lack of sleep. Ever since her son and daughter-in-law had left over a year ago to find work in Los Angeles, she woke up before five o'clock every morning to tend to the house and three young children they left in her care. At sixty years old, Josefina made the daily trip to sell the beaded necklaces and bracelets that she expertly strung together in the spare moments between cleaning, cooking, and caring for her grandchildren. She was married to one of the longtime replica vendors and was the only female vendor from Arrazola at Monte Albán. We sat in silence and waited for the young woman in charge of ticket sales to announce the bus's departure.

A dozen or so tourists milled about the lobby, some clutching guidebooks, others armed with overpriced bottled water purchased from the hotel's small concession stand. Scattered among the German-, Italian-, Japanese-, and English-speaking mix of tourists was a handful of local men, some of them from Arrazola. I made eye contact with an older man sitting on a bench across the room, whose face I recognized from the village but whose acquaintance I had not yet made. He must have recognized me, too, because he acknowledged me with a slight nod of his head. On his lap he held a small, dusty duffel bag that I assumed contained items he would sell that day. I glanced sideways at Josefina, who, overcome with drowsiness, appeared to have nodded off in her upright position. As if by force of habit, her eyes suddenly blinked open as the young woman from the ticket desk announced that we could now board the bus. Josefina hoisted her bag, heavy with the weight of the stone jewelry, onto her small frame and we made our way out to the bus.

During the twenty-minute ride to the archaeological zone, we twisted through the narrow, and at times dangerously steep, streets of the neighborhoods situated between the city's southwestern perimeter and the hill where Monte Albán majestically towered. We passed through the gritty, working-class neighborhoods of San Martín Mexicapan, San Juan Chapultepec, and Colonia Monte Albán, which presented a sharp visual contrast to the graceful colonial architecture and quaint cobblestone streets of the city's downtown hotel zone. Around us, many of the tourists chatted nervously, perhaps sharing my own ever-present fear of flying off one of the hairpin curves and landing in the precipice below. The poverty evidenced by some of the homes did not go unnoticed, and in fact, seemed to be a source of voyeuristic curiosity for some of the people on the bus. An English-speaking woman sitting behind me commented to her male traveling companion that "the neighborhood is lookin' pretty rough" and said she was glad they had decided to take the bus instead of walking all the way to the site, as some ambitious tourists did.

I asked Josefina why the bus took this old road up to Monte Albán, rather than the new highway just to the west, which was more carefully maintained and bypassed the urban sprawl of the *colonias*. She reminded me that many of the people who worked at the site, including vendors, lived in these neighborhoods and depended on this bus route for transportation to work. The city bus ran only as far as Colonia Monte Albán, and they relied on the tourist shuttle bus to make up the remaining distance. It was true; since leaving the hotel we had already picked up nearly a dozen passengers waiting on the side of the road along the bus route.

We finally pulled in to the site's lower-level parking lot, and once the bus stopped the passengers filed off one by one. Before taking her leave of me, Josefina made sure I had packed a bottle of water and gave me a piece of fruit from her bag, concerned that I might get hungry and be forced to seek out food in the convenient but expensive café housed inside the visitor center. Josefina, a member of the vendors' association, did not enter the site to sell her merchandise but instead combed the lower parking lot with dozens of stone necklaces and bracelets looped over her arm. She approached tourists as they boarded and unloaded from the green hotel bus as well as the privately charted buses that daily filled the dusty lot. On a nonholiday weekday like today, she might earn anywhere between 20 and 150 pesos (approximately U.S.$2–15) over the course of a six-hour sales period. However, having spent numerous mornings with her while she worked, I knew that on some days sales could be so slow that she would not even be able to recoup the approximately two dollars in bus and taxi fare it had cost her to get to Monte Albán.[1] After thanking her for the fruit, I wished her luck and joined the pack of tourists heading up the dirt footpath that paralleled the final stretch of road leading to the site entrance.

CHAPTER FOUR

Crafting the Past in the Present

The man in Oaxaca still makes [replicas]. A beautiful piece came out here one day—brought by a woman with a baby. It was made by the man. His father and his uncles made them too. He grew up in the profession, but he's better than either of them ever were. . . . I was told about a piece in Ocotlán that someone told me was a first epoch piece. But I had seen the man making it—a stupid piece—a rain god. It was made by these brothers, the father and the uncle. One, the father, was blind in one eye, but I had seen his brother making the piece. Worked in their backyard and used bonfire firing. . . . I used to go to their place with some frequency. Sometimes they would send for me and you always had to go. Otherwise you would never know if you would miss something. They never minded me seeing them make these things. They knew I wouldn't buy one but they didn't mind me watching. I knew them for years, but I never knew their names.

HOWARD LEIGH, FROM "STORIES OF A COLLECTOR"

THE ABOVE EXCERPT COMES FROM HOWARD LEIGH'S unpublished 1979 memoir, in which he reflected on a lifetime of studying and collecting Oaxacan antiquities.[1] Leigh was an American scholar of Mixtec language and culture who spent the bulk of his life in Mexico and, together with his associate Ervin R. Frissell, amassed one of the most impressive collections of Zapotec and Mixtec ceramics on the continent, today housed at the Frissell Museum in Mitla, Oaxaca. In his quest to find unique artifacts, over the years he purportedly learned to distinguish between ancient pieces and those crafted by modern-day artisans such as the family described above. Like other collectors of his stature, Leigh possessed a self-proclaimed eye for the authentic—for instance, he boldly declares an important pre-Hispanic sculpture in Oaxaca's Rufino Tamayo museum to be as "false as a three-dollar bill." On the common practice of "fakers" using ceramic facial molds he writes, "Fakers sometimes made molds for the little heads, but you usually can tell because there are no broken surfaces. They smooth that over and don't reproduce the broken surfaces of the head. But they churn out the little heads" (Leigh 1979: n.p.). The memoir's overall tone reveals the air of someone too experienced to be fooled by the common techniques of a replica artisan.

In *Faking Ancient Mesoamerica*, Nancy Kelker and Karen Bruhns assert that many of the pieces in Leigh's collection (some of which also appear in the 1966 book by Boos mentioned in the preface) are "forgeries" (2010:227). What the authors do not make clear is that Leigh was not simply a dupe to the "forger's" art, but rather occasionally reveled in the aesthetics of what we might call modern pre-Hispanic art. In one case he reports having purchased an unusual ceramic figure, the body of which was original, but whose head he recognized as being recently molded and attached, giving the illusion of a perfectly intact artifact. He evidently found the modified sculpture too intriguing to pass up despite its dubious pedigree. Leigh's purchase and his written acknowledgment that replica makers occasionally produced "beautiful" and "handsome" pieces indicate some degree of appreciation for the contemporary craft (Leigh 1979: n.p.). What is unclear is whether Leigh knew that the family of ceramicists he mentions above, whose home he often visited but whose name he never bothered to learn, was a major supplier of replicas sold at Monte Albán from the 1960s into the early 1980s.

As described in the preceding chapter, Arrazola men engaged in unregulated vending at Monte Albán as early as the 1940s, first offering original fragments to a handful of inquiring tourists, and later, around 1960, introducing copies of originals into the site. However, it was not until 1984 that replica production emerged as a cottage industry within the community. Prior to that time, the vendors purchased nearly all of the replica pieces that they sold from the family of artisans identified by Leigh only as a man blind in one eye, his son, and the man's brother. This chapter describes how Arrazola vendors made the transition from purchasing these premade pieces to producing ceramic replicas themselves in the mid-1980s. This created a craft industry parallel to the wood-carving trade, which was established as the community's primary economic activity at roughly the same time. I examine the further expansion of replica crafts at Monte Albán, including the introduction of nonlocally produced objects into the site. Included is a discussion of the material and social dimensions of replica crafts as they are today produced in Arrazola and marketed at Monte Albán. I contrast these conditions with wood carving in order to illustrate the motivations for participation in this alternative craft trade even as wood carving began to take shape as a commercially successful artisan form.

EARLY REPLICA MAKING IN SAN JUANITO

In 2003 Leopoldo Montes, the partially blind replica maker described by Leigh, still lived on the south side of Oaxaca in San Juan Chapultepec, a working-class neighborhood referred to by locals as San Juanito. The eighty-four-year-old man, along with his brother, was the ceramic artisan responsible for producing some of the earliest replica pieces sold to tourists at Monte Albán. The brother had retired completely from replica making but Montes still made ceramic pieces as his declining health allowed, and vendors from Arrazola made regular visits to his home workshop to buy figurines that they later resold at Monte Albán. The artisan had passed on his knowledge of ceramic techniques to his sixty-year-old son, who also worked making replicas that he sold himself at a small stand at the entrance to Monte Albán.[2]

Montes was born into a family of ceramic makers in the town of Santa Cruz Mixtepec, a community approximately forty-eight kilometers to the southwest of Oaxaca. The family later relocated to the city in search of work opportunities when he was a young man in his early twenties. Montes eventually set up his own household in San Juanito and began sharecropping corn, beans, and squash on nearby lands, which had yet to give way to the sprawling rows of concrete and corrugated tin houses that today dominate the neighborhood. Notably, a portion of San Juan Chapultepec's communal lands are located within the officially designated boundaries of Monte Albán, accounting for 2 percent of the total archaeological zone (Robles García 1996:115–117). Montes discovered that the land he worked contained ceramic fragments of pre-Hispanic pieces. He was particularly intrigued by the *caritas* (small facial forms) and instinctively began to collect them. It was only a matter of time before he stumbled into the lucrative market for pre-Hispanic artifacts, fueled to a large extent by private collectors such as Howard Leigh and Ervin Frissell. Already familiar with pottery-making techniques, he recognized the potential of applying the craft to the production of archaeological replicas.

To be clear, Montes was not the first person to make replicas of pre-Hispanic artifacts in Oaxaca. Leopoldo Batres, an archaeologist who worked during the Porfirio Díaz administration (see previous chapter), published a monograph in 1909 on archaeological forgeries in Mexico that specifically mentions falsified objects from Oaxaca (see also Kelker and Bruhns 2010).[3] Moreover, innovations in pre-Hispanic ceramic design and techniques for contemporary commercial markets have been observed in other parts of Mexico and Central America (Nash 1993). In Chihuahua, for example, the production of the now-famous Mata Ortíz pottery began in the 1970s when a self-taught woodcutter by the name of Juan Quezada was inspired to create pottery based on ceramic fragments he found at the nearby Casas Grandes (also known as Paquimé) archaeological site (Smith 1998).

Montes acquired the necessary raw materials and, aided by his brother, began to experiment with various sizes and designs. To expedite the sculpting process, he cast simple molds from the *caritas* that he found. This enabled him, in Leigh's words, to "churn out" the small faces, which were either sold as individual fragments or attached to full-sized figures whose bodies he crafted by hand. He established a network of buyers in and around Oaxaca with whom he regularly dealt. According to his son, who began making his own pieces in 1958, the family was neither secretive about its craft nor ever involved in the traffic in original archaeological artifacts. This contradicts information provided by one Arrazola vendor who claimed that Montes had sold the occasional artifact, as had others who lived around or worked at Monte Albán during that period. Nevertheless, Montes's son was unwilling to disclose any information about the clients with whom he and his father had done business over the years, except to say that they had produced pieces for local expositions, including events sponsored by Oaxaca's state-run craft store, ARIPO. Apart from the pieces destined for such events, in which the ceramic crafts would have been knowingly displayed and sold as replicas, it is difficult to know precisely how transactions with other Oaxaca buyers transpired.

Montes's client base expanded beyond his contacts in the city as the tourist trade began to take hold at Monte Albán itself. Early on, he brought samples of his work up to the main areas of the site with the intention of selling them, and eventually connected with men from Arrazola and other neighboring communities similarly interested in tapping into the archaeological souvenir market. In this way, replicas made by the San Juanito brothers started to enter the site around 1960.[4] An Arrazola man who began vending at Monte Albán in the early 1970s asserted that the family maintained a monopoly on the production of the ceramic replicas for several decades. He said,

> They grew beans, there below the highway [to Monte Albán], and they would find ceramic faces on the ground. So they came up with the idea that they could do that, and they started to make them—and they had a very good business, they have nice houses, those people! Because all of us would buy replicas from them back then, everyone from Arrazola. When I started to go up to Monte Albán in 1972, I would buy a lot of figures from them and every day I would sell them all. Their pieces were very rustic looking, but since no one else was making them in those days the tourists bought them. It wasn't like it is today.

With a steady stream of clients arriving at his home workshop, Montes no longer needed to directly market his wares at Monte Albán. Vendors oftentimes would stay and chat with him as he worked, seemingly fascinated by the way in which amorphous lumps of clay took shape under the artisan's hands. More curious individuals inquired about particular techniques or designs, and even offered suggestions as to the types of pieces they believed would be popular. These vendors became some of his best clients, and the growing tourist presence at Monte Albán seemed to bode well economically for both maker and sellers.

COPYING COPIES

Arrazola resident Guillermo Avila was among the customers who frequented the San Juanito workshop during the late 1970s and early 1980s. He got his start vending replica crafts in 1976 at the age of eleven, assisted by an older brother and some friends who were already successfully selling at Monte Albán. Every day after school and on most weekends, Avila and a classmate combed the archaeological zone looking for potential buyers, always working as a team to avoid being spotted and nabbed by INAH guards. The afternoons at Monte Albán were doubly productive; he fulfilled his duty of pasturing the family's goats while earning extra money to cover school expenses that his cash-strapped family could not afford.

Avila's inventory initially consisted of random ceramic fragments he found on the ground along with stone masks that he purchased from other Arrazola vendors, who brought them from the neighboring state of Guerrero (see discussion of masks below). The masks sold well enough, but he personally found them unattractive, not to mention less convincing to tourists who were looking to acquire "real" archaeological pieces. He later switched to exclusively selling ceramic figurines and soon was making frequent visits to the San Juanito artisans' workshop to purchase merchandise for resale.

Over the next eight years, Avila, along with an older and younger brother who also sold replicas, was an almost daily fixture in the archaeological zone. In that time he finished *secundaria* (roughly equivalent to middle school in the U.S.) and married his wife, a woman from a nearby *rancho*, who gave birth to their first child. In 1984, at nineteen years old and with a new family to support, he felt increasing economic pressure but faced limited job prospects in his hometown. A relative of his, Manuel Jiménez (discussed in chapter 2), was by then a successful wood-carver, and several other men in town were working to establish themselves in the trade, but wood carving was not yet perceived as the economic panacea that it would be just a few years later. Plus, he did not relish the idea of working at home every day, isolated from his peers. It occurred to Avila that by learning to make his own ceramic wares, he would be guaranteed all of the profits minus the cost of his raw materials.

Having observed the San Juanito artisans over the years, Avila had a basic idea of the molding and firing techniques for ceramic-making. He knew, for instance, that the clay they used was a mix of at least three types. What he did not know was the exact ratios of the materials or how to procure them. He reasoned that the ceramic artifacts found at the archaeological zone were likely made of the same clay that could be found on the hillsides of Monte Albán. Eventually settling on white- and yellow-colored clays he found around the site, and adding black-hued soil from a nearby riverbed, Avila began to experiment with different designs that he thought would appeal to tourists. He used other replica pieces purchased in San Juanito to cast his own molds for making faces in addition to crafting some from scratch. He cleared a spot for a large fire pit in the courtyard of his home and cooked the clay pieces by simply placing them in the flames, as he had seen San Juanito artisans do. When his first few batches exploded, Avila revisited each step of the production process until he determined that the problem resided in the clay, which, unsifted, contained granules that acted like gunpowder when heated. Rather than perform the time-consuming task of collecting and sifting the soil himself, Avila contacted a supplier in Atzompa, a neighboring village famous for its green-glazed ceramics. The Atzompa clay not only came pre-sifted but was already blended in the correct proportions for pottery-making.

Avila's finished replicas sold well. The originality of his designs set his pieces apart from those sold by the other vendors, who continued to buy from the San Juanito workshop and another artisan family who had more recently starting producing replica crafts in their home in Colonia Monte Albán, a small settlement located on the outskirts of the archaeological zone. His older brother started making his own replicas, and as word of their artisan activities spread, several other Arrazola vendors also decided to try their hand at replica making. Others approached the brothers about buying finished pieces to resell, offers which they mostly declined.

In 1985 Avila's younger brother, Martín, started selling his brothers' pieces to help cover the costs of attending *preparatoria*. Determined to complete his studies, for three years Martín Avila spent his vacations and nearly all of his free time at Monte Albán. Yet despite his persistence, he found that he lacked the marketing skills that his older brothers seemed to naturally possess. He described his personal discomfort with selling in a 2003 interview:

> I never really liked selling, you know? I always felt ashamed when I would go up to Monte Albán with my figures. Believe me, when someone approached me, if they were foreigners or gringos, French, Italian, whatever, at times I wouldn't feel so embarrassed. I would show them what I had and sometimes they would buy from me. But with the Mexicans, well, with anyone who spoke Spanish, I felt very ashamed. . . . I hardly sold anything. I often stayed until one in the afternoon without selling a single piece. Seriously, when it comes to selling I'm a complete failure!

After observing his frustration at having sold not a single replica, a friend suggested that Martín make the pieces and that he would buy from him instead of the San Juanito artisans. The idea appealed to him, and he set to the task of making figures. He needed little coaching in ceramic techniques, having spent time around his brothers while they crafted their pieces, and he diligently set to work. Within a few weeks, he had enough figures to fill two duffel bags—far more pieces than his friend could possibly sell at one time. One Saturday he packed up his wares and carried them to Monte Albán, where he debuted them among the vendors but away from the watchful eyes of the guards. To his surprise they purchased all of the pieces and requested more.

THE CONTEMPORARY REPLICA TRADE

As I neared the stone staircase that led up to Monte Albán's tourist center, the handful of Arrazola vendors that had accompanied me up on the bus veered off from the group of tourists and disappeared around the right-hand side of the hill into the brush. Another vendor, who owned his own car and drove to Monte Albán daily, pulled up and parked his car under some shade trees. He locked his car and followed the other vendors into the site. As mentioned in the previous chapter, one of the criticisms lodged against the vendors by INAH staff was that they entered the site daily but never paid the 35 peso weekday admission fee required of most visitors.[5] The vendors, in turn, felt justified in not paying the fees because Monte Albán was their place of work, and so continued to discreetly enter the site from the back way.

On the steps, groups of men and women were setting up tables and makeshift displays of straw hats, jewelry, T-shirts, ceramic statues, and other items they hoped would catch tourists' attention. Of the sixty-nine vendors who sold merchandise outside the ruins, twenty-two of them belonged to the same association as the forty-one men who sold replica crafts inside.[6] The remaining individuals formed part of a group that went by the name *Dani Di'paa*. This group reportedly had fifty members, but I never counted more than thirty present on any given day. No one from this group sold replicas in the interior portion of the site, although some offered stone masks and ceramic pieces, the latter obviously cast from molds, on the steps.

The on-site manager told me that *Dani Di'paa*, in addition to being more recently established, lacked the organizational structure and legal recognition of the Arrazola group. I also knew that there existed some tension between the two groups; *Dani Di'paa* resented what they viewed as the Arrazola vendors' monopoly over sales within the interior portion of the site, while many Arrazola vendors believed that *Dani Di'paa* was not a legitimate organization and that it did not work to defend selling privileges for all at Monte Albán. One Arrazola vendor described it as a "phantom group" and not a legitimate organization, headed by a single woman named Gloria who controlled a larger network of souvenir stalls throughout the city. The man suspected that all of these stalls were run by members of her extended family or friends, and he alleged that she had grown quite rich off of the earnings. I, too, found the group to be "phantom"-like; all of the *Dani Di'paa* vendors I approached declined to talk about their organization, as if mandated by a higher authority, and my persistent requests to meet Gloria were always met with evasion (e.g., "Maybe she'll be here later next week").

I made my way past the two rows of tables that flanked the staircase on either side. At the top of the steps a group of guides milled about, hoping to drum up some morning business. They called out to tourists entering the site, offering their services in German, French, Italian, English, and Spanish. One crotchety old guide liked to blurt out phrases in Japanese, yet I never witnessed him holding a conversation in Japanese or guiding Japanese tourists. When tourists refused his services, he chastised them in the appropriate tongue: "So you think you know more than the guides, huh? You'll be sorry when you get inside!" The other guides would typically roll their eyes and then try their own carefully rehearsed hooks. Like the replica vendors, the guides had been drawn into the tourist industry out of economic necessity, although many also professed a deeper, personal interest in archaeology and history. Nearly all had trained for other careers—schoolteachers, bookkeepers, administrative assistants—but found they earned more working as tour guides than in the oversupplied, underpaid professions for which they had studied.

By the time I made my way inside, the replica vendors from the bus had already installed themselves in their respective selling areas within the site. As per the INAH mandate, they kept all of their wares hidden away in their duffel bags except for a piece or two that they held in their hands to show to tourists. The men generally favored a dispersed selling pattern so as not to create too much competition between vendors. For the most part, they milled around by themselves within defined areas, but occasionally came together in small groups of two or three to socialize or commiserate about the lack of sales. When the midday sun got to be unbearable, the men retreated to the scant patches of shade, where they would sit until a potential customer or tour group neared. Replicas in hand, they approached visitors with simple but direct sales pitches, usually in Spanish but occasionally in French, German, or English: "Do you want to buy a figure?" and "Zapotec figures." Some individuals simply held out the pieces for sale for tourists to inspect.

Those who sold replicas inside were nearly all men from Arrazola or Los Ibáñez, a smaller settlement located on the southern slope of Monte Albán that is connected to Arrazola by a one-lane dirt road running along a riverbed. About one-quarter of them crafted their own ceramic replicas, while others purchased finished pieces from the workshops in Colonia Monte Albán and San Juanito.[7] In recent years, vendors looking to purchase ready-made ceramic pieces have increasingly bought them from Martín Avila. Encouraged by the success of his early sales as a teenager, he was now established as a full-time artisan, surpassing the San Juanito workshop as the largest supplier of ceramic replica crafts to Arrazola vendors. He also occasionally supplied pieces to Arrazola wood-carvers, some of whom kept an assortment of tourist crafts on hand in addition to wood carvings.

Monte Albán administrators maintained a list of the men "permitted" inside the site (while stressing that they did not grant "authorization" for vending activities), but this figure did not accurately reflect the number of individuals present at any given time. Except for times when tourist traffic was at its peak, such as Christmas and Holy Week, the actual number of vendors inside Monte Albán was typically below the maximum number of forty-one. Like many of the wood-carvers described by Chibnik (2003), replica sellers typically exhibited a mixed income-earning strategy, integrating vending with farming, the painting and reselling of wood carvings, and periodic trips to work in the United States. One twenty-six-year-old vendor, for instance, studied business administration at the Universidad Autónoma Benito Juárez de Oaxaca (UABJO) and went to Monte Albán only when his studies allowed, usually on weekends or during vacations.

Martín Avila did not directly market his crafts to tourists, but his case is particularly instructive of the way in which participation in the replica trade was combined with outside economic and educational pursuits.[8] With his replica earnings, as well as money earned during a brief stint working in a meat-processing facility in Minnesota, he had managed to nearly complete a law degree at the UABJO. Despite this, Avila—a highly articulate, intelligent man by then in his mid-thirties with a wife and two young daughters—remained pessimistic about ever working in the legal profession. As he explained to me, most of his university classmates graduated only to end up working low-wage service or administrative jobs in the city. With a family to support, he believed that tourism was virtually the only growth industry in Oaxaca's otherwise sluggish economy, and so, at least for the time being, he opted for full-time artisan production, punctuated by occasional periods of work in the United States.

The gendered division of labor that Chibnik (2003) describes for wood-carving households in Arrazola (men typically carving, with women and young adults sanding and painting) is largely absent in the replica-production process.[9] The net output of replica pieces is significantly less than in wood carving, and nearly all the replica artisans I observed worked alone. Family members assist on occasion by tending kiln fires or polishing pieces. In Guillermo Avila's household, his wife regularly assumed these duties while he was out at the site, in addition to making smaller pieces such as pipes or acrobat figurines. In the after-

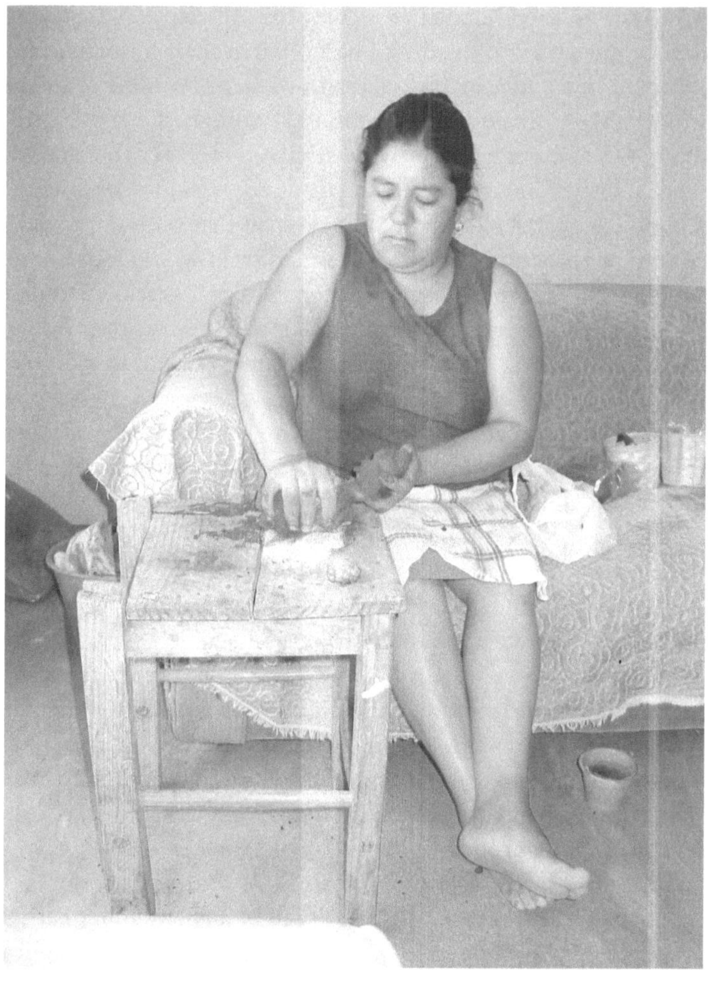

FIGURE 4.1. *Preparing clay for sculpting. (Photograph by author)*

noons after his return, the couple worked together in their living room, with his wife adding details and putting other final touches on her husband's sculpted pieces (fig. 4.1). The couple's teenage son and, less frequently, a daughter also made replicas. The son demonstrated a special talent for ceramic-making, and in his father's opinion the quality of his son's work matched or surpassed that of his own. Nevertheless, as in wood-carving households, the contributions of women and children, while deemed important and necessary, were generally viewed as supplementary to the work of male craftsmen.[10] Thus, while all of the male replica makers referred to themselves as *artesanos* (artisans), the women who assisted them tended to eschew this description, instead referring to their activities as "lending a hand" when their husbands required it.

Guillermo and Martín Avila both wished that none of their children would have to make their livelihood through the replica trade, even though they managed to provide relatively well for their families. This sentiment was shared by nearly all of the vendors who had young or school-age children at home. They hoped that with improved access to education and other resources their children would move on to better-paying jobs, perhaps in nearby Xoxocotlán or Oaxaca, instead of following in their footsteps. One man explained, "It's fine for a hobby maybe, to have something to do in their free time, but not as a career. There's no future in this." Wood carving, too, was viewed by some as a vocation with an uncertain future and was not necessarily encouraged as a full-time profession for younger generations. For instance, the wood-carver in whose home I lived during my fieldwork encouraged his exceptionally bright, then twelve-year-old, son to "keep working hard in school, so you get ahead, so you can choose what you want to do. Not like me, who didn't have the chance to study." While he would not have been disappointed if his son decided to become a wood-carver, he did not want him to experience his own regret and resentment at not pursuing his studies beyond junior high, when his family sent him out of state to Sinaloa to work picking tomatoes. The son later went on to win a statewide artisan competition while in high school but chose university study in computer and information science in Oaxaca; his father was undeniably proud of both accomplishments.

Chibnik reports that replica selling is ordinarily less remunerative than wood carving. He estimates that in 1996 vendors earned on average 100–150 pesos per day and that "almost all of the replica-makers in Arrazola in the 1990s were men older than forty-five" (Chibnik 2003:69).[11] This suggests that wood carving created a labor market that rapidly absorbed the community's young men who came of work age during the mid-1980s, and particularly during the 1986–1990 wood-carving boom. From this one might infer that older men already ensconced in the replica trade were less likely to leave their occupation and take up the relatively new wood-carving craft, even though it held the potential for generating higher incomes. Yet in my own 2003 survey of Arrazola men working as replica makers and sellers, I found that roughly half of them were under the age of forty-five, including Guillermo and Martín Avila, who were both in their thirties and widely held to be the best ceramicists in the community. In fact, younger men were more likely to make their own ceramic crafts than to buy them premade from workshops outside the village, the practice of most senior vendors who first started selling back in the late 1960s or 1970s. More importantly, it was Guillermo Avila who, at the age of nineteen, became the first person to make ceramic replicas in Arrazola, sparking a local cottage industry in the mid-1980s that chronologically paralleled the rise of the wood-carving trade.

If, as Chibnik maintains, wood carving was on the whole more remunerative than replica making and vending, then why would men in Arrazola choose to enter or remain in the replica business? Certainly more than one INAH official lamented the fact that the wood-carving trade was unable to attract all of the replica vendors with its promise of greater earnings and a "more dignified" position in the Oaxacan economy—one official only half-jokingly suggested that perhaps I could use my influence in the community to "get them to change their type of work."

In fact, nearly all of the men who came of work age (i.e., late teens or early twenties) just prior to or during the wood-carving boom at least tried their hand at wood carving, and five of them who once sold full-time at Monte Albán completely abandoned the trade in favor of full-time wood-carving careers. But other young replica vendors and artisans voiced a decided preference for their chosen occupation. Potential income was but one factor, albeit a crucial one. Both Guillermo and Martín Avila insisted that they liked making ceramics, and they found something genuinely satisfying in the creative process. Martín was the first to admit that their replica pieces simply came out much better than anything either one had ever carved.

> Look, we tried to [carve] once, but we really failed. The figures just wouldn't turn out right even though we tried to make different kinds, we couldn't even sell them. Not a single one! So we said, "Enough, this just isn't for us," and we went back to making these ceramic figures, but we tried to make them even better than before.

Others cited the fact that they would rather work outdoors at Monte Albán, in one of Oaxaca's most spectacular settings, than be confined to the home, as were most wood-carvers. A related complaint lodged by wood-carvers was that their sedentary lifestyle resulted in their declining health, citing increases in weight, high blood pressure, and diabetes. In contrast, Monte Albán vendors consistently did more walking and climbing as part of their daily job routine. One notably less ambitious man, who did not make his own replicas but instead bought them from other artisans, candidly admitted that he did not want to be bothered with the hassle of producing his own wares—with replica selling, he said, his only responsibility was to be at the site from 9 a.m. until about 2 p.m. and to periodically replenish his supply of replicas. Finally, it should be noted that by being able to occasionally sell replicas as "originals" (a strategy used by some, but not all), vendors may have been able to boost profits significantly over the figures reported by Chibnik.

Nevertheless, the most often cited reasons for entering or remaining in the replica trade revolved around the fierce competition that had come to characterize the contemporary wood-carving market. For the 1980s, when nearly every teenage and adult man in Arrazola attempted to participate in some aspect of wood-carving production, it is not difficult to understand the rationale for sticking it out in replica sales. Profits may have been more limited, but mechanisms for limiting competition—externally by INAH officials and internally by the vendors themselves—served to prevent market saturation of replica wares. The international demand for wood carvings rapidly tapered off at the end of the 1990s and into the new millennium. Wood-carving households that had prospered during the boom years suddenly found themselves without buyers. Only those who had long-standing relationships with galleries and collectors, such as Manuel Jiménez, or those workshops that were able to financially entice tour operators to supply them with clients did not feel the economic crush from the downturn in sales.

At the end of 2004, the male head of the household in which I lived in Arrazola, a talented and previously successful wood-carver, took up replica making in order to make up for the lost income from wood-carving sales. He carved in the morning and spent afternoons experimenting making ceramic figurines, which his father-in-law sold for him at Monte Albán (since that time he has also started to run a small grocery out of his house). One replica vendor optimistically predicted, "The wood-carving mania will eventually die down, as we're already seeing right here in Arrazola. At least at Monte Albán there will always be tourists!"

In addition to Arrazola, San Martín Tilcajete, and La Unión Tejalapan, carving is now done in the villages of San Pedro Cojonos and San Pedro Taviche, and in several workshops in Oaxaca. More recently, the wood-carving industry has been threatened by the offshore manufacturing of pieces in China, as North American wholesalers look to cut production costs (Alanna Cant, personal communication 2009).

MATERIAL AND SOCIAL ASPECTS OF REPLICA PRODUCTION

Chibnik (2003) has shown wood carvings to be highly varied crafts resulting from a complex, transnational supply chain of producers, intermediaries, and consumers, and he has illustrated that the total labor for producing a carving is often the sum of efforts by several individuals, even from different households. Indeed, in my experience it was rare that the same individual procured the raw materials for, carved, sanded, and painted a single piece. Women's labor in particular is completely subsumed in finished wood carvings, the overwhelming majority of which bear the signature of a male carver or other male household members who have contributed to the pieces. I also observed individuals selling carvings as their own handiwork when in fact they had been totally or partially made by someone else. On the distribution side, wood carvings are sold by villagers, Mexican and foreign wholesalers and retailers, tourists, and government agencies, including the state tourism office in Oaxaca.

Just as wood carving comprises a network of distributors, artisans, and individuals who may participate in only a portion of the production process, the replica trade demonstrates a more complicated organizational structure than is first apparent. Replica crafts vary somewhat in their stylistic elements but generally fall into two broad categories based on their materials: clay and stone. Most ceramic pieces are pre-Hispanic figural forms and small vessels produced locally, either in Arrazola or the aforementioned workshops in San Juanito and Colonia Monte Albán. Additional ceramic figures are occasionally purchased from suppliers who transport shipments of earthenware pieces from the neighboring states of Puebla and Guerrero.

Oaxacan-made ceramics are more likely to exhibit designs based on artifacts found at Monte Albán and other Oaxacan archaeological sites than are pieces produced out of state. Yet, as I discuss below, even these are more a product of their makers' imaginations than identical copies of original artifacts. Ceramic replicas imported from other areas of Mexico exhibit highly stylized characteristics that are less obviously identified with regional artifacts, while in practice vendors tend to classify these pieces as "Zapotec" or "Mixtec" when interacting with tourists, who may or may not be able to differentiate between regional Mesoamerican sculptural styles.

The visible markers proclaiming Arrazola's wood-carving trade to outsiders are virtually absent for its replica cottage industry. No hand-painted signs advertise "ceramics for sale," nor are replica crafts displayed alongside the assortment of wood carvings offered at the artisan market located on the town plaza. In contrast with the visual spectacle of wood-carving artisans, most of whom work outdoors in courtyards easily glimpsed from the street, ceramic artisans generally work in non-drafty, interior portions of their home where their clay is not subjected to the drying effects of sunlight and wind. Drop-in visits from folk art collectors and other potential clients are rare, as most people from outside the community are either unaware of or demonstrate little interest in visiting the home workshops of replica artisans.

Given the unprecedented commercial success of certain Arrazola wood-carvers, I was surprised to learn that wood carving was not necessarily perceived by village residents as a more lucrative or prestigious occupation than the making and selling of replicas. Although tourists rarely associate the replicas sold at Monte Albán with the wood carvings produced in Arrazola, the practitioners of these trades are often members of the same extended family and even the same household. The son of the famed originator of wood carving, Manuel Jiménez (see chapter 2), has worked as a replica seller at Monte Albán for over three decades. His sons, in turn, are successful wood-carvers with clients scattered throughout North America and Europe; they possess tourist visas and enjoy frequent travel to the United States to attend exhibitions, and one of their sons studied abroad there. The woman I lived with during my fieldwork is married to a wood-carver of modest commercial success while her father sells replicas. In addition to having served as the first president of the replica vendors' association, her father is a well-respected community member and former *agente municipal*, a town political office that confers a great deal of prestige. In some cases, vendors maintain wood-carving workshops in their homes, carving and painting during the evening when they are not at Monte Albán. In these households, it is also common for vendors' wives to paint or sand figures carved either by their husband or by other men in the community as part of their daily work.

The social interconnectedness of the two artisan forms within Arrazola has led most residents to view them as equally legitimate economic activities. Wood carving is uniformly perceived to be a more physically demanding task because it requires the practitioner to wield a machete and other sharp tools. But an individual's status in the community is not necessarily either elevated or diminished by making or selling replicas. Similarly, neither craft type was judged to be more traditional, culturally authentic, or visually attractive than the other. When asked to make such distinctions between the carvings made by her husband and replicas sold by her father, the woman above explained,

> For me, well, I would say that they're both *artesanías*. I like them both because each one has their own style. You know? It's hard to compare because the wood carvings are more colorful and they're more cheerful. I think that's why the tourists like them so much. But the replicas are more compelling. I think that they have more to do with the history of Oaxaca and the region because we live so close to Monte Albán.

Whatever social parity I observed between the two crafts in Arrazola, it was clear that the ceramic replicas did not enjoy the same publicity and prestige outside of the community as wood carving did—a fact not lost on the ceramic-makers themselves. Guillermo Avila brought to my attention a certain INAH sign located on Monte Albán's South Platform, part of a larger system of permanent, trilingual (Spanish, English, and Zapotec) markers located throughout the site interpreting the structures and history of Monte Albán. This sign was labeled "flora," and after a lengthy description of the area's wide array of pre-Hispanic plant life and its many medicinal and spiritual uses, the text directed the reader's attention to the village that could be viewed in the distance: "At the bottom of the valley one can see the town of Arrazola, where the famous handcrafted alebrijes are made; these figures, made from the wood of copal, represent fantastic animals" (fig. 4.2). Avila noted the irony in the sign singling out his hometown for its wood carvings while he and his fellow vendors from Arrazola, who were daily fixtures at the site and interacted with the very tourists for whom the sign was meant, warranted absolutely no mention. Though it clearly bothered him, he shrugged off INAH's omission, saying, "That's just the way it is, they're not very fond of us at Monte Albán." He then mentioned another INAH sign on the main plaza that I had missed on earlier trips to the site. This one instructed visitors in English and Spanish that it is against the law to "purchase archaeological objects or other items in this area." Although the federal law is technically designed to prohibit the sale of archaeological artifacts, one could easily interpret the mandate of this sign to include replica crafts as well.

Even though replicas produced in Arrazola have failed to achieve legitimacy within INAH's institutional structure, ceramic artisans take their craft seriously and have labored to consistently refine their products.[12] Artisans reported feeling pressured to come up with new de-

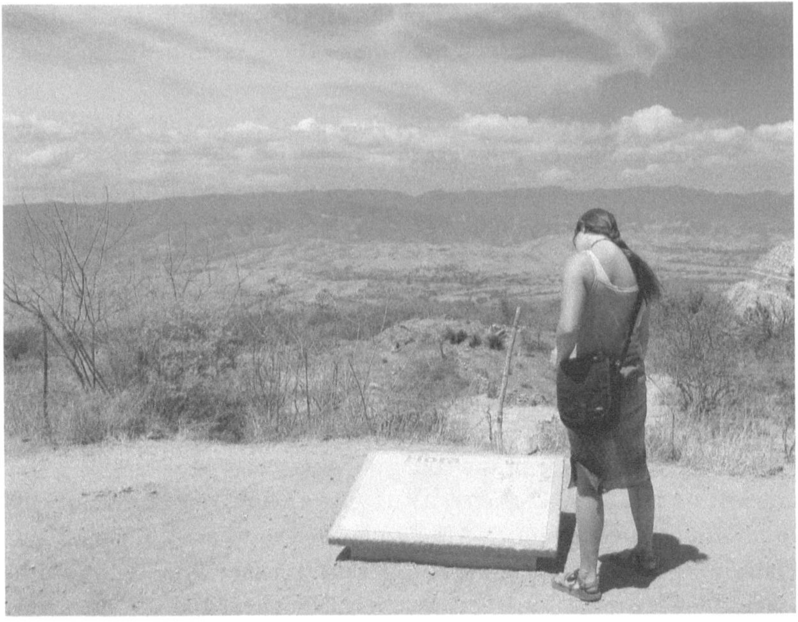

FIGURE 4.2. *An INAH sign informs visitors about the region's flora and directs their attention to the town of Arrazola in the distance. (Photograph by author)*

signs to distinguish their pieces from others', adding that the most popular designs were always at risk of being appropriated by others without permission, a phenomenon common in the tourism sphere (for discussions of other aesthetic appropriations, see Adams 2006; Colloredo-Mansfeld 1999; Kowalski 2009; Little 2004a; Meisch 2002; Wood 2008; Zorn 2004).

Anthropologist Andrew Causey (2003) witnessed similar efforts among Toba Batak wood-carvers from Sumatra, Indonesia, who produced newly carved "antique" religious objects for the contemporary tourist art market. Carvers literally kept photocopies of antique carvings under lock and key because competition to reproduce unique or unusual antique designs was so fierce. Furthermore, working within a genre based on aesthetic mimicry presents its own set of challenges for both Toba Batak wood-carvers and Oaxacan replica makers. Both groups of artisans must strike a fine balance between providing recognizable designs that signal "ancient" or "antique" to the purchaser while simultaneously keeping up with the moving target of tourist tastes and demands (fig. 4.3). Like archaeological replica makers in Oaxaca, many

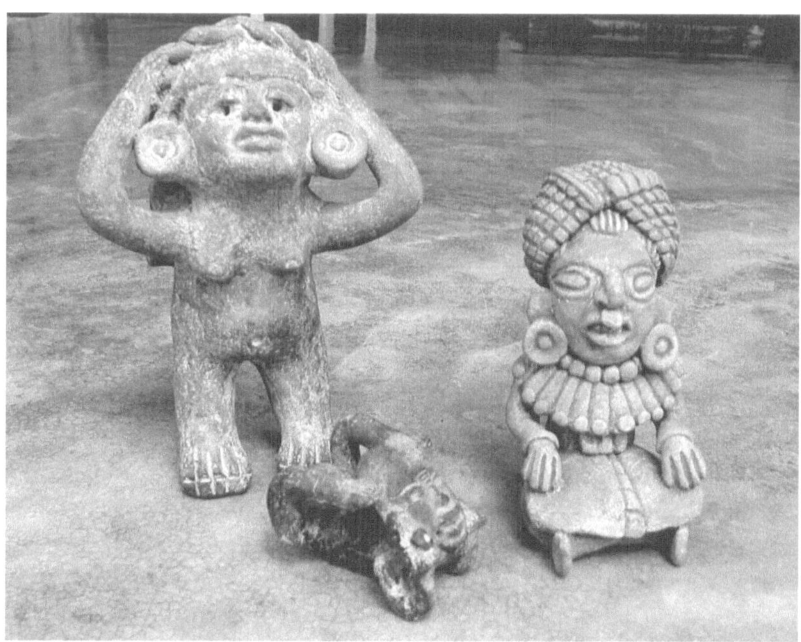

FIGURE 4.3. *A sample of ceramic replica designs. (Photograph by author)*

Toba Batak carvers find that "continuing the carving tradition means re-creating the same historical forms over and over, but others realize that westerners' uninformed interest in their work offers them an opportunity to innovate forms in the antique style, or to create imitation antiques" (Causey 2003:158).

Oaxacan replicas are not the same sort of hybrid forms, or "Maya modern artwork," observed by Quetzil Castañeda (2004a; 2009b) for sale at and around Chichén Itzá in Mexico's Yucatán Peninsula. Castañeda describes objects that are highly stylized renderings of Classic Mayan iconography and design; they are not intentionally made to look old, nor are they marketed as originals to unsuspecting tourists.

Initially I assumed replica artisans were working from photographs or drawings in Mexican archaeology books or other print media. After all, there is no shortage of commercial images of pre-Hispanic artifacts and iconography, as Monte Albán is featured on postcards, T-shirts, and souvenirs found throughout the city. I was surprised to learn that history textbooks published by the Mexican Secretary of Public Education (SEP) and provided free to elementary school children are some of the most-used visual resources. These texts convey the grandeur of the ancient past through the liberal sprinkling of illustrations of ruins, artifacts, and recreated scenes of pre-Hispanic life; the fifth-grade edition in particular focuses on Monte Albán and includes drawings of artifacts presumably found at the site. Artisans insisted that these stylized drawings (what amounted to cartoons) were useful not so much in that they served as exact templates, but rather because they represented basic stylistic elements such as facial features and expressions, symbols, and adornments considered to be Zapotec.

Although three artisans reported having acquired booklets or photographs dealing with archaeological artifacts from tourists at Monte Albán, Guillermo Avila was the only one I knew who consulted full-length, scholarly books on archaeology. It was not a question of artisans being opposed to utilizing such resources. Rather, most lacked the social and economic capital necessary to procure them in the various city libraries and privately owned bookstores, which catered primarily to university students, tourists, and middle- or upper-class Oaxacans. In my own experience, gaining access to Oaxaca library materials was certainly more difficult than in the United States. Books and other documents were generally not allowed to be checked out from the premises, and borrowers were required to show some sort of identification, preferably a university ID card. The library at the INAH-Oaxaca Regional Center, which houses many references on archaeology, was particularly well monitored and required visitors to prove some sort of university or research affiliation upon entry. It was during Avila's years as a law student that he became well acquainted with Oaxaca's libraries and its largest academic bookstore, the *Proveedora Escolar*. In addition to the legal textbooks required for his courses, the store carried an extensive selection of anthropological works on ancient Mesoamerica that proved useful in designing replicas, including the seminal 1962 text *Mexico: From the Olmecs to the Aztecs* by Yale archaeologist emeritus Michael D. Coe.

Whether working from grade school texts or from archaeology books, replica artisans all employ the same basic materials, tools, and techniques. They purchase premixed balls of clay weighing 10–15 kilograms each from neighboring Atzompa. The balls cost 100 pesos each and yield approximately 10–12 medium-sized figures (15–20 centimeters high). Artisan tool kits are simple and improvisational in nature; common implements include matchsticks, for making eyes and other round shapes; *carrizo* (a native plant resembling bamboo) sticks of various sizes, for scraping, making designs, and cutting bits of clay; and smooth stones, for burnishing. The sharp tips of nails are used to create

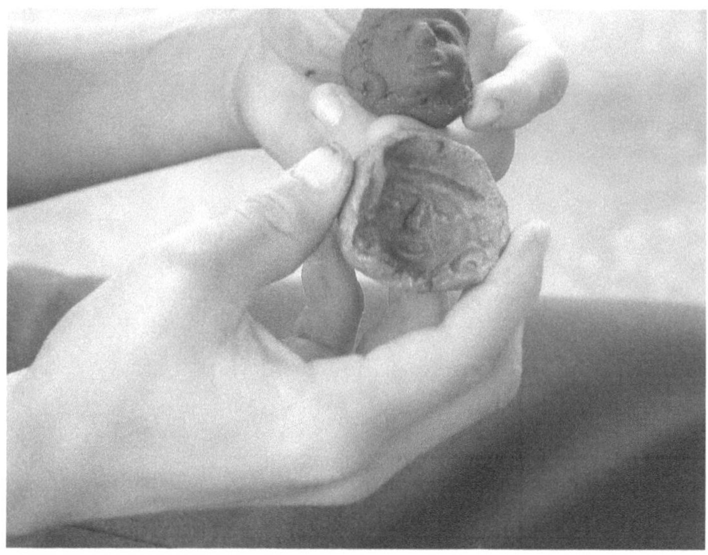

FIGURE 4.4. *Facial fragments known as* caritas *are usually cast from molds. (Photograph by author)*

rough surfaces on the clay where individually molded arms or other appendages may be attached.

To expedite the sculpting process, artisans employ molds cast from other finished pieces to form the faces for new figures, particularly for the small- to medium-sized replicas. Some men claimed to have molds cast from original artifacts, while others reported casting molds from other replica pieces that they or other artisans had made. The molds feature stylized facial characteristics that artisans generally classify as either Zapotec or Olmec, the latter distinguished by wide, full mouths and noses (fig. 4.4). Innovative or experimental facial designs are formed entirely by hand without the aid of a mold (fig. 4.5).

The sculpting process's simplicity is mirrored in the drying and firing techniques. Assessing contemporary production methods, Guillermo Avila pointed out that he and his fellow artisans were likely using "traditional materials" and "ancient techniques" similar to the ones employed by Monte Albán ceramicists centuries ago. Completed figures are allowed to dry over a period of several days or weeks. A man specializing in miniatures discovered that he could speed the drying process along by placing his figures on his wife's *comal*, a round, earthenware griddle used for making tortillas, and letting them slowly bake over an open fire (fig. 4.6).

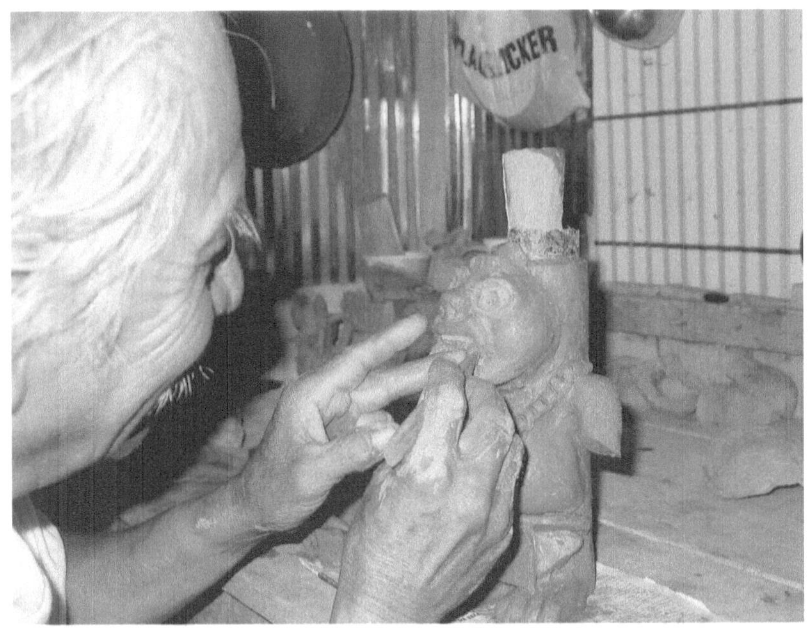

FIGURE 4.5. *Adding the facial details to a ceramic sculpture. (Photograph by author)*

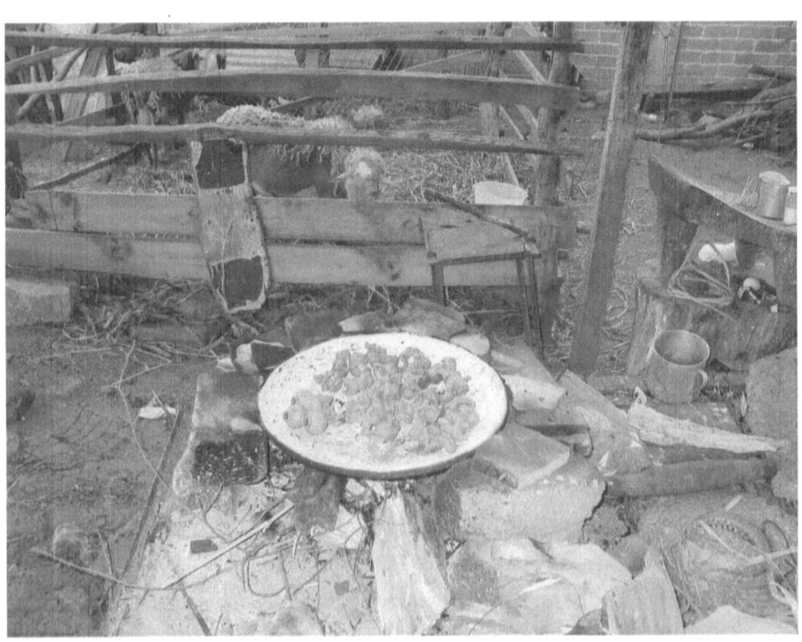

FIGURE 4.6. *Replicas drying on a* comal. *(Photograph by author)*

Once the pieces are partially dry (a stage referred to by potters as "leather hard"), artisans go over the pieces again, adding final details and polishing any remaining rough spots. For a smooth surface with a slightly glossy sheen, small pebbles may be used to uniformly burnish the entire piece. Finished pieces are fired in an open pit rather than in an enclosed kiln. The low-temperature method (500–1000° Celsius) results in an earthenware product that is much less durable than either stoneware or porcelain, both of which are kiln-fired at higher temperatures.[13] Pieces are typically left in their natural terracotta state and do not undergo the second firing required for glazed ceramics. The final step is to give newly made pieces the look of centuries-old artifacts though a variety of finishing techniques, a task that may be completed either by the ceramicist or by those vendors who buy premade wares.

Most men carefully guarded their methods, whether the purpose of these was simply to enrich the figures' earthy colors or to manufacture the patina of age that characterized recently excavated archaeological artifacts. The most commonly cited practice was to apply multiple coats of dirt (preferably obtained at or near the archaeological site) or corn husk ash to the pieces as they emerged warm from the fire and then again after they had cooled. Others applied a solution of potassium permanganate, said to deepen the pieces' color and seal the clay's naturally porous surface. An artisan in his early forties reported that he had briefly used potassium permanganate until learning about its toxicity, but added that "a lot of the old guys use it even though it might be harmful to them." Even more dangerously, one wood-carver who stocked a small inventory of stone and ceramic replicas in his workshop allegedly applied an acid-based solution to pieces he purchased from other artisans. As proof he offered up a stone figure that indeed appeared to have been eaten away in places, an effect he said he further enhanced by rubbing soil into those surface spaces. I also heard accounts of men burying replica pieces in the ground in corn husk ashes and even in piles of burro manure for months at a time in order to achieve a time-worn appearance.

Unlike ceramic crafts, which constitute a local cottage industry, nearly all the stone crafts sold at Monte Albán are distributed through Taxco, a city in the neighboring state of Guerrero. But this does not impede vendors from trying to convince customers that they completely handcraft all of the wares, including stone objects produced outside the region. Tourists described how they had been approached by men at the site who carried stone masks and figures, claiming that they had carved the stone and done the inlay work themselves. Trusting tourists believed these stories, especially when vendors offered up the scars on their hands and wrists as proof of injuries sustained while supposedly cutting stones—although they were more likely old wounds from misplaced machete strikes from wood-carving attempts. Other tourists were not so easily convinced. It was the presence of nonlocally made pieces that led one Australian tourist to conclude that vendors sold "stuff you could find at any archaeological site in Mexico" and a previous Monte Albán director to comment about the increasing serialization of replica crafts at the site (see previous chapter).

Stone objects became part of the standard collection of replica wares sold by Arrazola residents at Monte Albán in the early 1970s. One vendor in his late sixties recalled that he began getting requests in around 1973 from tourists who wanted to purchase masks like the ones they had seen on display in museums in Mexico City and Oaxaca. Several years prior, five men from the village had started experimenting with making their own figures and masks out of a purple-hued stone flecked with white and gray specks that they cut with machetes from the surrounding hills. The volcanic-looking stone ultimately proved difficult to cut with nonmechanical hand tools. More critically, the finished products, which one elderly man described as "too crude and very rustic looking," were not popular with tourists. They abandoned the idea and instead sought out a readymade stone product.

Inquiries with various shops and vendors in Oaxaca ultimately led them to Taxco, a city more commonly known for its silverwork but also a distribution center for stone crafts. One man recalled his desire to find a product that looked similar to a turquoise and shell mosaic skull discovered forty years earlier by Alfonso Caso. The piece, part of the famous Tomb 7 contents and emblematic of Monte Albán's archaeological treasures, was well known to tourists, who frequently asked for reproductions of it. They eventually located several distributors who were able to supply them with masks made in two styles: a single, solid stone, and mosaic inlay. These masks exhibited none of the finely crafted details of the original pre-Hispanic piece and resembled it only in the most abstract way. Yet the style was popular enough with tourists that by 1975 it had become a standard offering at the site.

One of the men who originally experimented with making stone pieces noted that their materials and the overall quality of the finished works had varied throughout the past thirty years. The early masks were typically made of blackish-green serpentine stone or the jadelike aventurine stone, and were considered by Arrazola vendors to be "the finest crafts" sold at Monte Albán at that time. When the availability of serpentine masks declined in the early 1990s, they were replaced by masks made out of granite, a lower-grade material that apparently did not appeal as well to tourists. Granite made a brief appearance before it was quickly replaced in 1992 by masks of soapstone, another inexpensive and easily carved material whose porous surface lent itself to painting. The soapstone masks, along with masks made of aventurine and mosaics of other materials such as rose quartz, tiger eye, mother of pearl, and malachite, are the stone items most commonly sold at Monte Albán today.

Prior to 1999 vendors made regular trips to Taxco to purchase stone wares. A wholesaler from there later began exporting pieces to Oaxaca himself, eventually relocating to Oaxaca, where he set up a distribution center in San Martín Mexicapan, a working-class neighborhood on the outskirts of the city in close proximity to Monte Albán. Vendors purchase mosaic and soapstone masks and stylized stone deities from the wholesaler, who sells an extensive variety of loose semiprecious stones as well as glass and plastic beads (the operation also supplies necklace vendors who work at Monte Albán and throughout the city). While the Mexicapan location is notably more convenient, the mosaic masks that vendors once purchased for 80 pesos or less in Taxco now cost them between 100 and 120 pesos per mask. Three other men from outside the region also made sporadic trips to Oaxaca to sell stone merchandise to vendors, but the Mexicapan outlet was the main supplier. Most common were masks composed of either a single, carved piece of soapstone or assembled from mosaics of relatively inexpensive stones. Less common were small figurines and vessels commonly made from quartz or other materials that take on a brilliant sheen when polished. Arrazola vendors commonly enhanced them with finishing techniques, or as they put it, by applying their own "original touches." As previously noted, this sometimes entailed dipping them in acid or other labor-intensive treatments designed to give the pieces added brilliance, durability, and sometimes a different color.

For the Arrazola vendors, the soapstone masks represent the most labor-intensive crafts apart from the locally produced ceramic pieces. While mosaic masks may be sold in the same condition in which they are obtained (vendors occasionally added an additional layer of clear synthetic gloss to seal the stones and heighten the shine), the soapstone masks require finishing treatments before they can be sold to tourists. In their natural state soapstone masks are a rather unassuming gray-beige color. To achieve the eye-catching turquoise and jade colors that many tourists associate with the original pre-Hispanic pieces on display

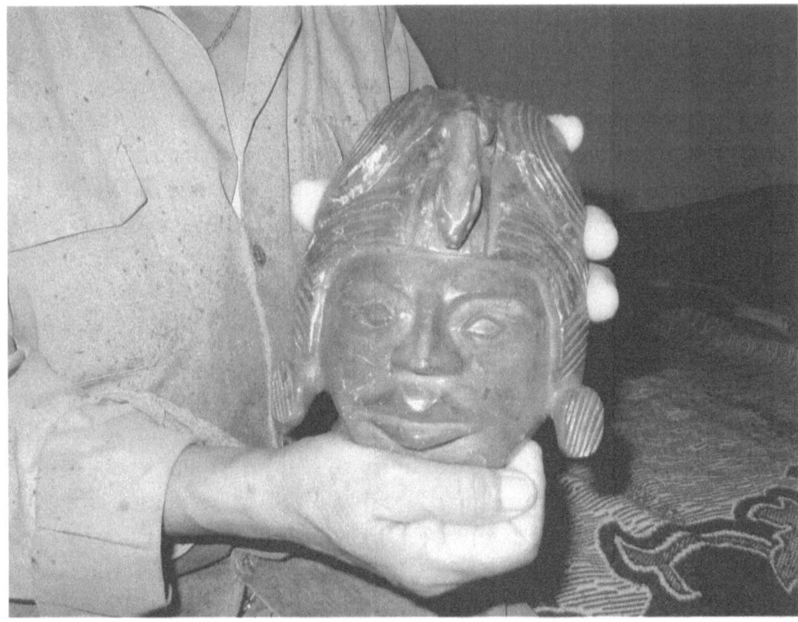

FIGURE 4.7. *Soapstone mask. (Photograph by author)*

in Oaxaca's museums, vendors apply two or more coats of synthetic aniline dye to the masks until they obtain the desired tone (fig. 4.7). After the paint dries, the masks are ready to be "cured."

The person I observed carry out this process coated each mask with a preparation of powdered potassium permanganate dissolved in water, which he had allowed to sit for three to four days in order to enhance its properties. However, he warned that if the solution was too strong or left on the mask too long it could actually dissolve the stone ("*se come la piedra*," or literally eat away at it). The chemical substance, which he referred to in Spanish as *permanganato*, was sold in hardware stores throughout the city. It was more commonly used to disinfect and heal surface wounds on livestock, but he explained that men in the community had discovered that it also served to set the dye and enhance the overall appearance of the stone pieces and ceramics that they sold. Without this step, the color was prone to fading and, worse yet, bleeding when exposed to moisture. He cautioned that one had to be very careful when handling potassium permanganate, as its powerful oxidizing effect made it extremely corrosive to human skin; the heavy apron and elbow-length rubber gloves that he wore as he worked underscored the danger. He used the same solution to cure the ceramic replica pieces made by his nephew as well as those he bought from San Juanito artisans, explaining that this extra treatment enhanced the clay's natural terracotta color and the stones' brilliance.

Arrazola vendors claimed to have developed these coloring and sealing techniques on their own. This is highly likely given residents' history of experimentation with other materials and craftwork; wood carving and ceramic making, both developed in the community within the past thirty years, are primarily self-taught forms. A resident who began vending at Monte Albán in 1972 recalled that he and several neighbors first experimented with extracts derived from local plants: "We would walk all over the hills around Monte Albán collecting any plant that we thought might give off a nice color when you boiled it. I knew what plants people here used to use for medicines but I had no idea what would work for dyes." After a string of failed attempts, he visited a hardware store in the city and asked how weavers from Teotitlán del Valle dyed the wool for their woven textiles. Thinking it to be a long shot, he brought home samples of the synthetic aniline dyes recommended by the Oaxaca storekeeper, the same dyes used to color the relatively inexpensive *tapetes* (woven rugs) found in many local shops and markets.[14] Over the course of several trial runs he achieved surprisingly good results.

The same man had bought dyes and potassium permanganate in relatively large quantities for years from the same small store in Oaxaca, where he routinely deflected inquiries about his purchases from overly curious employees. While the potassium permanganate was easily justified as a topical medicine for his burros, the aniline dyes were another story. He admitted, "Most store employees think we're weavers from Teotitlán, and that's why we need the dye." Indeed, the application of synthetic dyes and potassium permanganate were the two finishing processes that most Arrazola vendors were willing to openly discuss with me although there may have been others. In the interest of protecting the techniques that they had developed over the years, vendors necessarily maintained a certain level of secrecy when it came to the signature "*toques*," or finishing touches, that they gave their wares in order to enhance their perceived value or to give them the patina of centuries-old artifacts.

As I discuss in the next chapter, it is precisely this manufactured authenticity that makes Monte Albán replica crafts desirable to some and dangerous to others.

VIEWS FROM THE PYRAMID

The image of Mexico as a pyramid is one viewpoint among many others equally possible: the viewpoint of what is on the platform at its top. It is the viewpoint of the ancient gods and those who served them, the Aztec lords and priests. It is also that of their heirs and successors: the viceroys, the generals, the presidents. And, furthermore, it is the viewpoint of the vast majority, of the victims crushed by the pyramid or sacrificed on its platform-sanctuary. The critique of Mexico begins with the critique of the pyramid.

OCTAVIO PAZ, *THE LABYRINTH OF SOLITUDE*

I LOOKED UPWARD FROM MY POSITION AT the base of the giant stone staircase leading up to Monte Albán's South Platform. No matter how many times I climbed up those pyramid steps, I always arrived at the top feeling a sense of vertigo and as if my lungs were about to burst. I made my ascent in the midst of a pack of elementary school children all dressed alike in a favorite Oaxacan school uniform: white polo shirts along with navy slacks for the boys and navy skirts for the girls. Two female teachers trailed at the back, watching the mayhem unfold. Pushing myself up and over the last step, I leaned against a waist-high stone wall and stopped to catch my breath. One of the teachers yelled a last-minute warning about not climbing on rocks as the school group dispersed into bunches of shrieking children.

Just off to my left, partially obscured by some brush, I saw a vendor I had briefly met during my first few weeks at Monte Albán. Even though we had never talked at great length, Jorge stood out in my mind because I remembered that he was one of a handful of vendors who were not from Arrazola but was nevertheless a member of the vendors' association. Standing next to him was a smartly dressed woman who looked to be in her early to mid-thirties. His outstretched hand held a ceramic *pitao cozobi*, a ubiquitous and popular figurine sold at Monte Albán, which he apparently was trying to sell to the woman. I had heard guides at the site refer to this Zapotec deity in Spanish as the *dios del maíz*, or corn god, because of the corn-cob shapes that often adorned pre-Hispanic figural representations. Jorge glanced over in my direction but did not appear to recognize me.

I made my way over to where Jorge and his customer were standing. He continued with his sales pitch, seemingly unfettered by my sudden presence. I did not say anything, and was quite certain that he thought I was just another interested tourist. Closer to the figure in question, I could see that it was only about nine or ten inches high and, in my opinion, the quality of the work was actually quite high compared with similar pieces I had encountered for sale at Monte Albán. Well-formed features, strategically placed cracks in the ceramic surface, and just the right amount of dirt residue indexed antiquity to my untrained eye. In a hushed tone, Jorge assured the Mexican woman that this was an "original" and, indeed, a bargain at the 150 peso asking price. The woman cupped the figure in her palm and thoroughly inspected it from every angle. "Well, it's pretty nice. You can see all of the details on the face," she confirmed. She did not dispute the vendor's claims of authenticity. Fully aware that shopping was often construed as a competitive sport, I feigned interest in the piece and asked if I could hold it for a moment. She grudgingly passed it to me as if handing over a precious and fragile treasure. I remarked aloud that the figure possessed exquisite detail, tracing the contours of the idol's face with my fingertips. The Mexican tourist glared.

The seller asked us to follow him to a more secluded spot just around the corner, away from the tourist groups assembling at the top of the monument. In a barely audible voice, he explained to us that he was a tractor operator who tilled village lands at the edge of Monte Albán. He made a sweeping gesture with his arm and pointed in the direction of where the town of Arrazola sat below. He allegedly regularly unearthed small figurines and other archaeological fragments while on the job. He also swore that he was giving us an excellent price, even as, in the same breath, he lowered it from 150 pesos to 100.

The woman, obviously annoyed at my interest in the piece, could no longer contain herself and blurted out, "You can't legally take those back into your country, you know. They belong to Mexico. They can confiscate them at customs, or worse, they'll fine you or send you to prison." Not wanting to shatter the illusion but also not wanting to make outright false claims, I scrambled for an acceptable way out: "I've taken lots of those pieces home before—I just tell them they're replicas when I go through customs and they always leave me alone."

At that point, I could tell by the look on his face that it had dawned on Jorge who I was, and, more importantly, that I appeared to be helping him make a sale. He corroborated my assertion that I could safely transport replicas across the border into the United States, and proceeded to say that there were more pieces stashed in the bushes if we wanted to see them. The woman declined his offer, saying that she needed to find her husband. Perhaps I had been too convincing for my own good, I thought to myself.

I watched as the tourist walked back toward the enormous stairway that connected us to the main plaza below. Suddenly she was gone, with the optical illusion of her body disappearing over the edge of the pyramid as if into thin air. At that moment I took the opportunity to reintroduce myself to Jorge. Although he appeared genuinely pleased to see me, I could tell he was still distracted by what I presumed to be the failed transaction. Jorge, however, possessed a more nuanced understanding of tourist psychology than I and assured me that all was not lost. Pleasantries momentarily brushed aside, he instructed me to walk around the outskirts of the pyramid platform and then take my time circling back, making the return approach from the opposite side. I did as I was told and casually strolled off on my carefully prescribed path.

Looping back to my original point of departure I was surprised to see that the woman had returned and now stood talking with Jorge, who no doubt was telling her how much the "*güera*" (I managed to overhear that word, paired with a hand motion in my direction) wanted the piece.[1] Whatever he said, it must have been convincing, because she took out her wallet and handed over several bills. Transaction completed, the tourist walked away and Jorge came over to meet me. His ebullient expression and the spring in his gait conveyed to me that he was pleased by the sale, and he thanked me for helping. Before the conversation could progress any further, the same woman appeared again, this time with a male companion, whom I took to be the husband.

"Okay, I'll take that other piece you showed me, too. But," she qualified, "I'm only going to give you 100 pesos for it." Jorge did not argue, but rather produced the piece along with several crumpled sheets of newspaper from his duffel bag and wrapped it up before she could change her mind. Amused by his wife's tenacity in striking the bargain, the man good-naturedly joked about all the pre-Hispanic figures she had amassed, enough to "fill a small museum." He chided his wife, noting her inability to resist buying the objects for their home: "You just can't seem to pass those things up, can you?"

Both parties satisfied, the couple left. Jorge, his back slightly turned from me, discreetly made the sign of the cross. He wheeled back around on his heels and smiled. Not one to miss an opportunity, he asked, "So, do you want to buy a figure?" "Seriously?" I uttered in disbelief. Jorge sensed my amusement but nonetheless felt compelled to ask, "Are you sure you don't want to buy one? Because I've got the really good pieces over there in the bushes."

CHAPTER FIVE

Replicating Authenticity, Authenticating Replicas

> *The views from both the mountain and pyramids are spectacular. The area has underground passageways where one could give the illusion of being in one place, vanishing, and reappearing in another. It is believed that this trick was used by priests. When I was there, there were men being in one place, vanishing, and then popping up in another, but they were not Amerindian holy men. Rather, they were hucksters who would appear out of nowhere trying to sell me "authentic" relics. There were fertility figures, animals, and gods. All of these men swore that theirs were authentic and found, surprise, right under the ground at Monte Albán. After saying "no, no thank you, thank you but no, really no, I mean it, no" far too many times, I left the site and headed back to the city.*
>
> LEE ARNOLD, "DREAMING OF OAXACA"

TRAVELER LEE ARNOLD (2002) RECOUNTED HIS experience at Monte Albán on www.BootsnAll.com, a website billing itself as "the ultimate resource for the independent traveler." In contrast to the Mexican tourist discussed in the preceding vignette, Arnold portrays himself as too savvy to be taken in by the "discourse of uncertainty" (van der Spek 2008) maintained by vendors to incite the feeling of possibility: Could the recently crafted artifacts in fact be from pre-Hispanic antiquity? I previously discussed state interventions in replica makers and sellers' creative, and sometimes lucrative, use of Mexican cultural patrimony. Yet the full-scale suppression of the archaeological replica trade has never been realized, and vendors assiduously craft their own material and narrative interpretations of the pre-Hispanic past.

Drawing on the work of Bakhtin (1981) and Ricouer (1981, 1984), anthropologist Kathleen Stewart writes that "narrative is first and foremost a mediating form through which 'meaning' must pass. Stories, in other words, are productive" (Stewart 1996:29). From this insight it follows that archaeology's master narrative about Monte Albán may not be the only means through which the site's material vestiges are imbued with social meaning, even if archaeological discourse continuously works to assert its primacy. As such, here I am concerned with replicas as material nodes of meaning-making: sites for the proliferation of stories through which not only sellers but also guides, tourists, and others dialogically enact and circulate particular understandings of the past. What alternative ways of seeing and narrating Oaxacan material culture and patrimony are opened up through the practice of replica making and selling?

As mimetic forms, replicas derive their symbolic power from a hegemonic "art-culture system" (Clifford 1988) that is predicated on and privileges an authentic, consumable pre-Hispanic past and a folkloric, indigenous present. Yet—as neither genuine folk art nor artifacts in the eyes of some—pre-Hispanic replicas occupy an uncomfortable space somewhere in between these two realms of material culture, mimicking the symbolic and aesthetic codes of each. This is the power of the copy and why unauthorized replicas (even those explicitly marketed as such) frequently evoke co-mingling feelings of desire and anxiousness. In this chapter I take up how replicas' illicit representations of the pre-Hispanic past mediate between official narratives of patrimony and other modes of apprehending Oaxacan history and "culture," simultaneously evoking these discourses while working to destabilize them.

MATERIALIZING MEXICAN SENTIMENTS

Nationalist representations of pre-Hispanic culture are omnipresent in Mexico and draw on a wide repertoire of symbols, some faithfully reproduced from their original contexts and others that are highly stylized. Every day, Mexicans are reminded of their collective, indigenous heritage through a vast representational field of pre-Hispanic iconography, material remains, and linguistic references (street signs with Nahuatl names, perhaps trivial, are yet illustrative).

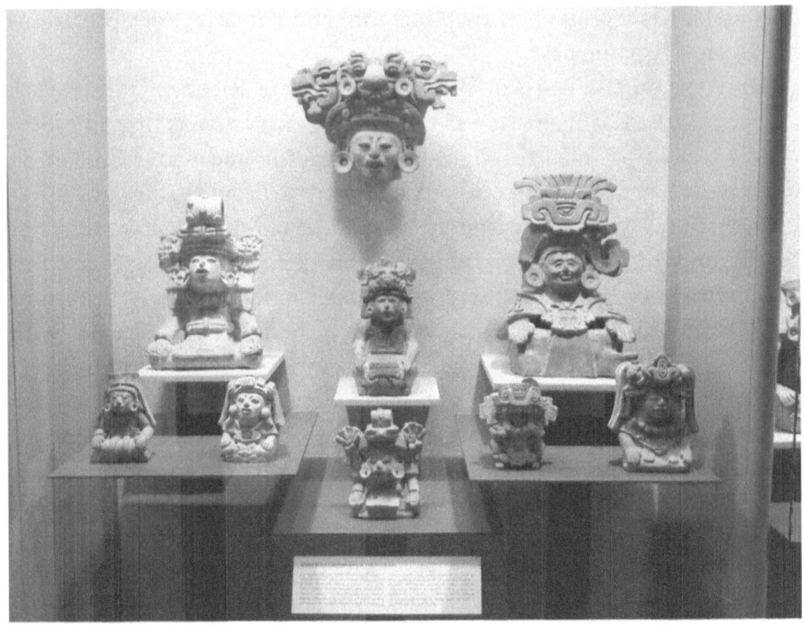

FIGURE 5.1. *A group of Oaxacan ceramic artifacts on display at the National Museum of Anthropology in Mexico City. (Photograph by author)*

Within this "revolutionary aesthetic statism," as Ana Alonso (2004) characterized it, museums and regional archaeological monuments represent the most elaborate staging of a Mexican pre-Hispanic past and serve as iconic national pilgrimage sites in their own right; visitation to INAH archaeological monuments and museums is encouraged by a national policy of free Sunday admission to anyone able to provide proof of Mexican citizenship. At these sites, the national narrative of pre-Hispanic grandeur, the bloody Spanish Conquest, and the subsequent process of *mestizaje* are enshrined and presented to the public through an assemblage of reconstructed archaeological material, artifacts, dioramas, and carefully crafted texts (Errington 1998; García Canclini 1995, 1997). The National Museum of Anthropology in Mexico City offers the nationalist pantheon par excellence, and includes a specially designated "Sala Oaxaca" (Oaxaca exhibit hall) where visitors may acquaint themselves with the diversity of pre-Hispanic sculptural forms from the region (fig. 5.1).

The message of these sites as a representational whole is further reinforced through a popular and widely distributed magazine, *Arqueología Mexicana*, published in conjunction with INAH and the National

Council on Culture and the Arts (CONACULTA) and available at newsstands and bookstores nationwide. Aimed at an educated, Spanish-language audience, *Arqueología Mexicana* frequently juxtaposes stories and images of archaeological monuments and artifacts with those of contemporary indigenous peoples, whose markets, foods, handicrafts, and other traditions are showcased in its glossy layouts. The magazine imparts a particular version of cultural continuity, as readers are visually and textually encouraged to draw connections between the Mesoamerican past and its contemporary manifestations.

Much to the chagrin of archaeologists and other cultural heritage boosters, replica crafts can be seen to be part and parcel of the same representational system that they themselves have created. In *The Plundered Past*, author Karl Meyer declares the prevalence of "fakes" to be "the venereal disorder of the illicit art market—the punishment for excessive desire and bad judgment" (Meyer 1973:108). However, his proclamation, delivered with unapologetic disdain, fails to examine desire itself as a productive social force (Deleuze and Guattari 2009 [1972]). Thus it is critical to see that the desire to represent and consume antiquity, in all of its various forms, is a generative force within the larger national machinery. From this standpoint, "fakes" do not stand apart from museums, magazines, heritage sites, etc. Rather, they affectively work on their producers and consumers only within this wider system of signification.

It is first necessary to explore the consumer base for Monte Albán replicas in greater depth. In my experience replicas were most frequently purchased by Mexican tourists. Americans, Europeans, and other foreigners also bought replica crafts, but not in the same quantities. And assessments by others who have some familiarity with Oaxaca's art and archaeological heritage market mirrored this observation. Former Monte Albán director Nelly Robles García, for one, felt certain that most replica-purchasers were Mexican tourists who got caught up in the "emotion" of being at such a massive and important heritage site. She said that large-scale archaeological monuments like Monte Albán were synonymous with Mexican archaeology for those outside of the field (with the negative consequence that lesser-known sites were financially neglected by the state and private donors). Mary Jane Gagnier de Mendoza, a Canadian expatriate married to a well-known Zapotec weaver with whom she ran a successful, upscale art gallery in Oaxaca, was more specific. She speculated that replica-buyers were likely "middle-class Mexican families out for the day with grandma." Notably, she singled out neither working-class Mexicans nor Mexican elites as consumers. This presumed market segmentation appealed to the notion that working-class Mexicans may not have the financial resources for purchasing objects with no utilitarian value.

On the other end of the spectrum, the wealthiest of Mexican tourists, in line with the assertions of Bourdieu (1984), exhibited a different code of aesthetics and taste that seemed to preclude an attraction to so-called pre-Hispanic fakes: Why buy a fake, after all, when you can have the real thing? As already noted, a flourishing high-end art market for original artifacts has historically guaranteed the availability of such pieces for those with the right contacts and large enough pocketbooks; in this regard, it seems, national and international efforts to police the sale and trade of pre-Hispanic antiquities have only been partially effective (Brodie et al. 2001; del Villar K. 1996; Messenger 1989).

Gagnier expanded her list of likely replica-buyers to include older Europeans, especially those participating in chartered tours. She imagined this type of buyer to be on his or her first "New World" tour and armed with a somewhat researched, if basic, knowledge of Mesoamerican archaeology. She observed that some Europeans still exhibited a "colonial mentality" toward Latin America, and that Mexico represented the rustic culture that had been lost in their own modern societies. She added that "people want the real thing. They want to be living that *National Geographic* article." She said that Oaxaca was perceived to be a "safe place to visit," unlike Mexico City, which boasted world-class museums and archaeological sites along with severe pollution and high crime rates.[1]

Gagnier believed that Americans—a group she estimated to comprise at least 70 percent of her own gallery clientele—also fancied Oaxaca as a safe and exotic destination. However, in her experience, American travelers were generally less well versed in the details of pre-Hispanic history and material culture, and were less likely to read books on Mesoamerican archaeology than their European counterparts. She did not see as much of a market for replicas among American tourists, and thus did not consider such items as appropriate merchandise for her store. She described replicas as "dangerous" because, in her words, "it is a very fine line between what's real and what's not." For the same reasons, she expressed anxiety about selling *retablos* and *ex-votos*, even though she always made it clear that the pieces in her shop were not originals, but designs based on original religious art.[2] She elaborated, saying, "Most people don't want to know because they like to carry the illusion of having bought an original." Monte Albán replica purveyors notably shared some of these entrepreneurial insights.

While Americans were generally less informed about pre-Hispanic culture and history than Europeans, they conversely exhibited a broader knowledge of Oaxacan handicrafts. The history of American patronage of Mexican folk arts—which stretches back to the 1920s—and the enduringly robust, commercial trade it set in motion (Delpar 1992; López 2010) mean that U.S. consumers have been primed for decades to appreciate classes of objects aesthetically encoded as Mexican folk art. Today, North American potential buyers may research regionally specific crafts before their visit by consulting such books as *Oaxacan Woodcarving: The Magic in the Trees* (Barbash 1993) and *Mexican Folk Art from Oaxacan Artist Families* (Rothstein and Rothstein 2007). Gagnier asserted that exposure to these publications and others like them significantly factored in Americans' purchase of local contemporary art and high-end folk art, such as the one-of-a-kind wood carvings she carried; Americans accounted for greater sales quantities than either Mexican nationals or European consumers.[3] Henry Wangeman, another foreign expatriate, reported a similar trend. For several years he and his Mexican wife ran an upscale folk art gallery attached to their English-language bookstore in Oaxaca. He said that for many Americans and Canadians, Oaxaca was a "crafts mecca," a place worthy of an annual buying pilgrimage.

Indeed, during the time that I lived in Arrazola, nearly all woodcarving purchases I witnessed were made by Americans. Mexican visitors frequently expressed their appreciation for the wood-carvers' technical skills but were less willing to spend money on objects that, in the words of one tourist, "don't have history." This apparent lack of "history" encompassed not only the relative newness of the woodcarving genre as it emerged in the 1980s, but also its lack of an overt historical referent such as pre-Hispanic iconography. Unlike replicas, with their unmistakable symbolism, the more experimental styles of many wood carvings did not always connote a typically Mexican aesthetic for national travelers. For instance, a woman from Mexico City on an organized tour to Arrazola said that she thought the wood carvings would "be fine to decorate a beach house, for instance, but they're not very Mexican."[4] On the other hand, pre-Hispanic replicas, because of their symbolic referent, appear to function in much the same way as the ubiquitous Aztec calendar stone, which has become synonymous with Mexico both within and outside of the country, and graces everything from T-shirts to coffee mugs.

I asked a guide at Monte Albán why he thought Mexican tourists might be drawn to replicas. The guide, who had studied anthropology and sociology at a local university, explained that the replicas "*les llaman*": literally, they call to the buyers. He said that many of his Mexican tour groups would stop and look at the pieces offered by vendors even if they did not intend to purchase anything—a practice that he found distracting as a guide trying to explain the site's history. He, too, noted that American and European tourists seemed less interested in replicas on the whole. His explanation was that replicas appealed to "*un sentimiento escondido*," a deep-rooted and perhaps unconscious sentiment that Mexicans possessed regarding their shared pre-Hispanic past. Including himself in this assessment, he declared, "After all, those are our ancestors. That's what we grew up reading about since we were kids." He did not, however, make the connection with the fact that many of the Monte Albán replicas' designs were quite literally inspired by the history textbooks from which Mexican schoolchildren learn about their nation's past. The guide's comments point to how a specific regional history becomes transformed into a Mexican collective self. The Zapotec and Mixtec peoples who once utilized Monte Albán, along with the Aztec, Mayan, and other well-known pre-Hispanic culture groups, collapse into a singular, unified Mexican ancestry.

Replicas serve as a medium through which Mexican tourists articulate an emotional investment in the past that vacillates between collective and individual fashionings of "antiquity." Philosopher Sándor Radnóti suggests that

> if we . . . return to the humble art of copying, then we shall see that any of the cheap copies on permanent display in the intimacy of people's home museums—even the commercially produced series—preserve or acquire some kind of an individuality lingering between personal memory and aesthetic experience. (Radnóti 1999:75)

Critically, as the following anecdote suggests, fidelity to a historically authentic "original" is not a prerequisite to the individual meaning-making associated with replicas and other representational forms.

In the spring of 2004 I met a retired married couple from the state of Zacatecas who had toured numerous Mexican archaeological sites, notably the Mayan ruins of Palenque and Chichén Itzá. On the day I interviewed them at Monte Albán, I inquired if they had purchased anything from the replica vendors inside the site. They said that they had not, but that in the past they had bought similar objects, including masks and ceramic fragments, at other archaeological sites. When I asked what made the replicas attractive, the man flatly replied, "Because they mean something [*Porque tienen significado*]." When pressed, however, he could not identify what their significance was in any precise archaeological terms. Rather, he summarily noted that "it's who we are" and that replicas represented "*lo nuestro* [that which is ours]," a phrase popularly used to denote Mexican cultural patrimony. I then asked him if a craft like Oaxacan wood carving had "meaning." He hesitated before replying that yes, wood carvings had meaning, but not in the same way. To illustrate his point, he lifted his hand to show me a ring on his right hand that he had bought on vacation in Peru. On it was engraved a figure that appeared to my eye to be some sort of pre-Hispanic warrior. The man identified it simply as "*un dios inca*," or an Incan god. He did not know what it meant or specifically which god it was, but that did not seem to matter much; he liked the apparent symbolism.

The conversation shifted. Issuing a sort of rhetorical challenge, the man said, "You don't have culture like this where you come from, do you?" He of course meant the United States. He continued, "I went to the United States on vacation two years ago, to San Antonio, Texas. Well, we saw the Alamo but other than that there wasn't much else to see except for the Riverwalk." I had heard similar comments during my fieldwork—usually in the context of Monte Albán—from Mexican tourists, guides, or others somehow connected to the tourism industry. The U.S. was perceived by many Mexicans across the class spectrum to be culturally devoid—"nothing but malls and fast food [*puros malls y comida rápida*]," as one Arrazola friend put it after returning from a two-year stint working in Oregon and California. Unlike Mexico, I was told, the U.S. had never been the home to any "great civilization" like the Aztecs or Zapotecs. For many, the contrast with Oaxaca was notable, and it was not uncommon to hear aficionados of indigenous culture and history (be they visiting tourists, American expatriates, or Oaxacans themselves) proclaim that "Oaxaca may be poor, but culturally it's the richest place in Mexico." This in mind, I agreed with the man that the U.S. did not have many archaeological ruins of the same magnitude as Mesoamerican sites like Monte Albán, but noted that there were many indigenous groups living in what is now the U.S. at the time of the Conquest. Brushing aside my answer, he continued, "Well, the Spanish may have destroyed everything, all the pre-Hispanic idols. But we Mexicans continue to be idol worshipers." He again thrust his ring my way, as if to provide evidence of his own idolatrous tendencies.

The fact that replicas mimic or pass for authentic cultural patrimony, while pleasing to some Mexican tourists, is nevertheless a source of anxiety for others. One middle-aged man from Mexico City expressed his disapproval of the unauthorized vending taking place at Monte Albán, but his comments also revealed a particular notion of right to ownership as well as a desire to possess. He said, "They shouldn't sell it because it's national patrimony! But I wouldn't buy anything from them anyway because they don't have the good pieces." I took "good" to mean perhaps well-preserved, fairly intact, or stylistically interesting "real" archaeological pieces, as his comments seemed to suggest that he believed the pieces sold by the vendors to be original archaeological artifacts. The man continued on to say that his brother-in-law knew where to find good pieces near his hometown in the state of Veracruz and had managed to collect quite a few. He himself had gone along on several of these excursions, usually to unmarked places in the countryside, but he never found anything bigger than pottery fragments. He admitted that he did not know exactly where one would have to go to find real archaeological artifacts in Oaxaca; he imagined that the area around Monte Albán was extremely picked over.

His earlier comments had led me to believe that he thought the replicas sold by the vendors were in fact original archaeological pieces. I was therefore surprised when the man took a moment to enlighten me about the vendors. "Look, those are just copies made with plaster that's made to look like stone. Don't believe it if they tell you that that mask or whatever they have is real. I bet if you dropped it on the ground it would turn to dust. Poof! Just like that." With the wave of his arm, he gestured to a replica vendor lingering around the monument's base, awaiting a tourist group's approach:

> See that guy down there? When I walked past him on my way up here he told me that he was selling pieces made of jade. But I could tell that that little statue he's carrying around isn't jade because I touched it. It didn't weigh enough, see? It's too shiny, it doesn't look natural. It's obvious that they polish those things, maybe even put varnish on them, so that they look more attractive. The only thing they're here for is to trick people.

What I had initially read as his objection to the selling off of cultural patrimony was, in fact, an objection to the vendors' claim to have authentic artifacts when in reality they just had "copies." However, he did not appear to have any problems reconciling his position that vendors should not be selling off national patrimony (even if only copies of it) with the fact that he and other family members searched for archaeological pieces as a pastime.

Still other Mexican tourists reacted to what they perceived to be the increasing seriality of replicas and the overall decline in their workmanship. In August 2003 I met an extended family of Mexican expatriates—who now made their homes in the United States, France, and Chile—as they congregated on the uppermost steps of Monte Albán's South Platform. They had come to Mexico that summer for a family reunion and were traveling in Oaxaca for a week. Despite the fact that none of them lived in Mexico (although they may have held Mexican citizenship), they all strongly identified as Mexican and said they preferred to spend most of their vacations in the country. One of the men, who lived in an upscale suburb of Houston, Texas, had been to Monte Albán fifteen years earlier and pronounced it his favorite place in all of Mexico. He recalled purchasing a replica from a boy on that previous trip, but claimed that he would not buy replicas being offered today. He said, "Before the figures they sold were rustic, like something you might actually find in the ground. Now they are very commercial. A long time ago they at least looked handmade; now they look like they come from some sort of factory or something." I asked him how he felt about the vendors being inside the ruins. He replied, "Don't you know that it's forbidden for them to be in here? Didn't you see the signs? They make it very clear that they shouldn't be here." His niece, who looked to be in her early twenties and lived in France, chimed in, "It's the same stuff you see all over Mexico, probably even the same stuff they sell in Peru, like at Machu Picchu, except there they just try to make it look more Incan."

The issues of collective identity and right to ownership bound up with pre-Hispanic material culture and its modern-day representations extended to non-Mexican individuals as well. In November 2003 I interviewed an American expatriate who had been living in Oaxaca since 1992. She earned her living guiding English-speaking foreigners around Oaxaca City and its environs in addition to running a small downtown cafe. Because her clients typically wanted to tour "some combination of ruins and Indian markets," she frequently planned tours so as to take advantage of the close proximity between central Oaxaca's artisan villages and archaeological sites. One of her most popular excursions was an all-day trip that included visits to Arrazola, Monte Albán, the ceramic-producing community of Atzompa, and, if it were a Thursday, the weekly market in the town of Zaachila. While she was fully aware that most of the replica sellers hailed from Arrazola, she believed that few of her clients ever made this connection. The woman espoused a personal predilection for replica crafts but objected to the sales practices of some vendors:

> I absolutely love the replicas! Some of them just have so much personality. I just wish those guys wouldn't lie and say that they're originals. I don't think most people believe that anyway. I mean, I'll buy one if I like the way it looks, but not because they're feeding me some story about how they found it in their field or whatever.

She and the other local tour guides (who were mostly Mexican, but also North American and European) did not want to see Mexico's "cultural heritage" destroyed or removed from the country and thus considered replicas to be a "compromise."

As the conversation progressed, her comments moved so seamlessly back and forth in addressing replica crafts and archaeological artifacts that at times I was unsure to which objects she referred; she talked about them interchangeably. So when she mentioned that a lot of guides she worked with had "huge collections of stuff," I at first assumed that she meant the replicas. However, her subsequent statement clarified the point: "The artifacts link you to the people. It's such a find, to know that a little Zapotec hand made that piece 1,400 years ago." As guides, she said, she and her colleagues felt an overwhelming sense of proprietorship with regard to Monte Albán's material culture. This was not only what she did for a living, she asserted, but it was who she was. And being able to show her clients artifacts up at Monte Albán made her job "feel real . . . like you're not just babbling some history lesson." As with the Mexican tourist above, I did not point out the contradiction in guides serving as stewards of national patrimony and at the same time clandestinely amassing their own private collections of artifacts. Instead, I noted that much of what was visible in the interior portion of the monument zone—where, I observed, visitors spent most of their time at the site—was actually the work of modern archaeology.

Writing about Chichén Itzá, another iconic Mexican archaeological site, Quetzil Castañeda (1996) invokes Baudrillard's notion of the simulacrum (Baudrillard 1988). According to Baudrillard, we live in a world constructed on the representation of representations, in which we have lost all ability to distinguish between truth and artifice; these simulations exist to fool us into thinking that an identifiable reality exists. Castañeda thus describes Chichén Itzá as a simulacrum of monumental proportions:

> The ruins are clearly an artifact of (primarily) Western science. They are a representation of the ancient city, constructed

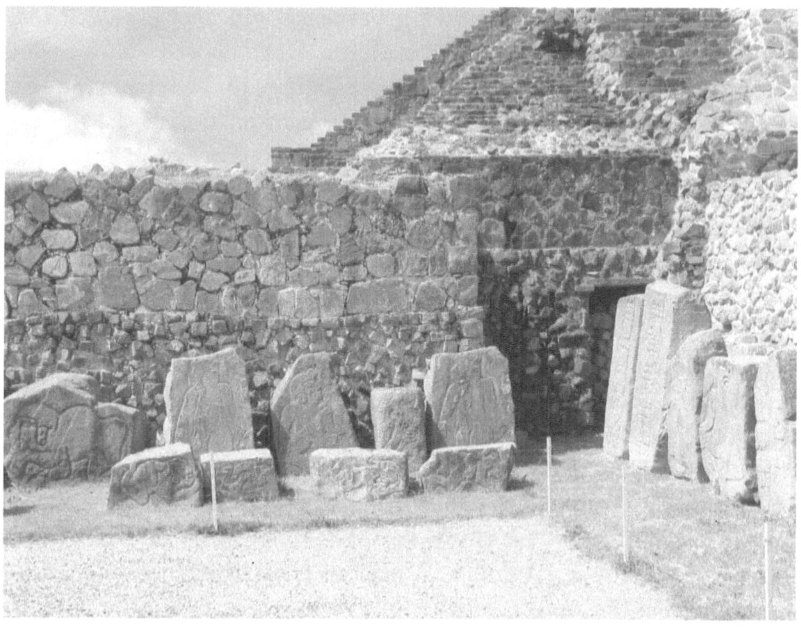

FIGURE 5.2. *Reproductions of the* danzantes *(dancers) and* nadadores *(swimmers) are a popular attraction for tourists at Monte Albán. (Photograph by author)*

> through the techniques of early twentieth-century archaeological science. Chichén Itzá is a life-size scale-model replica of "itself": it is *hyperreal.* The traces of the constructed authenticity of Chichén are scandalously and continuously concealed and effaced in memory even as they are brought to consciousness. (Castañeda 1996:104)

Nearly all of Monte Albán's visible structures demonstrate signs of reconstruction. For instance, I learned from guides that the impressive carved stone monoliths known in Spanish as the *danzantes* (dancers) and *nadadores* (swimmers) are reproductions and not the original pieces. These artifacts are named for the imagined activities of their humanlike figures (although archaeologists are not necessarily in agreement with these attributions) and counted among the oldest carved stone monuments found in Oaxaca (Winter 2002 [1989]). Reproductions of the monoliths are grouped together below the wall (parts of which also evidence signs of reconstruction) they supposedly occupied in the southwest corner of the Main Plaza and are a stopping point for all guided visits at the site (see fig. 5.2).

It is also critical to note that while in the past visitors were able to see some of the tombs and chambers at Monte Albán, most are now sealed off from the public, presumably to avoid damage to the remains and/or injury to visitors. Tourists walking the interior portion of the site encounter very little evidence of pre-Hispanic sculpture or painting, except for the aforementioned reproductions of carved stone monoliths. Some original artifacts are on display at the permanent exhibition inside the visitor center, but much of the material has been moved to private INAH storage facilities or is on display at off-site locations such as the Santo Domingo Museum in Oaxaca. The visitor experience at Monte Albán, then, is crafted around present-day representations or reproductions of the past as much as authentic material culture. To what degree have these interpretive efforts come to stand in for or signify the pre-Hispanic past for Monte Albán visitors? Viewed within this framework, replicas, too, may be positioned within this system of simulation.

During our conversation, the American expatriate mentioned above suggested that the Monte Albán experience was in fact the sum of its many parts: the reconstructed temples, ball court, and the INAH museum; the placards with their explanations written in English, Spanish, and Zapotec; the panoramic views afforded from the tops of the pyramids; the explanations by guides like herself; and even the replica vendors, who offered their own stories about Monte Albán along with their tourist souvenirs. Without these mediating elements, she assured me, visitors would have a vastly different experience at the site. She explained,

> Your job is to make people feel how it was, how the people who lived there were. You're the link. I try to make people understand that the people who built Monte Albán weren't that different from us, and once you get past the human sacrifice the connections are easy to make.

In this regard, she explicitly viewed herself as an extension of the institutional apparatus whose function it was to interpret the past and "make it real for people who may or may not know anything about archaeology."

Of course, the saturation of contemporary representations emanating from both within and outside of state archaeology proved frustrating to some. An undergraduate student from the University of Michigan, in Oaxaca for three weeks with a college study abroad program, frankly expressed his disappointment with the site's authenticity and that of Oaxaca more generally. I asked the young man, a media studies student, and his female companion about their impressions of the replica vendors and their wares. The woman said she "sort of liked the masks," and that she might buy one for her dad, "since he's really into masks." She found the ceramic pieces less appealing because the vendors tried to pass them off as originals by saying "that they had found it in the mountains." While she did not believe their claims, she found the sales tactic amusing and admittedly played along with one vendor who had tried to sell her a "cheesy acrobat" figurine, though she bought nothing in the end. Her classmate was less willing to suspend disbelief and revel in replica sellers' storytelling. Unlike other tourists discussed here, the young man was less concerned with whether these were "real" or "fake" archaeological artifacts—it was obvious to him that they were not the real thing. He instead focused on the fact that vendors were selling crafts that lacked any meaning in a present-day cultural context: legitimate cultural objects should not only represent the past but demonstrate the sellers' cultural continuity with it. On this matter the students' opinions diverged.

> *Male student*: Well, I don't blame them, but I don't trust them either. I doubt a lot of them have those masks up in their houses and it doesn't seem like they probably use them anymore for rituals. For me it just doesn't have the cultural currency.
> *Female student*: Yeah, but wouldn't you say that part of their culture is *being* an artisan? They still make the stuff themselves even if they're not using it personally. I mean, they're still putting some creativity into it, and I like that.
> *Male student*: I try to buy things that are descended from things that still exist or at least once existed. Still, I know this is modern Mexico and this is the situation. I'm sure they're probably just poor and need the money.

The young man continued, citing another instance of disillusionment during his Oaxaca travels:

> It's sort of like they want you to see the significance in everything. We had this assignment where they took us to see a demonstration of a guy wood-carving while his wife painted, I don't even remember the name of the town, it was somewhere out of the city. Anyway, the point was, we had to figure out what the

> painting meant. So, this girl in our group asks the woman why she was painting whatever she was painting, I think it was some flowers or something, and she was like, "Because we have to sell it."

Notably, he did not appear to make any connection between the woodcarving artisans and replica sellers, who may in fact have been from the same town.

"WHAT WE DON'T KNOW, WE INVENT"

Víctor and I stood in front of the makeshift display of souvenirs that he erected every morning on the steps overlooking the parking lot of Monte Albán. Up until a few years ago, he had sold his ceramic figures inside the main structures of the ruins. But personal differences with other members of the vendors' association eventually forced him to leave the group and take a spot among the row of outside sellers who lined the stairway leading up to the main entrance. His inventory that morning consisted of perhaps fifteen ceramic replicas of various sizes and styles, which he had neatly lined up on a large swatch of fabric that he draped over the rock wall. Rounding out the offerings were leather key chains, pens, bobble-head wooden animals, clay whistles, and small pyramids stamped "Monte Albán," the ambiguous plastic forms just as easily signifying any number of pre-Hispanic pyramids were it not for the gold-embossed place-name.

The hordes of tourists that had descended upon Monte Albán a couple of weeks earlier during Holy Week were gone now and business was slow. Unlike busy days, when my presence might have been a nuisance or perhaps even interfered with sales, that day Víctor seemed genuinely glad to have my company. I hoisted myself up on the rock wall, being careful not to disrupt his display. Víctor leaned up against the wall and lit a cigarette. He took a long drag, and then asked, in an offhand way, if I liked to run. As it turned out, Víctor, who I guessed to be in his mid-fifties, was an avid runner in spite of the cigarette that dangled from his lip, and had recently competed in an organized city race. He had not placed among the top finishers, but was now training for another race. He started to detail his training regimen, which included hill work on the slopes of Monte Albán, but before he could finish an English-speaking couple escorted by a Mexican guide approached us.

Víctor positioned himself to one side of the display so that the merchandise was clearly visible. Except for the polite greeting he issued the visitors, he remained silent. The guide and his clients paused in front of the clay replicas, all crafted by Víctor in his home workshop. The guide directed the couple's attention to the largest piece. In English that betrayed only a hint of a Spanish accent, the guide proceeded to utilize Víctor's work as a pedagogical tool. "Look right there. That large piece you see in the middle? That's an excellent example of a piece that was found by archaeologists inside of tomb 104. It represents the god that the ancient Zapotecs called Cocijo, you may have heard of it. Archaeologists have discovered that he was the god of both rain and the corn." The guide pointed to the small clay representations of corncobs that Víctor had attached on both side of the figure's trunk. "See the corn? That was one of the most important foods of the Zapotecs at Monte Albán. And as you can see from many of our dishes, corn is still one of the most typical foods we eat in Oaxaca."

The replica was composed of multiple images and symbols, and I was curious to hear the guide's interpretation of its components. "What do those other designs mean?" I interjected, much to the guide's surprise. His didactic tone replaced by open annoyance, he responded, "As anyone can see, they're other important gods of the Zapotecs!" Unwilling or unable to offer more in the way of an explanation, the guide did an about face and marched off, the tourist couple in tow.

I turned to Víctor in order to gage his reaction, worried that he would be upset at me for scaring away potential customers. The upturned corners of his mouth let me know that he was more bemused than angry. "What did you say to that guy anyway? I understood some of it, but I didn't catch everything. He looked pretty pissed off." I replied, "I just asked him what he thought the different parts of the statue represented." He tried to put me at ease. "Don't worry about it. They weren't going to buy anything anyway. I could tell even before they even walked up. The ones on tours don't buy that much because the guides don't give them enough time to look. That guide probably didn't know what to say and felt embarrassed since he's supposed to be an expert on Monte Albán. You know, a lot of them, especially the ones from the *centro* [Oaxaca City] who aren't regular guides up here, they act like they know everything."

He said that he had seen the original piece from tomb 104—up until about three years before, the tomb had still been open to the public—on which his own rendition of Cocijo was based. He later allegedly saw the same likeness in the Santo Domingo Museum in Oaxaca, but he believed it to be a copy since it did not look the same as he remembered. He in fact thought several of the pieces on display in Oaxaca museums were copies, but whether the archaeologists displayed them knowingly or unknowingly was another question. The thought crossed my mind that perhaps he had recognized his own work or that of his fellow vendors displayed in official venues.

I still wanted to know what all of the elements represented. One by one, he worked his way around the piece, which he said had taken two hours for him to make, explaining the individual designs. He claimed that the figure reproduced certain stylistic elements from the original but that it also deviated from it in other aspects. The large face at the center of the statue, for instance, was similar to the one on the original. But where the original also had two smaller jaguar heads, his only had one in the middle. He also gave his jaguar ear spools because the Cocijo head had them and he liked the way they looked. The leaflike designs radiating out from the top piece were his own creation but he felt that they were in keeping with the style of the original. A small bag held in the left hand symbolized a bag of copal, while the opposite hand was outstretched. He said that the first time he had seen the original it held a bag in its hand, but he later heard from a guard at Monte Albán that this part of the sculpture had been broken off when someone attempted to steal it while it was still on display at the site.

Nearing the end of his explanation, Víctor pointed to a tiny mask-like face at the bottom of the figure embellished with leaves, which he said represented fertility. I did not understand what the face had to do with fertility so I asked for a clarification. "Well, it represents a woman, doesn't it?" he replied. I let the issue drop and asked him where he gathered the information for all of these design details, apart from having briefly seen original pieces at the site or in city museums. He hesitated for a moment, and I thought perhaps he would cite the SEP elementary school textbooks (discussed in chapter 4). Instead, he matter-of-factly explained, "What we don't know, we invent."

Working in the context of one of Mexico's most famous archaeological sites, replica makers and sellers were aware of their crafts' representational potential and, conversely, that the objects depended on the narrative power of the site as national and international cultural patrimony. As such, Víctor's replicas were meant to mimic the materials and designs of original archaeological artifacts. Whether their sellers chose to market them as original pieces or replicas, the objects' consumer appeal depended on their ability to convincingly reference Monte Albán's material culture as well as a more generic pre-Hispanic or ancient past.

Yet as previously noted, replicas rarely, if ever, exactly reproduce the archaeological artifacts. I offer this detail to suggest that replica makers and sellers are engaged in their own interpretive work, which has both a material and narrative dimension. As demonstrated in this book's epigraph, Sándor Radnóti (1999) argues that "art forgery" and other unauthorized acts of copying entail their own hermeneutics, which may supersede while critically commenting upon established or dominant frameworks for interpretation. The "rogue" aesthetics of replicas, following Radnóti, pose the possibility of different and, more importantly, unauthorized interpretations of Oaxaca's cultural past. Within the wider field of cultural production (Bourdieu 1993) such interpretations point to the ongoing struggle over the forms history should take; fears of other ways of knowing, seeing, and profiting off of the past take hold.

Replica pieces sold at Monte Albán, especially the ceramics, can be said to rely on what their makers imagined to be similar types of materials, techniques, and designs used by pre-Hispanic artisans thousands of years earlier. Guillermo Avila, for instance, was emphatic that he used only clay that came from Atzompa, where he guessed that pre-Hispanic artisans from Monte Albán would have gathered their material. His few homemade tools, such as brushes or scrapers, were made from *carrizo* and animal hair, mainly from his goats, he pointed out—thereby representing technologies that have easily been around for hundreds of years. From time to time, he wandered a riverbed near the town of Cuilapan looking for stones for burnishing and polishing ceramic pieces. He said that during his forays he sometimes even came upon what he believed were simple tools once utilized by pre-Hispanic inhabitants of the area. One day as I watched him work he showed me a black stone that he used exclusively for polishing. The stone was perfectly rounded and so shiny that it looked like glass. He told me, "I found this stone when I was walking. It was the only one that looked like this, there weren't any others. Sometimes you get lucky and find pieces, things that, maybe, were part of a hatchet or another tool." Whether the odds and ends he collected and used in making his own replica pieces were truly leftover from Monte Albán's pre-Hispanic craftsmen I cannot say. What is important here is the way in which Santiago *imagines* himself in relation to this particular place and its material culture through his own artisanry.

This creative imagining is predicated on reproducing pre-Hispanic techniques and designs with a certain degree of fidelity to both form and content. Yet at the same time there is innovation: replicas evoke the originality and authenticity of cultural patrimony but do not faithfully reproduce it.

For Miguel, a seventeen-year-old Arrazola replica maker whose uncle taught him the craft, replica making was undeniably more of a hobby than an occupation. In fact, his long-range goal was to attend a local university and study accounting once he finished *preparatoria*. He nevertheless found himself engaged in the hermeneutic process, creating and (re)presenting his version of the past, a history that had fascinated him from the time he began to learn about Monte Albán in school. As he explained, "Ever since I was thirteen or fourteen years old, I would walk up to Monte Albán, every Sunday I'd go. Sometimes I'd find little pieces, little faces, nothing valuable. I'd walk along imagining what it must have been like in those times." He made this comment as he sculpted the ceramic figure of a woman bent over a *metate*, a large stone tablet traditionally used for grinding corn. With a small mold loaned to him by his uncle, he cast the woman's head but then shaped the body and *metate* by hand. I asked him if that was a design he had seen someplace else, since he had previously mentioned taking ideas from school textbooks. In this case, he said, he was just designing the piece as he went along, having actually never seen an archaeological piece featuring a woman bent over a *metate* in such as manner. After he completed the figurine he set it on a table to dry. We happened to be sitting in his cousin's wood-carving workshop, where by chance he had left some of his freshly painted carvings to dry. Miguel carefully positioned his still-damp piece next to a brightly colored porcupine complete with individually painted toothpick spines. He then suggested that I take a photo of "Arrazola's two *artesanías*," a request that I was happy to oblige (see fig. 5.3).

Critically, none of the Arrazola replica makers pretended to possess the same level of skill as the pre-Hispanic craftsmen whose work they emulated, nor did they claim to understand the meaning of the designs in the same way. Moreover, all the artisans I spoke with practiced their trade, admittedly, out of economic necessity. In a self-deprecating moment, Martín Avila remarked,

> In truth, they were true masters of sculpture, true artists. We're simply artisans. But them, at least from the pieces I've had the chance to see, I tell you, I can't begin to compare my work with theirs. Still . . . well, we do it to survive, right? But we still give our work our own touch. Our own ideas, we put our own thoughts into the work . . . That's why I don't like using molds, even though that's the way some people do it. This is a way of making a living, but at the same time you have to feel it. To make a piece you have to feel it too. You should live what you're doing. Because if you're just doing it to do it, bam, bam, it's not going to come out, it won't come out well at all.

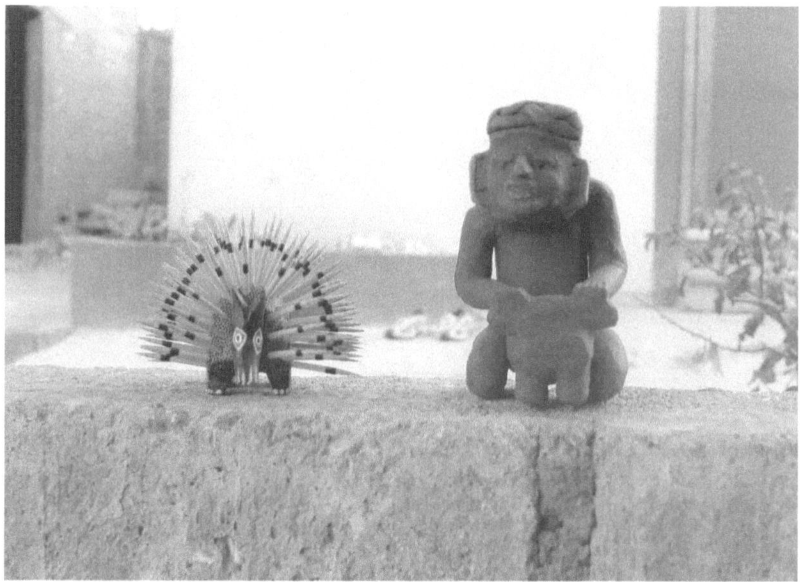

FIGURE 5.3. *"Arrazola's two* artesanías*": A wooden porcupine and a ceramic replica sit side-by-side in an Arrazola workshop. (Photograph by author)*

Despite his professed status as a mere "artisan," of all the replicas I observed, Martín Avila's work, in addition to being the most technically impressive, showed the greatest degree of stylistic innovation. Unlike some of the other replica makers and sellers described here, Avila would be recognized as a craftsman, if not artist, had his pieces been viewed in another context. He constantly experimented with new designs, and not only because others in and outside of Arrazola had begun to copy his work. His innovation was also tied to the fact that tourists at Monte Albán got tired of seeing the same old pieces over and over; he likened it to wood carving, in which the evolving tastes of the art market pushed carvers to come up with new themes. The pieces sold better, he noted, when they had both a utilitarian and a decorative function. When possible, he constructed figures in such a way that they could hold pencils or other small desk items.

Notably, his original designs—the ones that most dramatically deviated from Monte Albán archaeological artifacts—were among his bestsellers. According to Avila, tourists especially liked any figural representation that combined human forms with jaguar heads or bodies (fig. 5.4). In previous years he had introduced variations on two different thematic pieces that also proved to be popular, neither of them

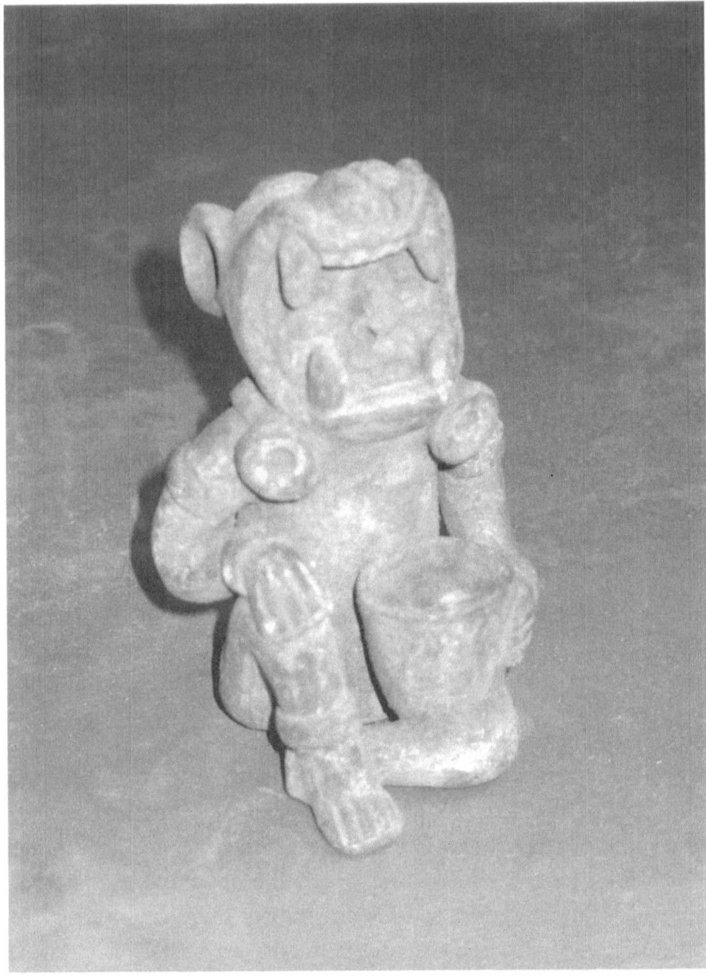

FIGURE 5.4. *Jaguar motifs were cited as one of the most popular design elements with tourists. This "Jaguar Warrior" is an original design featuring a human form wearing a jaguar mask. (Photograph by author)*

taken from a book or specific preexisting artifact. One was what he referred to as a "water carrier." This was a male form with what appeared to be a large urn or pot strapped to his back. He said he was inspired to make this style after he had read that water had had to be ported up to the top of Monte Albán by human carriers since there was no natural water supply and no pack animals. His other design was what he simply referred to as a "ball player." This male figurine's popularity undoubtedly stemmed from the tourist fascination with the reconstructed ball court area inside Monte Albán but also took its cue from the present-day sport *pelota mixteca*, or Mixtec ballgame, which some men in Arrazola played.[5]

Other elements from contemporary life found their way into Avila's work. One day he showed me an exquisite ceramic piece of a woman bent over a *metate* that he had just finished molding and set out to dry before firing. The first thing that caught my eye was the woman's hair; it looked more realistic than any hairdo that I had ever seen on an archaeological artifact or another replica, as though you could see the individual strands of hair. He explained the inspiration for the piece:

> This one is a Zapotec woman, a *molendera* [a woman grinding]. But I gave her a braid for hair—you would probably never find an original that had a braid exactly like that. But I see here, in Cuilapan, in Zaachila, here in Arrazola, you know, there are a lot of women who still wear their hair like that. So, you have to imagine how the women wore their hair back then.

I suggested that his replica in fact might not really be a replica at all but rather a modern commentary on how he and the tourists who purchased the pieces envisioned the past to look. Avila was in agreement: "Exactly. We never would have imagined it, but here we are modernizing the past, just a little bit, so that it's more appealing."

Radnóti writes that "forgery is the democratic satire and parody of the aristocracy of art; in the carnivalesque horseplay of parody and miming, forgery annihilates the uniqueness of a work of art by way of the implicit criticism of copying" (Radnóti 1999:14). His comments may be directed toward cultural forms normally designated as "classical" or "fine art" (i.e., European sculpture, painting, and literature), but they have important implications for the replica trade at Monte Albán. Radnóti asserts that in the rogue act of copying or mimicking aesthetic objects resides an inherent critique of "art" as a historically determined social category.

The Arrazola replica artisans and sellers I have described likewise go to great lengths to create and market objects that consciously mimic the stylistic elements of authentic archaeological artifacts—objects that exist under the modern rubrics of "cultural patrimony" and "pre-Hispanic art"—while at the same time they do not strictly model the past. Furthermore, I have shown in preceding chapters that the replica trade is governed by a system of production techniques, labor organization, and marketing networks in much the same way as other Oaxacan folk art such as wood carving. As their makers and sellers insist, replicas are *artesanías* (i.e., handmade and, for the most part, locally produced) despite the fact that they do not conform to officially sanctioned ideas about Oaxacan folk art.

Radnóti provides a partial genealogy of the modern notion of art, tracing it to ideas about beauty and originality that first emerged during the European Renaissance. Drawing on Benjamin (1968), he claims that originality, also understood as historical authenticity, tends to be the dominant mode for perceiving the value of a human creative work within the modern system of art and aesthetics (Radnóti 1999:53–54). The assumed historicity of aesthetic objects (particularly those designated as antiquities) is as important, if not more so, than their outward appearance. The original work of art derives its aura from, in Benjamin's words, "its presence in time and space, its unique existence at the place where it happens to be" (Benjamin 1968:220). Benjamin expresses both fascination and apprehension about what he sees as the destructive potential of technologies of reproduction; he famously posited that copying undermined the authority and diminished the aura of the original. He referred primarily to reproduction in the context of European arts made possible by the advent of mechanical technologies like film and photography, but as anthropologist Christopher Steiner (1999) aptly demonstrates, reproduction figures heavily in the creation of ethnic and tourist arts as well. Seriality and copying point to the commodity status of these cultural forms even as the consumer logic of the folk art and crafts market emphasizes the handmade or preindustrial aspects of their production.

Efforts to theorize tourism and cultural patrimony have shown that authenticity serves as a polyvalent organizing principle for those both visiting and working at heritage sites (e.g., Bruner 2004; Castañeda 1996; Di Giovine 2009; Little 2004a). Postmodern sensibilities may allow us to increasingly revel in the semiotic free play of theme parks and other built environments like Las Vegas (see Kirshenblatt-Gimblett 1998; Urry 1990, 1995), but this does not mean that the expectations of getting behind the simulacra are necessarily diminished. In Oaxaca, a place oftentimes billed as the "real" Mexico, tourist pleasures are not physically or metaphorically built in quite the same way upon the Disney-esque, fantasy landscapes that became standard objects of postmodern critique (e.g., Davis 1997; Fjellman 1992; Gottdiener 2001). It is precisely because the idea of Oaxaca and all that it entails stands in relation to the "not real" Mexico (ostensibly border towns and beach zones) that visitors arrive with pre-saturated desires, whose inflections are manifest in practice.

Within the space of Monte Albán, where the grand narration of Mexico's past intertwines with tourist desires, it is perhaps not so surprising that the unauthorized production and marketing of replicas has come to be regarded as a "threat." Not coincidentally, "dangerous" is a word I heard used on more than one occasion in reference to replica crafts and the vendors themselves, even though neither poses any sort of physical threat to those working at or visiting the archaeological site. Instead, the sense of danger appears to stem from the way in which the replica trade depends upon and plays with notions of authenticity and originality, the way the replicas hold the dialectic tension between reality and imagination, inherent not only in the object but also in the general apprehension of an archaeological site's materiality.

Visitors to Monte Albán are left wondering: Are these indeed real artifacts unearthed in the fields surrounding the site? If not, do these itinerant vendors make the pieces themselves, as some of them claim, or were these serially produced objects, "churned out in some factory God-knows-where" and distributed to archaeological sites throughout Mexico? Are the replicas becoming "too generic" or "less rustic," and therefore less "charming," than the ones sold at the site in past years? Are these exact copies (and what do the designs "mean" anyway?) or just made-up styles that only mimic authentic archaeological pieces? In contrast, the authenticity of other Oaxacan cultural patrimony is for the most part taken for granted. Artifacts displayed in local museums, for example, are presumed to be the legitimate expressions of pre-Hispanic belief and aesthetic systems—even though archaeologists frequently complain about the "fakes" that have managed to sneak undetected into collections for years. Likewise, as I demonstrated in chapter 2, the abundance of folk arts for sale in and around Oaxaca, including Arrazola's wood carvings, are often assumed to be locally made by indigenous communities and even to form part of a long-standing tradition of artisan production with roots traceable back to pre-Hispanic times.

Indeed, replicas are perceived as dangerous by some because they claim to represent exactly what they are not: the original archaeological artifacts associated with the pre-Hispanic culture of Monte Albán. It is the fetish of cultural patrimony that creates the consumer desire for replicas in the first place. But in rising to meet this demand, the replica trade threatens the authority of patrimony, which García Canclini suggests forms part of a sacred national discourse that is above scrutiny.

> Precisely because the cultural patrimony is presented as being alien to debates about modernity, it constitutes the least suspicious resource for guaranteeing social complicity . . . it occurs to almost no one to think about the social contradictions that they express. The perennial character of these goods makes us imagine that their value is beyond question and turns them into a source of collective consensus, beyond the divisions among classes, ethnic groups, and other groups that fracture society and differentiate ways of appropriating that patrimony. (García Canclini 1995:108)

Just as replicas reveal the fissures in the discourse of cultural patrimony naturalized by state institutions and the tourism industry, the ambivalence surrounding the identities of the replica sellers themselves reveals the instability of discourses of race and ethnicity in Oaxaca. I take up the question of "Indianness" in the context of replica vending at Monte Albán in chapter 6.

DISCRIMINATING TASTES

"No McZocalo!" and "We don't want McDollars!," read protesters' signs. In 2002 the city of Oaxaca made headline news in the United States and throughout the world for what many regarded as a milestone victory for the anti-globalization movement. After multiple protests and rounds of failed negotiations, the American fast-food behemoth McDonald's ultimately abandoned its plans to build an outlet on the *zócalo*, the downtown plaza considered by many to be the heart and soul of the historic city. A number of city officials and developers had initially supported the plan, but the negative publicity and the threat of lost revenue from tourists seeking a quainter Mexico than one dominated by the Golden Arches finally put a halt to the project.

A series of well-organized demonstrations, led by one of Oaxaca's most famous residents, contemporary artist Francisco Toledo, was key to winning the battle. In reference to the plaza, Toledo himself famously declared, "This place is not for McDonald's. This is a sacred space."[1] Although I arrived in Oaxaca to do my fieldwork as the issue was being laid to rest, I knew that the plaza demonstrators strategically handed out free tamales and *atole* (a thick corn drink), two foods they perceived to be emblematic of a noncommodified, local cuisine. By all accounts, it seemed that David beat Goliath in the standoff between the local and the global, and that, at least for the time being, the architectural, culinary, and cultural integrity of Oaxaca was to be preserved.[2]

Never mind that the average Oaxacan could not afford to eat on the *zócalo* anyway, I thought, as I sat at one of the outdoor cafés that ring the plaza. At 25 pesos per beer and 65 pesos for a plate of mole enchiladas, a local delicacy for which Oaxaca is rightly famous, the cost of my meal, which came to 100 pesos with tip (roughly U.S.$10 at the time), was more than double the Oaxacan minimum wage of 45 pesos per day. I, too, usually eschewed eating on the *zócalo*. But that day I was with an American friend, who had come to Oaxaca to visit me and experience the Day of the Dead festivities, and she expressly wanted a prime spot for people watching. And a prime spot it was. I scanned the sea of mainly fair, somewhat sunburned faces that filled the café; the space was a cacophony of Italian, French, German, English, and Mexico City Spanish.

At the table next to us was a family of well-dressed Mexican tourists. They appeared to be the only nationals in the outdoor portion of the café, with the exception of the waitstaff and the constant stream of candy and craft vendors who wove their way through the maze of tables; a private security guard, a familiar fixture in nearly all the *zócalo* cafés, stood stoically nearby in case the itinerant vendors became too insistent with the customers. The close proximity of the table permitted me to overhear the Mexican tourists' conversation. The teenage daughter complained to her mother that there was "nothing to do in Oaxaca" and that she would rather be at the beach with friends. The mother's impatience was obvious, as she silenced her by saying, "Oaxaca is not for having a good time, it's for cultured people [*Oaxaca no es para divertirse, es para gente culta*]."

Beyond the limits of the sidewalk café, in the middle of the plaza, was a different version of Oaxaca, the Oaxaca which most of us sitting in the café presumably had paid money to see. This space was inhabited by stooped old men sitting on iron park benches; families unpacking midday snacks of beans and tortillas taken from market bags; indigenous Trique women, dressed in their distinctive red *huipiles* (traditional women's shifts), with their children in tow; construction workers taking a break, enjoying popsicles in the shade of the giant laurel trees. Aside from the special tourist police, who routinely made rounds throughout the crowd, the *zócalo* seemed an idyllic and self-contained lifeworld. Somehow, even the demonstrations against human rights violations, political corruption, and labor abuses, an ongoing spectacle on the plaza, appeared quaint—in fact, one Canadian tourist I met felt that they "added to the festive atmosphere of the place."

The Oaxacan culture for which we all had come (anthropologists included), the "real" Mexico that the guidebooks had assured us was not to be found in dusty border towns, seemed to shine especially bright during the numerous religious and civic celebrations that punctuated the calendar year. The Day of the Dead festival, celebrated during the first two days of November, was no exception. Seasonal items such as sugar skulls and *pan de muertos* (bread of the dead) lined the aisles of the city's market stalls, while families cleaned and elaborately adorned the local cemeteries in preparation for nighttime vigils honoring their deceased. This time of year was highly anticipated by all Oaxaca residents, but particularly the hotel and restaurant owners, tour operators, taxi drivers, gallery owners, and artisans who depended economically on the mass of tourist visitors who descended upon the city to experience this uniquely Mexican celebration. In addition to the various cemetery and market tours, a number of tourist-oriented businesses offered special book readings, art exhibits, and dance performances (for more details on tourist promotion of the Day of the Dead in Oaxaca see Norget 2006).

On the first night of the celebration, I attended a book presentation hosted by a local bookstore widely considered to have the best selection of English-language publications in Oaxaca. I arrived about twenty minutes before the talk was to begin and in the meantime leafed through a Mexican cookbook by author Diana Kennedy. A store employee soon announced that the lecture room was ready and that we could go in and be seated. That night's featured guest was photographer Judith Cooper Haden, who had earlier that spring published a visually stunning collection of images, many of artisans, in a book entitled *Oaxaca: The Spirit of Mexico* (Haden and Jaffe 2002). A flyer posted at the store entrance praised Haden's photography for its ability to "capture and exalt individual elements that combine to create the poetic song that stirs the Oaxacan air."

I quietly took my place near the back and then made a quick survey of the room. The packed audience overwhelmingly comprised middle-aged, what appeared to be Euro-American men and women, with a sprinkling of college-aged individuals and a couple of young children. I recognized several Americans who formed part of Oaxaca's rapidly expanding expatriate community. Many of the women in the audience were dressed in regional indigenous clothing and jewelry, and judging by the numbers, the Amuzgo *huipil* (a blouse worn by indigenous women in areas of the Oaxacan coast) seemed to be the hands-down favorite.[3] The energy in the room was palpable, and conversations in English buzzed all around me. The owner of the bookstore made his way to the front of the room. By way of introduction, he commented on the qualities that, in his opinion, made Oaxaca a "transcendental place," the nodding heads and smiling faces in the audience confirming a shared sentiment. At that point, he turned the floor over to Haden, who, as it turned out, was one of the *huipil*-clad women sitting in the front row.

After providing some brief autobiographical information, Haden described Oaxaca as a "craft mecca" and stated that her overarching goal was to document the work of aging folk artists, a noble cause by anyone's measure.[4] She noted her special affinity for the folk art of Oaxaca, with its clear connections to the pre-Hispanic craft traditions of the region, and reminded us that her work played an important role in preserving those traditions. Visually documenting Oaxacan artisans and their work was particularly enjoyable from a photographer's perspective, she added, due to Oaxaca's "magical light," imbued with the same qualities as the light illuminating the equally photogenic, artistically inclined city of Santa Fe, New Mexico.

Her accompanying slideshow featured a number of the skillfully composed, visually striking images from the book. As she went through the pictures, many of them using the city as a backdrop, she noted her dislike for the telephone and electric wires that could be seen crisscrossing in front of the colorful downtown buildings, in essence ruining the illusion of a colonial cityscape. "Fortunately for us," she said, "Oaxaca is working hard to put those wires underground." Power lines and all, Haden found provocative material for her visual art in the juxtapositions between the so-called modern and traditional. One image she identified as being among her favorites depicted an elderly woman walking in front of a wall emblazoned with a Coca-Cola advertisement. Referring to the photo as one of her many "anti-globalization images," she directed our attention to the woman's braids. She pointed out that, for her, this Oaxacan hairstyle signaled continuity with the pre-Hispanic past.

The photographer worked her way through the rest of her slides, most of which featured artisans as their subject matter. Those familiar with Oaxacan folk art recognized the images as a veritable who's who of the region's artisans, many of whom had gained international acclaim: Dolores Porras, a master ceramicist from Atzompa; Issac Vásquez, a weaver from Teotitlán del Valle credited with reviving the use of natural dyes; Manuel Jiménez, the Arrazola resident responsible for beginning the wood-carving tradition. Among the lesser-known artisans photographed by Haden was a pair of elderly sisters who made elaborate sculptures with dried flowers. Haden paused at this slide, mentioning the unwavering cheerfulness of the flower artisans during the photo shoot "despite their humble conditions."

During the question-and-answer session, an audience member raised his hand and asked whether the subjects of Haden's book had minded being photographed, as he had heard that many locals, especially the indigenous people, did not like having their pictures taken. At that point, Haden offered a piece of her biographical information that had been omitted from her earlier introduction. Yes, in fact, a lot of people did object to having their photos taken by outsiders. However, in her case she was able to mitigate the issue by purchasing pieces from each of the artisans featured in the book, which she in turn sold in the Mexican folk art store that she owned in Seattle, Washington.

The following evening, I again found myself at the bookstore, this time to hear a talk by Christine Mather, author of *Santa Fe Houses* (1986) and *Santa Fe Style* (2002), given to a packed audience that looked virtually identical to the previous night's. The author opened by informing us that although her talk would focus specifically on the homes of Santa Fe, we should not lose sight of the many parallels between that city and Oaxaca. Both were colonial cities (Oaxaca being an example of a rich colonial center, and Santa Fe a poor one), and the Pueblo Indians, like the native inhabitants of Oaxaca, had their own distinctive dress and craft traditions. She said that she was personally drawn to the distinctiveness of Oaxaca, particularly its art, architecture, and culture, much as she had been drawn to Santa Fe, where she currently made her home.

The fact that so many Santa Fe homes were "handmade, not cookie-cutter" dwellings had inspired Mather to document the various architectural and design elements that made Santa Fe style so unique. She credited all the intellectuals and artists who moved to Santa Fe in the early twentieth century with forging the creative, artistic sensibility that could be seen in her community today. During the slideshow she directed our attention to particular features of individual homes, any one of which could have graced the pages of *House Beautiful* or *Architectural Digest*; hand-carved ceiling beams known as *vigas*, adobe stoves, and hand-painted Mexican *talavera* tile mingled with large (and I imagined) expensive collections of Southwestern and Latin American art. Pausing at a slide of a well-furnished living room with several intricately woven rugs hung side-by-side on the wall, Mather pointed out that while those pieces had been woven in New Mexico, similar but substantially less expensive weavings by Zapotec artisans could be purchased in stores in Oaxaca.[5] Commenting on no one home in particular, she praised Santa Fe style for its ability to create "a tranquil fortress" that offsets the fact that "we are besieged in our everyday lives." More importantly, the sense of intimacy fostered by the diminutive architecture of Santa Fe homes was especially suited to the vast openness of the New Mexican landscape, which could at times feel "formidable and too huge."

I felt ambivalent about my own awe (tinged, I suspect, with a hint of envy) at the amazing parade of homes we had just witnessed. Having at one time lived just thirty miles north of Santa Fe in the town of Española, a largely working-class Hispanic community, I knew that this tour of homes presented a highly selective version of northern New Mexican domestic spaces. Nowhere in any of this were the crumbling adobes, government housing, and mobile homes that increasingly dotted the New Mexican landscape. These were the structures that housed the area's poorest residents, many Native American and Hispanic, whose material culture was apparently the artistic inspiration for Santa Fe's upper-class, predominantly

Anglo homeowners. In fact, rising home costs and the lack of affordable housing—trends directly related to the influx of wealthy artists and entrepreneurs from other parts of the country—were two of the most pressing socioeconomic issues for Santa Fe city officials.

I evidently was not alone in my concern about the high costs associated with achieving "Santa Fe style." A gentleman three rows ahead of me raised his hand to comment. "The homes you just showed are absolutely amazing. But it seems like it would take a lot of money to decorate a house like that. I mean, how could the average homeowner achieve that look on a smaller budget?" The author, perhaps having fielded that question before, answered, "It's not about money; it's really all about taking risks." Such risk-taking, we were told, involved experimenting with unusual color palettes, the strategic placement of ethnic handicrafts, and opening oneself up to the possibility of new textures, fixtures, and lighting. Noting that we were running out of time, she took several more questions from the audience before issuing her final nugget of advice to those aspiring to capture the Santa Fe style: "Anyone can do it, so get out there in Oaxaca and start collecting!"

CHAPTER SIX

Replicas and the Ambiguity of Race and Indigeneity

I stood at Monte Albán with Alberto, an artisan, and his customer. Alberto tried to close the sale as I strategically remained a few feet away as. His asking price was 100 pesos (roughly ten U.S. dollars) for two small figurines representing a Pre-Hispanic acrobat and a "jaguar god"—designs loosely based on Oaxacan archaeological motifs. I recognized the pieces from Alberto's home workshop in Arrazola, where I had seen him firing them less than a week ago. The Mexican tourist persisted in haggling over a difference of 10 pesos; the vendor expertly split the difference and began to wrap up the pieces in crumpled newspaper before the buyer could change his mind. As the replica seller rummaged through his pocket looking for change, the tourist asked for clarification on the pieces he had just purchased.

"So are these Zapotec or Mixtec?" he wanted to know, referring to the two pre-Hispanic cultures typically associated with Monte Albán.

Alberto, who seemed used to this sort of inquiry, replied, "Those are Zapotec. You can tell from the faces. See?"

He pointed to the face of the acrobat figure. I was not sure what stylistic elements distinguished the piece as Zapotec but the tourist did not press for details. He drew another connection instead.

"Zapotecs, like you guys [vendors]."

Alberto nodded and answered simply, "Yes, like us."

THIS CHAPTER EXAMINES THE MULTIPLE AND sometimes ambiguous ideas about race and indigeneity that are articulated within Oaxaca's overlapping craft and tourism economies, and illustrated by this encounter at Monte Albán. These spaces constitute part of a Oaxacan "touristic borderzone" (Bruner 1996; Little 2004a) where transnational processes of cultural and economic exchange related to tourism entail a reworking of ethno-racial classifications. Of concern here is how categories such as "Indian,"[1] "indigenous," and "mestizo" and ethnic classifiers, including "Zapotec" and "Mixtec," among others, are experienced and enacted locally by artisans, vendors, tourists, and anthropologists.

Anthropologist Les Field notes that "artisanal production, the authenticity of artisan productions and indigenous peoples are historically intertwined in Latin America" (Field 2009:511). Scott Cook and Jong-Taik Joo (1995) locate Oaxacan artisans' long-standing position more specifically, within a Mexican nationalist paradigm that equates rural craft production with indigeneity, a connection which very much comes to the service of the ethnotourism market. Taking this assertion as a point of departure, I will examine the production and circulation of ideas about ethno-racial identity vis-à-vis Arrazola. As discussed in chapter 2, Arrazola's wood-carvers are frequently assumed by outsiders to be indigenous and, more specifically, Zapotec. However, in a contradictory fashion, residents from the same community may be marked as non-Indian or mestizo in their roles as archaeological replica makers and sellers. It should be noted that I do not seek to prove or disprove Arrazola residents' indigeneity. In fact, that would be contrary to the point I wish to make. Rather, following de la Cadena and Starn, I wish to illustrate how community members navigate the "tense dynamics of being categorized by others and seeking to define themselves within and against indigeneity's dense web of symbols, fantasies, and meanings" (de la Cadena and Starn 2007:2).

I first refer briefly to the institutional framings of race and ethnicity in Oaxaca today in order to situate the tendency of some anthropologists and INAH representatives to discursively cast replica makers from Arrazola as predominantly nonindigenous mestizos or campesinos (rural farmers). Next I describe how community members ambivalently identify and dis-identify with ethno-racial categories such as indigenous, *indio*, and Zapotec within the cultural and economic matrix of tourist encounters. I then discuss tourist notions of indigeneity and Oaxacan cultural continuity, which Arrazola residents negotiate in their everyday lives as high-profile artisans and craft vendors. The concluding portion of the chapter highlights the ambivalence of ethno-racial classifications in Oaxacan craft tourism through one artisan's reflection on his position within this economy.

ARRAZOLA AND THE PROBLEM OF RACE AND ETHNICITY IN OAXACA

Through their work in the wood-carving or replica trade, people from Arrazola are in regular contact with tourists, journalists, anthropologists, and state officials. Outsiders frequently try to pin down the ethno-racial status of Arrazola residents through direct questioning or tacit assumptions. When I arrived in Arrazola to conduct fieldwork, I found that questions structured around an indigenous/nonindigenous dichotomy did not seem to resonate much with community members. Asking people if they were indigenous or asking them if they considered themselves Zapotec or a member of any other Oaxacan indigenous group generated a plurality of responses, revealing indignation, pride, and even confusion over terminology.

For instance, Alberto (the replica seller in the opening scenario) told me that tourists frequently asked him if he was an indigenous Zapotec "because that was the most important civilization here at Monte Albán, besides the Olmecs and the Mixtecs.[2] Since we're here inside the ruins with our handicrafts, they think we must be the descendants of the original Zapotecs." He agreed that allowing tourists to draw these connections lent a decidedly more authentic feel to the archaeological replicas that he sold. Another Monte Albán vendor, also from Arrazola, advantageously used the semantic slippage around the term "native" in his dealings with tourists at the archaeological zone:

> A lot of the tourists who come here think we're Zapotecs. Sometimes they ask me where I'm from and I tell them, I'm native to this place [*Yo soy nativo de aquí*]. They take it to mean you're from right here, from the ruins of Monte Albán, even if I show them my village just over there.

Arrazola residents' double position within the tourist economy, as wood-carvers and as purveyors of archaeological souvenirs, has significant implications for perceptions of ethnicity and race both within and outside of the community. Certain questions invariably arise. Is Arrazola to be considered an indigenous community? More specifically, can the archaeological replica vendors at Monte Albán legitimately claim a Zapotec identity, or are they exploiting this identity because ethnicity sells, as some Monte Albán employees allege?

Anthropological scholarship on indigeneity and identity politics in Oaxaca reveals such questions to be misguided, as ethno-racial categories are contingent and mutable (Campbell 1996; Feinberg 2003; Kearney 1996; Nagengast and Kearney; Stephen 1993; Whitecotton 1996). The problematics of racial and ethnic formation, membership, and mobilization have been thoroughly interrogated from multiple angles throughout the Americas: from Mexico's Yucatán Peninsula (e.g., Castañeda 2004b; Hervik 2003; Loewe 2010) to Central America (e.g., Field 1999; Gordon 1998; Hale 1997, 2002, 2006; Little 2004a) and South America (e.g., de la Cadena 2000; Guss 2000; Sansone 2003; Weismantel 2001). And this only begins to scratch the surface. But even as scholars present local identities as historically dynamic, Latin American state and popular interpretations still "involve a discourse about origins and about the transmission of essences across generations" (Wade 1997:21). This is true in Oaxaca, where both state tourism and private tourism (and not infrequently local politics) represent indigeneity as evident and unchanging.

Ana Alonso (2004) writes that in regard to Mexican nationalist ideology, space serves as a "boundary marker of ethnoracial identity in Mexico. The South and the rural are coded as 'Indian,' whereas the North and the urban are coded as 'Mexican'" (Alonso 2004:469). Scholars working in Oaxaca must contend with the state's location within this paradigm, while at the same time dealing with the local organization of race and ethnicity around various urban regional centers. This is no easy task given the historical complexities of these classifications. Social categories have shifted over time with Mexico's large-scale political and economic transformations, and contemporary identities stem as much from the colonial period and twentieth-century nationalism as from continuity with a Mesoamerican cultural past. For example, John Chance (1978) has shown how Oaxaca's colonial-era caste system gave way to a more class-based form of social stratification by the end of the eighteenth century as the region was drawn into developing systems of commercial capitalism.

Nationalist ideologies of *indigenismo* (discussed in chapter 1) and *mestizaje* still shape contemporary ideas about race and indigeneity even as neoliberal multiculturalism entails their reworking at both individual and institutional levels.[3] "*Mestizaje*" refers to the racial intermixing of Indian with European, a supposedly biological process that was to ultimately create a singular, mestizo nation. The official *indigenista* narrative largely omitted indigenous groups as historical agents, casting them instead as "living reminders of the nation's glorious Pre-Hispanic past, which is presented as the heritage of all Mexicans" (Feinberg 2003:72). As noted, ethnically marked handicrafts and archaeological monuments remain celebrated national symbols even as the populations associated with them struggle to achieve socioeconomic parity with middle- and upper-class Mexicans (Bonfil Batalla 1996; Errington 1998; García Canclini 1993, 1995, 1997).

What, then, defines race and ethnicity in Oaxaca today? The confluence of state-sponsored *indigenismo*, ethnotourism, and anthropological investigation—both national and foreign traditions—has had the net effect that Oaxaca is construed as a region where indigeneity can be safely viewed, studied, and consumed. Often, indigenous "culture" is equated with quantifiable characteristics such as native-language use and sociopolitical organization. In fact, Mexico's federal institutions as well as some scholars tend to rely on native-language retention and other census data as the standard measure for identifying indigenous communities.[4] But while speaking a native language or self-identifying as indigenous may be an obvious marker, anthropologists have argued that ethnicity in Oaxaca cannot be reduced to a laundry list of specifically indigenous characteristics (Cook and Joo 1995; Feinberg 2003).

In the Central Valleys of Oaxaca, the cultural practices and forms of sociopolitical organization such as *tequio*, *mayordomía*, *guelaguetza*, and *usos y costumbres*[5] that are deemed characteristic of Zapotec-speaking communities may also be found in monolingual Spanish-speaking communities, including Arrazola. Economic differences between native language–speaking and Spanish-speaking villages, too, are often minimal (Chibnik 2003; Cook and Joo 1995). Moreover, as recently as the 1980s some Oaxacan communities designated as indigenous by outsiders did not necessarily self-identify as such; rather, individuals stressed their village-based affiliations over ethnic-based identities (Dennis 1987; El Guindi and Selby 1976). Even communities where indigenous languages were widely spoken may not have perceived themselves as belonging to an ethnic group (Zapotec, Mixtec, or otherwise) or, certainly, to a larger pan-Indian collectivity. As Joseph Whitecotton perceptively remarked about the valley of Oaxaca, "Until anthropologists and linguists told them that their language was Zapotec, most villagers thought of it simply as *idioma*, the native language of their town; to them the notion of Zapotec as a single language was not important" (Whitecotton 1996:10).

These findings reveal both Mexican and American anthropology's perhaps unwitting hand in the fixing of racial and ethnic categories, even as the discipline has come to terms with the "de-centering" of the classic sociological subject (Hall 1996) by postmodernist/poststructuralist thought. Although the fact remains that anthropologists are drawn to Oaxaca because they want to work in identifiably indigenous communities, this is not a problem in itself. However, we should be cautious in making authoritative pronouncements about a community's "Indian" or "mestizo" status that fail to account for the historical trajectory of ethnic/racial formation in relationship to recent mobilizations of identity within an economic, social, and political matrix.

For instance, in recent decades social movements in Oaxaca have coalesced around emergent conceptualizations of indigeneity; these include the COCEI, a radical leftist Zapotec coalition formed in the Isthmus of Tehuantepec (Campbell et al. 1993; Rubin 1997). Kearney (1995) describes the consolidation of Mixtec identity through the struggle for migrant labor rights in California, while the effects of the 2006 teachers' strike and the subsequent formation of the *Asamblea Popular de los Pueblos de Oaxaca* (APPO), a broad coalition with representation from various Oaxacan municipalities, unions, NGOs, and other social organizations, remain to be seen, at least in terms of local identity politics. In Arrazola, community members are aware of indigenous social movements in the region and beyond, particularly the Zapatista struggle in Chiapas. However, like the Guatemalan handicraft sellers described by Little (2004b), they frequently view such organizing as unrelated or even at odds with their own material conditions as artisans and vendors. For instance, the massive decline in Oaxacan tourism resulting from the social unrest of 2006 mentioned above economically devastated many Arrazola residents, as well as others whose livelihoods depend on tourism. Most artisans and vendors I know found the nascent APPO movement a curse rather than the blessing heralded by left-leaning social activists.

In his study of Oaxacan wood carving, Chibnik broaches the issue of race and ethnicity in Arrazola and two other central Oaxacan wood-carving communities. He finds that while wood-carving artisans

> acknowledge their indigenous ancestry, they talk about themselves as residents of a particular community, the state of Oaxaca, and the country of Mexico. I have never heard artisans in these villages identify themselves as "Indians" or "Zapotecs." Very few speak an indigenous language. (Chibnik 2003:242)

In Arrazola, the historical narrative of the town's formation undoubtedly shapes residents' self-identifications. As discussed in chapter 2, the town is not a long-standing pre-Hispanic settlement, and it was officially recognized as an independent community only in 1937.

Before that time it functioned as a sugarcane estate, attracting rural workers from other regions of Oaxaca, many of whom spoke indigenous languages. Critically, while Arrazola residents are largely the descendants of unambiguously indigenous people, the present-day community does not demonstrate geographic continuity or blood descent from a pre-Hispanic settlement in this locality; and residents today do not display the obvious linguistic markers of indigeneity.[6]

ENTERPRISING MESTIZOS AND DISPLACED CAMPESINOS

As the federal institution responsible for developing and maintaining the Monte Albán site, INAH must figure into any discussion of ethno-racial identity in central Oaxaca. Not only does the monument zone present an interpretation of pre-Hispanic indigenous cultures that is operative in the present, but its staff and archaeologists are in regular contact with local communities that are culturally and economically invested in utilizing the site to different ends. Former Monte Albán director Nelly Robles García admitted that the so-called vending problem at Monte Albán was nowhere near as serious as it was at other prominent sites like Teotihuacán or Chichén Itzá (Castañeda 1996), but was reluctant to condone entrepreneurial activities outside the purview of INAH. Certain state employees took a more extreme position, presenting a seamless narrative of ethical right and wrong in which replica vendors' alleged sale of potsherds and other artifacts was offered up as proof of their ignorance of and disregard for the nation's past. I reiterate these points because denial of vendor requests to occupy the archaeological zone frequently entailed denying vendors' indigeneity as well, as illustrated by the following examples.

One employee characterized replica sellers as "enterprising mestizos" who possessed no historical or cultural connection to Monte Albán.

> They're not indigenous. They don't even speak an indigenous language. Some have money, and even nice cars. I'm sure you know that a lot of them drive up to Monte Albán every day. They're not fools [*No son necios*]. They're smart and they do very well for themselves.

Implicit in his statement was that "real" indigenous people spoke Zapotec or other native languages and rarely managed to move beyond the grinding poverty that still grips many communities in the region. In other words, to be indigenous, one must be poor and socially marginal, and perhaps even foolish or gullible. Such a perspective is remarkably in line with the Mexican state's view of its indigenous peoples from the early part of the twentieth century, in which they were said to exhibit dangerously "backward" characteristics that were viewed as impediments to the nation's modernization. On different occasions Monte Albán employees and guides explained to me that people from Arrazola "don't speak *dialecto*" (the term is a local way of referring to indigenous languages) and no longer maintain indigenous "customs [*costumbres*]."

Monte Albán's on-site administrator, who by all accounts got along well with the vendors and was respectful in his dealing with them, also voiced doubt that replica makers and sellers could claim to be indigenous or that they should be labeled as indigenous by outsiders. He told me that out of all the people working at the site, there was perhaps only one person he considered to be indigenous: a Trique woman who dressed in a distinctive red and white *huipil* and sometimes sold souvenir T-shirts at the site entrance. He also complained about what he considered to be a negative consequence of Monte Albán's designation as a UNESCO World Heritage site: that declaring the archaeological zone as world cultural patrimony mistakenly gave people like the vendors a feeling of ownership over something to which they had no legitimate right. In particular he was critical of vendors who tried to justify their presence at the site by saying that their fathers and grandfathers had worked under archaeologist Alfonso Caso or that they themselves were "born and raised at the foot of Monte Albán." Breglia (2006) observed similar space-claiming tactics by longtime Maya workers at Chichén Itzá, who believed that the site was theirs "not by right of cultural affiliation to the ancient Maya but by their twentieth-century presence living and working in the archaeological zone" (Breglia 2006:117). But whereas the Chichén workers have retained access to the site by asserting this modern linkage, keeping much-coveted INAH jobs within families over generations, Monte Albán vendors have not been as successful.[7] The on-site adminstrator, for one, remained unconvinced, concluding that "culturally speaking, these people have very little to do with Monte Albán."

At the higher levels of the INAH administration, Nelly Robles García and Eduardo López Calzada, at the time of my fieldwork the director of the INAH center in Oaxaca, offered slightly different takes on the identity of the replica vendors.[8] Perhaps because of their backgrounds in anthropology and their very public roles as INAH spokespersons, their criticisms of the sellers were couched in more diplomatic terms. In separate interviews, both took care to acknowledge the discrepancies between the celebratory presentation of Monte Albán's ancient history and the largely substandard living conditions of the people who lived on the fringes of the site, some of whom spoke indigenous languages and who by all standards of institutional measure could be considered indigenous. Indeed, one of the issues that Robles García faced during her directorship at Monte Albán was the flood of poor, often rural, Oaxacans into the city and the proliferation of makeshift housing encroaching on the site's boundaries (see also Robles García 1996). With regards to the town of Arrazola, both officials were well aware of its particular history as an agricultural estate, and attributed its involvement in the replica trade to a paltry land base, as well as the general lack of economic opportunities in Oaxaca outside of tourism.

López Calzada in particular was sensitive to the economic plight of the vendors, and during a 2003 interview he stressed that INAH was working toward a long-term solution that would be agreeable to all parties. Still, he suggested that vendors strategically utilized ethno-racial categories to market their products, and that they used similar tactics in their negotiations with INAH in order to remain inside the confines of the archaeological zone. He hedged when I asked him if he would describe Arrazola as an indigenous community, giving me the impression that he, too, felt uncomfortable imposing such definitive categories. He did mention, however, that the town itself had formed only in the 1930s and had not existed as a pre-Hispanic or even colonial settlement. Furthermore, Arrazola and its residents were increasingly incorporated into the Oaxaca urban configuration through tourism as well as jobs and schools located in the city. Yet he conceded that there were perhaps some residents who "could be considered indigenous." "Ideologically they see themselves as disenfranchised campesinos or indigenous people," he said. "They assume indigenous rights."

From his perspective, the group represented a displaced peasantry that had created an employment niche at the site. This placed INAH in a politically compromised situation. The vendors attempted to rally popular and media support for their group by asserting the grassroots or peasant origins of its members. INAH, in turn, felt pressure to meet vendor demands and offer assurances that the group would be allowed to remain at the site. On a more personal level, López Calzada said that the vendor presence created a moral dilemma for him and other INAH anthropologists, many of whom had built their careers conducting research in rural Oaxacan communities like Arrazola. How could INAH denounce the very people whose culture, in both its pre-Hispanic and its contemporary manfestations, it purported to document and protect?

Robles García appeared less conflicted about INAH's position on the replica vendors. Both in her 1996 dissertation on cultural resource management and in a 2003 interview, she maintained that replica vending was a subterfuge used by some in order to traffic in original archaeological pieces (Robles García 1996:286). In her dissertation she describes the vendors only as "part-time farmers (*campesinos*)" from Arrazola and nearby settlements (Robles García 1996:285), notably avoiding the use of any ethnic or racial categorization. In contrast, in the same document she describes the present-day inhabitants of Mitla, the town emcompassing the archaeological zone of the same name, as Zapotec. These omissions suggest that, for perhaps some of the same reasons cited by López Calzada, she did not consider the replica sellers to be indigenous, much less heirs to Monte Albán's cultural patrimony. Elsewhere she describes the replica vendors and other outside speculators as being driven primarily by financial incentives rather than a historical interest in or legitimate cultural connection to the pre-Hispanic history of the site, stating that "the cultural value of Monte Albán is alien to those groups" (cited in Holo 2004:220).

DISPLEASING TOURISTS

MacCannell employs the term "reconstructed ethnicity" to refer to the "kinds of touristic and political/ethnic identities that have merged in response to pressure from White Culture and tourism" (MacCannell 1992:159). The pressures associated with cultural performances for tourists are duly noted by Little (2004a), who insightfully captures the strategic (and creative) essentialism employed by Mayan vendors who market an array of ethnic handicrafts to tourists in Antigua, Guatemala. He writes, "Although vendors generally avoid telling tourists that they are Maya because they feel that tourists will not believe them, they are particularly frustrated when tourists do not identify them as *indígenas*" (Little 2004a:121). In this context, "vendors want tourists to consider them Indians, Mayas, or Kachikeles. In other words, they want to be Others in relation to tourists and to Ladinos. It is this difference that they hope will induce tourists to buy" (Little 2004a:119).

Lynn Stephen (1993) and W. Warner Wood (2008) likewise observe that artisans and merchants from the central Oaxacan weaving town of Teotitlán del Valle enact particular ideas about indigenous Zapotecs in their negotiations with tourists and others from outside the community. Yet these cases represent groups who express some combination of easily identifiable markers of indigeneity: wearing *traje* (indigenous dress), knowledge of a native language (Kachikel or Zapotec), and/or ties to a community accepted as having pre-Hispanic roots. What are we to make of artisans and vendors who do not readily demonstrate a particular cultural content that the state, tourists, or even some anthropologists designate as indigenous?

Returning to this essay's opening scenario, it is clear that Monte Albán vendors undertake similar calculations about how to present themselves and their wares in accordance with tourist desires. In fact, this is one of the primary critiques lodged by Monte Albán employees in their efforts to discursively undermine vendors' claims to utilizing the archaeological site as commerce space. This perspective largely maintains that replica artisans and vendors are mestizos performing indigeneity for tourists even though they have allegedly "lost" the cultural characteristics, such as language, that once made them indigenous.

The social contradictions expressed through interactions between local artisans and vendors and tourists are indicative of the highly charged class politics of Oaxacan tourism, which includes control over how the Monte Albán archaeological site is utilized. The majority of tourists are middle- and upper-class Mexican nationals, many from wealthy, urban-industrial areas such as Puebla and Mexico City; they are followed in number by upper-income visitors from the United States and Western Europe (SEDETUR 2001). The disparity in wealth between tourists and locals is striking and frequently breaks down along racial and ethnic lines. Both Monte Albán replica purveyors and wood-carvers experience and respond to the structural inequalities of the tourism trade on a daily basis.

Consider the following incident involving Tomás, another vendor from Alberto's community who had worked for nearly forty years selling archaeological replicas. In one of our conversations, Tomás acknowledged that he and some of the other vendors occasionally experienced problems with tourists. He singled out Spanish tourists in particular, noting that "the Spanish have very strong personalities. To us their manners are very sharp." One day while he was vending at Monte Albán, a Spanish tourist instigated a conversation with him as he walked around with his small duffel bag of replica crafts. Tomás's recounting of events revealed a verbal sparring match that evoked Mexico's colonial order.

The well-heeled tourist spared no amount of rudeness in asking Tomás, "*Oye*, ¡*coño*!, you're an Indian [*indio*], right?"[9] Although suspicious of where the conversation was heading, the vendor engaged with the tourist, replying that he was indeed an Indian.

"Well then, why do you speak Spanish so well?" the Spaniard wanted to know.

The vendor indignantly countered, "Look, unfortunately for me, the only things you Spanish left us were your language and your religion. You took everything that Mexico had in return. That's why I speak the way I do!"

The Spanish tourist feebly tried to defend himself. "Oh no, not all of us came here and robbed things!" he said.

Already incensed, Tomás paid him no heed and instead invoked his community's own colonial history. "It doesn't matter. They were the same people, from your same blood. And just so you know why I speak Spanish, where I was born, that was an estate owned by your ancestors who came from Spain. After they came here to exploit Mexico, a lot of them stayed. They robbed our lands—a Spaniard just like you still has lands in my village, in Arrazola."

"How can your village be called Arrazola? That's a Basque name!" retorted the Spaniard. But Tomás was done dealing with the tourist. "Basque or Spanish, it's all the same to me!" he said, and turned and walked away.

In this exchange, the replica seller is put on the defensive when the Spanish tourist assumes not that he is indigenous (*indígena*), but that he is an "*indio*," a term with a historically negative connotation in Mexico (Knight 1990). The tourist incites further indignation when he assumes that the vendor would *not* speak Spanish well. It is also telling that the vendor makes reference to the Arrazola estate heir, Arturo Larrañaga, as a Spaniard. Larrañaga (introduced in chapter 2) was born and raised in Mexico and resided in the city of Oaxaca. In my conversations with him, he acknowledged his Basque-Spanish ancestry but clearly considered himself to be Mexican. Yet Arrazola residents structurally viewed their relationship to the estate heir in colonial terms: he was the light-skinned estate heir who still owned lands in the village, and they were the help. Indeed, some of the men in the community sharecropped his lands, while an Arrazola woman was a domestic worker in his city home. In related fashion, Arrazola residents often referred to members of Oaxaca's business class (especially hotel, restaurant, and gallery owners) as "*españoles*" (Spaniards) whether or not those individuals had any recent connection to Spain, if any at all.

It is useful to recall Judith Friedlander's classic study of "forced identity" in the central Mexican community of Hueyapan, where "to be Indian . . . signified primarily that you were poor" (Friedlander 1975:75). She found little that distinguished villagers there from other rural Mexican populations. Many of their supposedly Indian traits, rather than being survivals from pre-Hispanic times, were actually of Spanish colonial origin. She concluded that

> Indian-ness is more a measure of what the villagers are not or do not have vis-à-vis the Hispanic elite than it is of what they are or have. . . . Consequently, despite the fact that the "content" of Hueyapan is always changing, the "structural" relationship of Indian to Hispanic remains the same. The villagers are still Indians by virtue of the fact that they continue to lack what the elite continues to acquire. (Friedlander 1975:71)

Jorge Hernández Díaz (1998) counters that this emphasis on class struggle precludes any discussion of real cultural differences that may exist within Mexico's heterogeneous population. And he is right that perceived ethno-racial difference is not simply epiphenomenal to class position. Yet Friedlander serves as a reminder that class must be reinserted into discussions hitherto dominated by *indigenista* frameworks of race and ethnicity, which have been, and continue to be, based on easily observable cultural traits such as native-language use (Cook and Joo 1995). More importantly, both Friedlander and Hernández Díaz suggest that the continued elite control of state institutions and its assertion of a Mexican national identity depend on the maintenance of the mestizo/indigenous dichotomy. The persistent structural inequalities and racial discrimination experienced by Hueyapan residents mirror the experiences of numerous Oaxacan communities, where the class of urban elites derives power in part from its ability to distinguish itself from indigenous populations (Montes García 1998).

A selective tradition, based on ethnically marked folkloric forms such as handicrafts, is crucial to the cultural hegemony of elite sectors not only in Oaxaca but throughout the country (García Canclini 1995; Williams 1977). The cultural tourism industry also benefits from the conflation of certain economic activities and their associated class markers with local ethno-racial identities. Murphy and Stepick (1991) argue that the authenticity so prized by visitors to Oaxaca is in large measure a byproduct of the region's underdevelopment. Even as indigenous and other poor Oaxacans work to acquire the material goods and amenities associated with a middle-class, urban lifestyle, outsiders pour into the region seeking bucolic scenery and culture unblemished by industry and new technologies.

CRAFTS AND TOURIST EXPECTATIONS OF CULTURAL CONTINUITY

People ask me all the time, "What happed to all the Zapotec and Mixtecs who lived at Monte Albán?" and of course I tell them that they're still living right here—all they have to do is look around them.

BRUCE WHIPPERMAN, TRAVEL WRITER AND AUTHOR OF THE *OAXACA HANDBOOK*

I sat in the audience in an English-language bookstore in the city of Oaxaca in 2003 as travel writer Bruce Whipperman delivered this commentary to a packed audience of predominantly Euro-American tourists. During his talk, the author stressed Oaxaca's indigenous roots as he described its must-see attractions, which included the ruins of Monte Albán and craft villages that were an easy day trip from the city. His comment illustrates the way in which many visitors, Mexicans and foreigners alike, juxtapose modern Oaxacans—particularly artisans—with the ancient Mesoamerican civilizations represented today by Monte Albán and other archaeological remains.

On another occasion, an American tourist in the city described Oaxaca to me as "a living *National Geographic*." Other scholars (Hervik 2003; Lutz and Collins 1993) have critiqued the magazine's representational technique of contrasting images of archaeological ruins with their so-called living descendants, and the tendency to view Oaxaca as one *National Geographic* article writ large is rooted in such juxtapositions. Discourses of cultural continuity between ancient Monte Albán and modern Zapotecs and other indigenous groups serve as a powerful subtext in the marketing of the region's diverse array of handicrafts. One of the ways this connection is elaborated is through commercial tours to Monte Albán and other archaeological sites that seamlessly fuse with visits to village craft markets and artisans' workshops.

Over the course of my fieldwork, I participated in numerous commercial tours in which the itinerary included stops at Monte Albán, the Thursday market in the town of Zaachila (described by the tour operator as a "traditional Indian market"), and craft workshops in Arrazola and the ceramic-producing town of Santa María Atzompa. Leaving the urban center of Oaxaca, where most visitors are concentrated, these tours create a series of physical and psychological contrasts: past/present, city/country, and indigenous/nonindigenous. Writing about the cultural production of Zapotec textiles and artisans, Wood (2008) notes the double articulation of Williams's (1973) country and city trope. Both urban and rural Oaxaca occupy peripheral positions within the larger nation; the city represents a present that is not yet complete and modern, while artisan communities outside of urban Oaxaca are associated with a rural, indigenous life way ostensibly characterized by a pre-Hispanic mode of production (Wood 2008:76).

Cook and Joo (1995) draw attention to anthropology's complicity in this reification of ethno-racial categories, as they have historically informed state and tourist discourses on Oaxacan handicraft production. In the Central Valleys, where handicraft production is an economic mainstay for multiple communities, artisans are frequently assigned indigenous (usually Zapotec) identities based on their craftwork. Cook and Joo do not dispute artisans' indigenous roots or their right to utilize ethnicity to market their products. However, they remind us that communities' participation in a craft economy does not necessarily mean that residents view themselves as ethnically or racially distinct from other groups.

> The assumption is pervasive that a direct linkage exists between craft production and indígena identity in Mexico regarding historical origin and contemporary participation at the village level. . . . The problem here is not that present-day artisans in Oaxaca choose to identify themselves and their products as Zapotec but that the anthropologists who study them often fail to consider the probability that such artisans have multiple identities deriving from their participation in an array of nested structures of social relations. (Cook and Joo 1995:49)

Employing Fredric Jameson's (1981) concept of "strategies of containment," Michael Kearney (1996) similarly takes to task ethnographers who participate in the construction of unitary, undifferentiated subjects. Rendering "the artisan" as anthropological subject has led to complex, individual identities being "contained and reduced in consciousness to that of distinct univocal others, for such cultural containment is integral to the constitution of the sociopolitical difference between First World self and the essentialized subaltern other" (Kearney 1996:167). He notably refers to Oaxacan wood-carvers and their art, both of which are thoroughly embedded in global systems of exchange. Discourses on Oaxacan village artisans obscure their status as transnational migrants working in a Chinese restaurant in Los Angeles or a meatpacking facility in Wisconsin—jobs variously held by Arrazola artisans I know.

As internationally acclaimed wood-carvers, Arrazola residents are accustomed to receiving reporters, filmmakers, and anthropologists in their community. They are also keenly aware of their celebrated yet economically and socially subordinate position within Oaxaca's field of cultural production. One Arrazola wood-carver, whose father-in-law sold archaeological replicas at Monte Albán, noted that while Americans in particular expressed admiration for his craft, they often seemed disappointed when they arrived at his workshop only to discover that he wore tennis shoes and soccer jerseys and drove an old but functioning Volkswagen. He said, "It's like they come here and they want to see you still wearing homemade clothes and living in an adobe house." He noted that Arrazola had in fact been more like that when he was a child in the 1970s, but that things had changed due to wood-carving, the growth of tourism at Monte Albán, and the influx of remittances from residents working in the United States. The same man spoke of participating in a state-sponsored craft exhibition in Mexico City several years earlier. Visibly agitated, he recounted to me how all of the artisans from Oaxaca were put up in rooms without beds. Whether the arrangement was intentional or merely an oversight, he experienced the situation as humiliating and discriminatory. In his reading, the officials in charge of the event wrongly assumed that "all Oaxacans were *indios* who slept on *petates* [woven palm mats] on the ground at home."

Situations like the one described above create a profound ambivalence in many Arrazola residents. On one hand, they knew that Oaxaca is characterized as a cultural gem and the most ethnically diverse place in Mexico, and that a particular cultural content defined as indigenous can be a valuable asset. They also recognize that they fit within this narrative of cultural continuity as wood-carving artisans and, perhaps to a lesser degree, as makers and sellers of archaeological replicas at Monte Albán. Yet the historical weight of dominant social categories, with their implications of poverty and, ironically, cultural backwardness, at times becomes unbearable.

One morning as I slowly drove my truck over the potholed back road that connected Arrazola to Monte Albán, I spotted a neighbor, Andrés, a replica vendor, walking in the same direction. The van he normally relied on for transportation to the site had refused to start that day, and so I offered him a ride, which he gratefully accepted. As we drove, I noticed that Andrés, normally gregarious and full of jokes, seemed unusually sullen. I asked him if he was sick. With this opening, he began to complain about a recent confrontation he had had with a Mexican guide, who was leading a group of English-speaking tourists at Monte Albán.

Although he normally worked alone when selling his replica crafts, that day he and a fellow vendor from Arrazola approached the tour group together. His friend, who understood some English from having worked several years in the United States, overheard the guide telling the tourist group that the vendors were, in Andrés's words, "poor Indians who lived off the crafts they sell." Incensed, he pulled the guide aside after her group had dispersed and confronted her in Spanish. "I asked her, 'Why did you tell those gringos that we were *indios*?' She didn't even say anything. So I told her, 'Look, I'm proud to be an Indian. Who do you think you are to put us down?'" Andrés claimed that he was not upset so much that the guide had called them *indios*, but that she had said it in a condescending tone that he felt expressed disdain and pity.

Paradoxically, the same discourses that ascribe indigeneity to Arrazola residents in certain instances serve to withhold it in others. While wood-carvers from the community are widely perceived to be indigenous Zapotecs by outsiders, replica vendors are subject to a different sort of scrutiny by tourists, as their economic activities are not as easily contained within master narratives of traditional Oaxacan artisans. Some tourists assume that replica sellers are indigenous, but others are less certain, as the following examples attest.

During my discussion with the University of Michigan student introduced in the preceding chapter, I asked him to describe the communities that he had visited during his stay, which included a number of "Indian artisan towns." The student explained that he liked "to look at people to see what they are ethnically," but hesitated when I asked him how he would characterize the men selling archaeological replicas at the site. Perhaps worried that he would give an incorrect response, he finally concluded that they were "possibly mestizo." He continued, "Sometimes you can tell from people's face structure and skin color what they are. But these guys [replica sellers] look better off than most."

An interesting, if not uncommon, conflation of popular notions of race, ethnicity, and class may be observed in the student's comments. First, he believes that indigenous Oaxacans may be physically distinguished from mestizos in much the same way that African Americans are seen to possess specific, racialized phenotypic traits. Second, the racial categories of "Indian" and "mestizo" may also double as ethnic categories, either standing in relation to or displacing more specific terms such as "Zapotec" or "Mixtec." Yet despite his assertion that identity may reside in a particular set of physical characteristics, in his assessment the student ultimately falls back on what appear to be class indicators (i.e., looking "better off than most"): the vendors may have looked poor, but not poor enough for the young traveler to classify them as indigenous.

In other instances, assumptions about the replica vendors are expressed primarily through the idiom of cultural tradition and authenticity. Take the middle-aged married couple from Minneapolis, Minnesota, whom I met at Monte Albán in 2003. Both schoolteachers, they spent most of their summers traveling and had timed their visit to Oaxaca to attend the Guelaguetza festival in the city during the month of July.[10] According to them, the replica crafts and the men who sold them lacked a "story." The man found it particularly unsettling that he had no clear way of verifying the vendors' identity, a problem that he considered exacerbated by their atomized selling strategy—in other words, their lack of a fixed location within the site. Motioning in the direction of a vendor, he said,

> That guy over there with the baseball cap could be anybody for all you know. I want to know that he's part of a community, that he's got an authentic product. You don't know where those things [replicas] come from. For all you know, there's some twelve-year-old kid in the city hammering those things out.

His wife attempted to clarify by adding that, "I think what he means is that you don't know if they're from a village or not. You don't know if it's traditional or something they just made up, like with the black pottery and some of the other crafts that have obviously been around for a long time." Ironically, the craft forms that are most iconic of Oaxaca today, wood carvings and black pottery produced in the town of San Bartolo Coyotepec, do not have the long histories that most tourists suppose. While San Bartolo and other communities have engaged in pottery making for centuries, the method for making black pottery was allegedly discovered by one woman, Doña Rosa, in the 1950s. The pieces are mainly decorative, since they are porous and cannot hold liquids—a major break with the original, utilitarian function of many ceramic vessels.

I suggested to the tourist that perhaps he would feel more comfortable if the vendors were set up in stalls or a co-op where shoppers could watch artisan demonstrations (much like in the craft villages) and learn about the history of the archaeological souvenirs. The man was enthused by this idea and was "willing to wager that guidebooks like Lonely Planet would jump all over it." He continued,

> We saw something like that in Mitla, they had a separate building where people could sell stuff, even though it wasn't really the kind of setup you're talking about. I think what you're seeing here is people just buying stuff on a whim from whoever happens to be there when they're about ready to leave, or maybe if they just want the guy [vendor] to stop following them around. You just don't know if these guys have a history of making crafts or if what they're selling has any link with traditions from the area.

The couple's comments suggested that they had difficulty placing the Monte Albán sellers, who do not operate within the confines of a well-defined artisan market or craft village. The woman insightfully related their desire for a narrative of the vendors' identity to the aesthetics of consumer society. She said, "I think in the U.S. we're really into labeling. We look for the story, whether it's for jeans, perfume, or whatever. Plus, we're used to having a lot of choices and the story is how you ultimately make a decision." What she did not explicitly state was that the story they were seeking was one in which authentic objects pair easily with ethnic producers.

Arjun Appadurai (1986) describes ethnic arts as a special class of commodities in which consumer desire for handmade, one-of-a-kind objects fuels a parallel desire to know the producers' biographies. Later in our conversation, the female tourist drew an analogy between Oaxaca and a recent trip to China. Her comments demonstrate how notions of authenticity and tradition inform, and indeed fuse with, perceptions of race and ethnicity in the tourist encounter:

> We went to China on vacation last year as part of a tour, and I think the government there really has the right idea. In the tourist areas they make sure to distinguish the ethnic Chinese from the Han Chinese by labeling the stores and stuff. They'll actually have a sign that tells you. That way you can tell who's who. It's not like they discourage you from going into the Han shops and buying souvenirs or anything, but they want tourists to be informed. You always know when you're getting something from

an ethnic Chinese because it's clearly marked, you don't have to second-guess it.

Monte Albán vendors were the first to admit that being perceived as indigenous could be a boon to sales, but most did not use indigeneity as an overt marketing strategy in the way that has been observed by Little (2004a) in Antigua, Guatemala, where market vendors strategically speak Kachikel and women wear *traje*, key features that distinguish them as Maya. In the Oaxacan community of Teotitlán del Valle, woolen rugs and textiles are marketed as ethnic handicrafts and indigeneity is a crucial component of what Wood (2008) calls the "Zapotec weaving complex" (also Stephen 1991, 1993; Whitecotton 1996). But it is much easier for Teotitlán and the nearby weaving community of Santa Ana del Valle to mark themselves as Zapotec when marketing their crafts. Both communities boast a high number of Zapotec speakers, and as noted earlier, native-language use continues to be an important criterion (at least by state measures) in determining who is and is not indigenous. From a less commercial perspective, both Teotitlán and Santa Ana have their own ethnographies, written by American anthropologists Lynn Stephen (1991) and Jeffrey Cohen (1999), respectively. While perhaps not read by the same tourists who purchase local textiles, these ethnographies serve to validate these towns' Zapotec identities within the academic community.

Few would question the ethno-racial status of the two weaving communities mentioned above; they are long-standing settlements that retain native-language use and other cultural features marked as indigenous. However, other Oaxacan craft villages that do not demonstrate the obvious linguistic markers of Teotitlán and Santa Ana are also frequently perceived by outsiders (especially tourists) to be indigenous by virtue of their artisan production—this is certainly the case for Arrazola. In the market for wood carving, residents are represented as Zapotec or having Zapotec roots, even if they claim other backgrounds, such as Chatino or Mixtec, or no specific ethno-racial identity at all. I am less familiar with how residents of other nearby, well-known craft-producing communities such as Santa María Atzompa, San Bartolo Coyotepec, and Santo Tomás Jalieza self-identify, but on multiple occasions I have witnessed tourists, guides, and officials from the state tourism office refer to them as indigenous communities.[11]

In contrast, the nature of replica craft sales—conducted inside of Monte Albán—makes it difficult for visitors to ascertain the origins of the vendors and their wares. It is not always clear to tourists that most of the men positioned around the ruins are from Arrazola, although they are proud to claim their hometown when people take the time to ask. Tourists also express uncertainty about who makes the replica crafts. The vendors are therefore more hard-pressed to present, or to be contained by, the seamless narrative of belonging to an ethnic artisan community than are their family and neighbors involved in wood carving. The fact that their replicas are unauthorized by Monte Albán officials and have almost no market outside of the archaeological zone also means that they lack the well-structured representational system (websites, books, gallery venues, etc.) by which information about other Oaxacan crafts circulates. Unlike the residents of Teotitlán, who often speak Zapotec with one another during transactions with tourists (see Wood 2008), I never observed Arrazola replica vendors utilizing an indigenous language. While these details may resist common state and anthropological constructions of indigeneity, they do not necessarily preclude vendors from claiming indigeneity in certain situations, nor does any of this keep some Monte Albán visitors from assuming that vendors are indigenous.

The dialogic process by which Arrazola replica sellers negotiate indigeneity may result in individuals' simultaneous negation of such identities, pointing to complex, internally differentiated subject positions. In my conversation with one replica artisan, he alternately described himself as Zapotec and mestizo. When asked to self-identify, however, he articulated a personalized version of the nationalist discourse of *mestizaje*. He, like other community members I interviewed, talked about Arrazola's colonial history as a hacienda, where he assumed Spaniard landowners and indigenous workers mixed to produce new mestizo subjects, the town's present-day population. Whether or not the owners of the prerevolutionary Arrazola estate were intimately involved with their workers is not documented, nor did anyone in Arrazola offer personal anecdotes from family histories that would support such claims.

Important here is how the national narrative of *mestizaje* has been refashioned to make sense of local experiences by means of ethno-racial categories. The same man said,

> Here, we're the product of *mestizaje*, but we still have indigenous blood, more than anything else we're the descendants of those cultures. . . . If we were indigenous we would have the privilege of speaking the languages, of speaking our mother tongue, Zapotec for example, in addition to Spanish. No, we're not in-

> digenous because of the fact that, until now, we've been on the margin of all the development taking place in indigenous communities. There are communities that receive government support. But here in Arrazola we've remained separate from a lot of that. It's only in the last few years that the town's started to get the most basic services, water, electricity, we don't even have a real drainage or septic system here. What we do have, we've done it through our own efforts.

Here is yet another articulation of ethno-racial identity vis-à-vis economic status. But where Friedlander (1975) posits that being indigenous in contemporary Mexico is to be poor, this speaker suggests that Arrazola has remained poor precisely because it is *not* indigenous within the Mexican state paradigm. In other words, Arrazola is rarely the target of government programs aimed to alleviate poverty in officially designated indigenous communities. To be clear, I am not suggesting that Oaxacan indigenous communities have achieved social and economic integration at the expense of towns such as Arrazola; in fact, many of Oaxaca's poorest residents are indigenous. I include this anecdote as an example of how Arrazola residents are effectively prevented from participating in a specific brand of state-acknowledged politics of indigeneity that would enable particular forms of economic development.

A PARTING TAKE

The vendor who went by the name "*el Mole*" and I sat in the shade of a large laurel tree on the site grounds. I was interviewing him about his experiences selling archaeological replicas at Monte Albán. I asked him how he earned his nickname, which referred to one of Oaxaca's most celebrated gastronomical creations: a rich, dark sauce made of ground chiles and chocolate, among other ingredients. Sheepishly he replied, "I don't know, that's just what they call me." "They" referred to the other Monte Albán vendors. I would later find out that he was dubbed *Mole* due to the darkness of his complexion, apparently resembling the deep brown color of the sauce by the same name.

First and foremost a shrewd businessman, the thirty-seven-year-old vendor agreed to be interviewed for no more than thirty minutes so as not to squander time that could be more lucratively used for selling. I found out that he had married a woman from Arrazola and learned the replica trade from his father-in-law. Prior to working at Monte Albán, he had made a living as a wrestler in local *lucha libre* events, Mexico's hugely popular, stylized wrestling competitions. The man was in the middle of describing his procedure for sculpting and firing ceramic figurines when I heard the unmistakable ring of a cell phone coming from his backpack. He motioned for me to shut off the tape recorder, took the call, and then nonchalantly tucked the phone back in his bag. My face must have indicated surprise, prompting him to declare, "*El indio ya tiene celular*—why don't you put that in your *pinche* thesis!"[12]

"The Indian now has a cell phone"—was the artisan claiming indigeneity? Maybe, but the irony of his comment, evidenced by the challenging tone with which he delivered it to me, an Anglo anthropologist from the United States, suggested something more. His self-reference to being "*indio*," as opposed to *indígena*, was telling. His words parodied one of the assumptions that tourists at Monte Albán commonly made about him and that he thought perhaps I shared. For some tourists, it was imperative that he be indigenous as they tried to make sense of the reconstructed, modern Monte Albán landscape. In fact, the vendor was providing his own astute commentary on the complex nature of ethnoracial identification within Oaxaca's tourist complex.

The historical dimensions of Mexico's racial hierarchy may be distinctive, but the new forms of "cultural racism" that Charles Hale (2006) argues characterize ladino–Indian relations in Guatemala are also evident in Oaxaca.[13] Hale observes that "while overt biological justifications of inferiority are on the decline, ladinos still regularly note cultural differences between themselves and Mayas, and often point to these differences in explaining why Indians have remained in inferior social positions" (Hale 2006:210). He further argues that the rise of official multiculturalism has had the effect of making racial hierarchy ever more resilient, and that the "growing ethos of cultural equality and multicultural citizenship among dominant actors does not necessarily signal the elimination of racism" (Hale 2006:223). Instead, ladinos demonstrate a profound racial ambivalence, marked by a growing support of indigenous culture and inclusion with a simultaneous unwillingness to concede their long-standing racial privilege.

Hale's analysis is primarily concerned with Maya ascendancy within the political sphere, but it is not a stretch to recognize that state recognition of cultural difference is effectively synergistic with the tourism enterprise, both in Guatemala (Little 2004a; Little 2004b) and in Mexico. In Oaxaca, a selective tradition based on racially/ethnically marked folkloric forms is crucial to the hegemony of elite sectors: government officials, urban business owners, and tour operators alike celebrate while economically profiting from a seemingly benign multiculturalism.

Arrazola's production and marketing of two distinct craft forms has led to divergent and even contradictory discourses about the community. As a village of wood-carvers, Arrazola is considered to manifest Oaxaca's indigenous cultural heritage, part of a national public culture comprising not only artisan traditions but also archaeological vestiges. Alternately, through their production and marketing of archaeological replicas, Arrazola residents are positioned within a contemporary archaeological semiotic system in which they may also be construed as the direct, modern-day descendants of Monte Albán's pre-Hispanic population (see also Ardren 2004; Hervik 2003). Yet as I have argued here, these same practices may alternately serve to render the vendors as nonindigenous from the perspective of outsiders. The significance of these social categories is heightened at a site like Monte Albán, a master symbol of Mexico's indigenous past and its "survival" into the present.

Drawing on a broader theoretical model, Joseph Whitecotton (1996) suggests that Oaxacans' understanding and strategic use of ethno-racial categories are constituted in dynamic relationship to national and international socioeconomic structures; identities grow larger and more complex to meet the onslaught of globalization more effectively. Writing over a decade ago, he anticipated emergent identities in Arrazola in recounting the following incident:

> A prominent wood carver in Arrazola showed me a video about his work narrated by Vincent Price on the VCR in his home. This video called the carvers of Arrazola "Zapotec" even though they themselves make no such claim; at present they associate being "Zapotec" exclusively with speaking the language which no one in their village does. Perhaps in the future, the North American equation of biological heritage and ethnicity, plus incentives for sales, will create self-proclaimed Zapotec wood carvers in Arrazola. (Whitecotton 1996:23)

In touristic border zones such as Antigua (Little 2004a) and Oaxaca, the primacy of transnational processes of tourism in contemporary ethno-racial formations is evident, colluding with and even supplanting other processes of identity negotiation.

The ambiguity of racial ideology in Oaxaca is, according to Deborah Poole, what "lends it its singular power to mobilize older social prejudices and modes of understanding difference, reworking them to fit the exigencies of changing social and political landscapes—always present but never quite the same" (Poole 2004:39–40). Racial and ethnic categories are constituted in relation to overlapping and ever-shifting ideas of biological essence, historical process, cultural identity, and national subjectivity. Like many people in Oaxaca, Arrazola residents undoubtedly share in a collective, regional history that predates European arrival, but at the same time they are the inheritors of a postrevolutionary project that aimed to incorporate them as national mestizo subjects.

That Arrazola artisans and vendors today both reproduce and refute ethno-racial categorizations should not come as a surprise; the individuals' presented here are attempting to rework them from within, against the grain of history, and through new modes of tourist consumerism. As such, the conflation of artisanry with indigeneity in the tourism market may prove a generative force in artisans' self-identifications and articulations. There is power, and perhaps slippage, but no lie in the assertion, "*Yo soy nativo de aquí.*"

CHAPTER SEVEN

Why Fake Jaguar Gods Matter

Revealing hidden assumptions about the past they claim to stem from, fakes advance our understanding no less than the truths that expose them.

DAVID LOWENTHAL (1992:190)

AS CONCERNS MOUNT THAT GLOBALIZATION IS eroding the distinctions that give places their unique character, Oaxaca retains its aura of cultural alterity even as it experiences the penetration of multinational capital and flows of visitors from around the world. Mexico City–based writer and travel columnist Barbara Kastelein describes a network of social actors and institutions that continuously work to submerge those aspects of Oaxacan lived experience not in line with tourist expectations. Although her comments evidence a dualistic notion of cultural authenticity, they are still perceptive:

> While Oaxaca is not yet inundated by plastic trinkets and "airport art"—sights its ideal tourist does not want to see—Wal-Mart, catsup, norteña music, and Choco Krispis are part of the contemporary spectacle that tourism promoters, cultural defenders, and travel writers are reluctant to acknowledge. (Kastelein 2010:345)

Oaxaca is lauded as a repository of traditional indigenous or "peasant" culture as it is manifested through its most folkloric elements (handicrafts, festivals, and folk religious celebrations such as the Day of the Dead); these forms reinforce notions of cultural continuity and rustic authenticity at the same time that they contribute to the promotion and packaging of Oaxaca by state and private interests for an ethnotourism market. Wood carvings and replicas, then, are necessarily bound up in the same logic of cultural authenticity. To borrow from David Brooks (2001), this logic sustains the "bourgeois bohemian" sensibility that bemoans a McDonald's on the city's downtown *zócalo* but seems not to notice when wealthy foreigners and Mexican outsiders snatch up nearby historic properties, transforming them into boutique hotels and restaurants catering to tourists.

Discourses about Oaxacan culture are in part constructed around the strong presence of locally produced *artesanías*. Crafts are widely promoted and perceived as being rooted in pre-Hispanic modes of production regardless of their historical specificities. Yet, as García Canclini (1993) cogently argues, the notion of handicrafts as manifesting continuity with the pre-Hispanic past may have as much to do with *indigenista* state ideology and the demands of modern consumer society as with actual nonindustrial technologies and patterns of production. García Canclini's Gramscian approach posits an understanding of crafts as historically situated cultural forms where the struggle for cultural hegemony is constantly being waged and whose meanings are dialogically fashioned out of shifting social relations.

The wood carvings made in Arrazola are a specific example of how a craft and its producers may be contained within discourses of Oaxacan handicraft production based on ideas of cultural wholeness and continuity with a pre-Hispanic past. Although Arrazola is located at the base of the ruins of Oaxaca's largest pre-Hispanic settlement, the town itself is the result of colonial patterns of land usage and subsequent reforms by the postrevolutionary Mexican state. Its present-day residents do not identify simply as indigenous or Zapotec, and in fact may claim different ethnic and/or mestizo identities depending on the context. The wood-carving craft, too, is a relatively recent development. Prior to the 1980s there was no community-wide history of wood carving, and the whimsical, animal-inspired pieces that today are associated with the genre have always been produced for an outside market. But the stakes are high for wood carving as one of the bestselling Mexican folk arts in the United States and as a craft representative of Oaxaca both within and outside of Mexico. For marketers of the crafts, which may include artisans themselves, it is advantageous that the public associate wood carvings with long-standing, indigenous folk traditions.

Still, wood carvings resist being completely subsumed by discourses that construct contemporary Oaxacan handicrafts as premodern survivals. This is demonstrated by their limited appeal among Mexicans, who have a different historical relationship to handicrafts as objects symbolically linked with state-sponsored nationalism. Mexicans often acknowledge the skill and craftsmanship that go into wood carving and recognize it as symbolic of Oaxaca; but they do not generally situate wood carving on the same historical trajectory as other crafts from the region such as textiles and ceramics (although these crafts, too, have their own complex, modern histories). Thus despite its iconic status, wood carving may not always be perceived as a fully authentic cultural form (i.e., one exhibiting a long-standing history of local production) for certain classes of Mexican consumers, at least in terms of national patrimony.

Neither replica crafts nor those who sustain the trade conform to prescribed notions of appropriate or authentic cultural production in the same way as wood carving. Paradoxically, replicas share many of the same qualities commonly associated with other Mexican handicrafts. Ceramic replicas are handmade locally by self-taught artisans, and stone pieces are partially finished by the men who sell them. The pieces function as souvenirs, objects that remind their travelers of their Oaxaca trip and their visit to Monte Albán. It is not a stretch to assume that replicas, like most other Oaxacan handicrafts, have a decorative function inside purchasers' homes. Perhaps more importantly, the Arrazola residents who make and sell replicas consider them to be *artesanías* having no less of a craft tradition or vocation as wood carving within the community. Still, judging from the comments I heard from tourists at Monte Albán, some would say that they do not count as real folk art at all, since they do not apparently represent any long-standing community function or artistic tradition. Replica making, for example, is not part of the public spectacle of artisan work that now serves as a tourist attraction in its own right. In fact, most tourists are unaware that many of the replica sellers they encounter at Monte Albán live in Arrazola, a town that is almost exclusively associated with wood carving.

Jacques Derrida (1974) famously theorized the instability and partiality of the sign, arguing that efforts to secure a fixed, universal meaning for a text are merely an imposition of arbitrary power that ultimately constrains its interpreter. Following this insight, I want to suggest that replicas reveal the instability and openness of the archaeological sign, an assemblage of textualized material remains whose meaning is condensed and heightened in the individual artifact. As cultural forms replicas appear to stand in relation to what they are not: real archaeological artifacts. The meaning and value of pre-Hispanic replicas is therefore constituted in relation to original artifacts, at the same time that they legitimate the artifacts themselves (it stands to reason that if you have something that is "real" then there must be something outside of it that is not). Replicas' value stems from their ability to evoke the material referents of pre-Hispanic history that are manifest in the ruins of iconic archaeological monuments such as Monte Albán.

In this way, replicas cling to the nationalist and tourist narrative of Oaxacan prehistory and culture at the same time that they exist at its margins. The polyvalence of these discourses is evidenced by the fact that tourist consumers perceive replicas in different manners. Mexican tourists, and to a lesser degree Europeans, may be willing to overlook their manufactured authenticity. My observations suggest that the overwhelmingly Anglo, middle- and upper-class North Americans who travel to Oaxaca are generally put off by something they perceive to be "fake," even if it symbolically references the pre-Hispanic past.

Complicating the interpretative understanding of replicas is the fact that they occasionally pass as original pieces. It is in these moments that replicas are perhaps most successful, much to the consternation of Monte Albán archaeologists, who have a huge stake in maintaining what they perceive to be the historical integrity and accuracy of the site. In these instances we witness the overcoming of the fake/genuine dichotomy, as replicas take on the same value and meaning as the archaeological pieces on which they are modeled. Replicas harness the power of cultural patrimony to represent the Mexican national past—a power that is by and large controlled by the state apparatus through the national organ of INAH. In other words, replicas make archaeologists nervous for good reason.

Replicas have the potential to illuminate the social conditions surrounding their existence, and they demonstrate the contradictions of the "real things" that they supposedly replicate. Moreover, their "real" referents lend them their power and, thus, a sort of authenticity. When I observed the making of these so-called fakes by supposed counterfeiters, I saw the handcrafting of skilled artisans. Moreover, the vendors' playful assurances that their goods are "originals" (meaning originating with them) render the slippage and subversion of the original and replica near complete. In such contradictions and collusions we glimpse the competing desires to possess and represent, as well as sell and consume, images of Oaxacan culture.

The purpose of this book has not been simply to valorize a practice of which many archaeologists and art historians are undoubtedly critical, yet I hold firm to the conviction that it is important to document the stories and voices of those who inhabit UNESCO "heritage-scapes" (Di Giovine 2009) but do not equally share in the power to consume and (re)interpret such sites as they see fit. Refusals of a paradigm in which heritage is for the benefit of all may take implicit or more overt forms, such as the following comment by an Arrazola artisan:

> All this about Oaxaca being the cultural patrimony of humankind, it's not true. It's nothing more than the cultural patrimony of a handful of people, a few who are able to live off of it, those who have economic and political power. If you look at all of Oaxaca it's the same thing. Just look at the downtown, the owners of a lot of those businesses aren't even Mexican. They're all Spanish, French, other foreigners. What we Oaxacans are good for is selling our labor at the cheapest price possible. We're just the employees for all of this.

Elucidating the potential of material culture as a site of social analysis, Fred Myers states that "in objectification, cultural objects externalize values and meaning embedded in social processes, making them available, visible, or negotiable for further action by subjects" (Myers 2001:20). In Oaxaca, archaeological replicas thus provide a lens for understanding how archaeological science and the tourism industry effectively delineate a field of cultural production and determine how "culture" as a resource is to be preserved and disseminated.

REPLICA, COPY, SOMETHING ELSE?

Gilles Deleuze wrote that

> the simulacrum is not degraded copy, rather it contains a positive power which negates both original and copy, both model and reproduction. It doesn't even work to invoke the model of the Other, because no model resists the vertigo of the simulacrum. (Deleuze 1983:53)

Without delving too deeply into Deleuze, let it suffice to say that his reading of simulacra does not harbor Baudrillard's (1988) pessimism about living in society that privileges images—pure surface—over real meaning and depth. Rather, he sees the opening up of potentialities:

simulacra as a positive force that offers the possibility of overthrowing the categories that collectively assert dominant orders of knowledge. According to Deleuze, simulacra subvert binary distinctions (e.g., real/fake), so that the "privileged point of view has no more existence than does the object held in common by all points of view. There is no possible hierarchy: neither second, nor third" (Deleuze 1983:53).

I have hinted throughout this book that perhaps replicas are not really replicas or copies all, although they may take on some physical semblance of material culture from the past. If we accept Deleuze's position, then perhaps they are something else, some other order of representation, whose work is "not to become an equivalent of the 'model' but to turn against it and its world in order to open a new space for the simulacrum's own mad proliferation" (Massumi 1997: n.p.).

What is certain is that replicas push at, often surpassing, the limits of the possible interpretations of Oaxacan cultural history and the acceptable modes for conveying them; the material objects as well as the stories told about and through them signal the contradictions and ruptures within the cultural system—even when they appear to reproduce the categories and logics of the system itself. "Fake" jaguar gods do matter, and not because they are material frauds waiting to be unmasked by experts. Rather, they reveal that all is not what it appears, that there are multiple stories to be told about Oaxaca's cultural past and present.

Notes

CHAPTER ONE

1. SEDETUR is the Spanish acronym for the *Secretaría de Desarrollo Turístico.*

2. The creation of the term "alebrije" has been credited to Mexico City papier-mâché artist Pedro Linares (1906–1992). Linares reportedly made up the term to describe his fantastical, monsterlike papier-mâché creations inspired by his dreams (Masuoka 1994). The word "alebrije" has been widely appropriated by the state government and the art establishment in the promotion of Oaxacan wood carving, apparently because some of the wood carvings exhibit fantastical designs similar to those of the papier-mâché alebrijes. Few wood-carvers actually use this term in reference to their own work.

3. The same individuals may also refer to their objects as *ídolos* (idols), a curious invocation of Spanish colonial discourse that casts native peoples as idol worshipers.

4. The *pícaro* is a specifically Iberian tradition, but is analogous to the trickster and clown figures that are found in narrative and performance genres throughout the world.

5. Since Benedict Anderson's seminal work *Imagined Communities* (1983) was published nearly three decades ago, there has been a proliferation of works on nation-states and national identity that address this topic from both generalist and region-specific perspectives. Some have focused on the role of archaeology in nationalist ideology (e.g., Díaz-Andreu and Champion 1996; Jones 1997; Meskell 1998; Smiles 1994), while other have explored folklore's relationship to nationalism (e.g., Abrahams 1993; Handler 1988; Herzfeld 1982).

6. Under Díaz, Mexico developed modern infrastructure such as oil refineries, railroads, and factories. However, the rural peasantry bore much of the cost of modernization, as capital and land became increasingly concentrated in

the hands of the elite. The ensuing revolution of 1910 was in part a response to the rising civil unrest brought about by Mexico's growing social and economic divide.

7. The *porfiriato* is the Spanish name given to the period of the Díaz regime.

8. "*Lo mexicano*" refers to things that are "typically Mexican," and may encompass everything from material goods to perceived aspects of the national character, such as the inherent fatalism described by Mexican Nobel Laureate Octavio Paz in his classic text *The Labyrinth of Solitude* (Paz 1985); the original text was published in Spanish in 1950.

9. His *Consideraciones sobre el problema indígena* was published in 1948 by the Interamerican Indigenist Institute.

10. Such negative stereotypes were undoubtedly bolstered by journalistic and literary representations of the oppressive Díaz regime and the bloodshed of the subsequent revolutionary period. Here I am referring to works such as John Kenneth Turner's *Barbarous Mexico* (1911) and D. H. Lawrence's *The Plumed Serpent* (1926).

11. Kahlo was especially fond of textiles from the Isthmus of Tehuantepec in Oaxaca, and many of her self-portraits feature her wearing indigenous clothing from this region.

12. *Mexican Folkways* was a bilingual English-Spanish journal published by folklorist Francis Toor, an expatriate who lived in Mexico City and published extensively on Mexican popular culture.

13. The Institutional Revolutionary Party (PRI) was formed in the wake of the Mexican Revolution and controlled national political life for more than seventy years. The PRI lost control of the presidency in 2000, with the election of rival PAN candidate Vicente Fox.

14. In addition, in 2009 Robles García was named as the head of the INAH *Consejo de Arqueología*, the national archaeology council. She served as the director of Monte Albán during the time that I carried out the fieldwork for this project. The archaeologist Miguel Angel Cruz González succeeded her in this position.

15. This scholarly neglect likely stems, in large part, from the fact that tourism itself only became a legitimate anthropological topic in the late 1970s, with the publication of Valene Smith's now-classic text *Hosts and Guests: The Anthropology of Tourism.*

16. Barbash does discuss the endemic poverty he encountered in Oaxacan wood-carving communities, particularly in the early days of the craft in the 1980s, when few artisans had attained substantial economic success. His subsequent publication (2007) on wood carving in Arrazola and the other Oaxacan wood-carving communities sensitively portrays the socioeconomic transformations and challenges facing residents after the wood-carving boom of the preceding decades.

THE SKULL OF BENITO JUÁREZ

1. "Gringo" is a commonly used and at times pejorative term for an American. The Sierra Norte is a mountain region that runs through the northern portion of the state of Oaxaca. Benito Juárez, Mexico's first indigenous president, was born in the mountain town of Guelatao in 1806.

CHAPTER TWO

1. It is important to note that the criteria used to define crafts, folk art, and art are not fixed and may vary from one context to another. Oaxacan wood carving, for example, is generally described as a folk art or craft, but it occasionally crosses over into the fine art market and is frequently sold in upscale galleries and museums in the U.S. Alternately, Oaxacan wood carving may fall into the tourist or "airport art" category, depending on when and where it is acquired and the perceived quality and originality of the piece. The final category, as Graburn suggested in his early work on ethnic and tourist arts (1976), may entail a devaluing of the work by identifying it as a somehow less authentic, commodified form. Of course, all of these classifications are problematic and reflect intersecting discourses historically conditioned by class, racial, and gender ideologies.

2. The term "*hacienda*" has also been used in reference to the Arrazola estate (e.g., Velasco Rodríguez and Aguilar Sánchez 2000), but it generally denotes an estate of larger scale. For example, Oaxacan *fincas* at the turn of the twentieth century rarely were greater in size than 200 hectares, while *haciendas* could encompass thousands of hectares of land. In keeping with the archival records and other scholars who have written about Arrazola (Chibnik 2003; Serrie 1964), I employ the term "*finca*" here. However, it should be noted that current residents of the community typically refer to the "*ex-hacienda*" when speaking about the estate that existed prior to the founding of their village.

3. The *encomienda* system was key to the settlement of New Spain after the Conquest. Spanish *encomenderos* received the tribute and labor of indigenous peoples in return for overseeing their conversion to Christianity as well as their general welfare. In practice, indigenous peoples were essentially slaves and suffered tremendous abuse at the hands of the *encomenderos*.

4. These stores played a critical role in maintaining the dependency of the worker on his or her *patrón*. Although goods could be bought on credit, the overly inflated prices for necessary household goods often meant that employees were forever in debt to the company store.

5. When the other districts in the Central Valleys are included (Etla, Oco-

tlán, Tlacolula, and Zimatlán), the number of haciendas in 1910 totaled sixty-seven (Velasco Rodríguez and Aguilar Sánchez 2000).

6. Land was communally held under the *ejido* system. Sometimes it was reapportioned to individual community members for their own use, and at other times it was worked by the community as a collective.

7. The state of Oaxaca organizes communities according to a multitiered system of political and legal jurisdiction. Arrazola is an agency of the larger municipality of Santa Cruz Xoxocotlán, which in turn pertains to the central district of Oaxaca State.

8. As part of the postrevolutionary land reforms, Arrazola also received a small allotment (about 53 hectares) from the former Candiani and La Compañía *haciendas*, which were owned by the Sodi family and were located on the southern edge of present-day Oaxaca City (Velasco Rodríguez and Aguilar Sánchez 2000); this was in addition to the *ejido* lands surrounding the village. Today the village retains about 10 hectares of this land. In recent decades, residents have been faced with declining agricultural productivity, the result of shifts in climate, soil erosion, and an overall decrease in available water resources.

9. The government sent teachers to provide rudimentary instruction prior to this date, but their presence in Arrazola was sporadic. Víctor Martínez Vásquez (1994) offers a more specific account of the role of *indigenismo* in the development and implementation of rural Oaxaca's educational system.

10. An original pay sheet (*lista de raya*) from July 1932 indicates that most laborers were paid 1.5 pesos, and that all worked seven days per week at the height of the excavation season. This pay sheet was on display as part of a 2003 exhibit, "*Arqueología: Diálogos con el Pasado*" (Archaeology: Dialogues with the past), at the Monte Albán museum and visitors' center.

11. Jeffrey Cohen conducted fieldwork in Santa Ana del Valle and Lynn Stephen in neighboring Teotitlán del Valle. Both are Zapotec-speaking communities that are centers of woven textile production.

12. Under the initial agreement, which was to be facilitated on the U.S. end by Wells Fargo Bank, the fund was to be set up and administered by the Mexican National Bank of Agricultural Credit. In 1975 the bank merged with two other financial institutions to become Mexico's National Bank of Rural Credit, known as Banrural.

13. Chibnik notes that census data at this time was recorded at the level of the municipality. Therefore, exact population totals were available for the municipality of Xoxocotlán, to which Arrazola belongs, but not for the village of Arrazola itself.

14. Within the *compadrazgo* system, it was and still is very common for individuals of greater economic and social status to act as sponsors or godparents for children of lesser means.

15. Sanding is considered the most tedious stage of the wood-carving process, and the one requiring the least amount of skill. For that reason, it is the

task most often assigned to children and teenage helpers who are unable to carve or paint.

16. From the beginning, carving has been a male-dominated activity. I spoke with women in Arrazola who had tried their hand at it, but most deemed it to be too dangerous and to require greater physical strength than they could muster. Having tried to carve myself and seeing the many cuts and scars on wood-carvers' hands, I fully agree with their assessment.

17. The demand for wood carvings has tapered off significantly from the levels it reached in the late 1980s and throughout much of the 1990s. Arrazola families still earn a substantial portion of their income from the sale of wood carvings, but many are now sending family members (typically, but not exclusively, male) to work in the U.S. In the year that I lived in Arrazola (2002–2003), even some of the more established and well-known wood-carvers found that they were unable to make ends meet and left to work in the U.S.; many of them temporarily relocated to the Los Angeles, California, area.

18. *Barro negro*, or black pottery, is produced in San Bartolo Coyotepec, a community located just south of the city of Oaxaca. The pottery, along with rugs from Teotitlán del Valle, has been long considered to be one of the crafts most emblematic of the Oaxaca region.

19. The material gains of the wealthiest households did not necessarily result from wood-carving sales alone. More commonly, a combination of successful wood-carving sales with remittances from family members working in the U.S. allowed these households to acquire more consumer goods, many of which are purchased in the U.S. In other cases, the male heads of households held outside jobs that were relatively stable and economically lucrative, such as the town mayor, who worked as a manager at a Ford auto dealership in Oaxaca.

20. The article, entitled "These Magicians Carve Dreams with Their Own Machetes," appeared in the May 1991 edition of *Smithsonian* magazine.

21. Here I refer to articles such as the one that includes the opening quote to this chapter, which was written by journalist Susan Ferriss for the *Austin American-Statesman* (Oct. 4, 1998, D6). Incidentally, I do not know any carvers from Arrazola who use hallucinogenic mushrooms to enhance their creative abilities. This assertion may have resulted from outsider journalists' conflation of the craft tourism in Oaxaca's Central Valleys with the mushroom tourism described by Feinberg (2003) in the Sierra Mazateca region of the state.

22. Works by Michael Kearney illustrate that anthropological representations of Oaxaca have dramatically shifted over the past thirty years. His early book, *The Winds of Ixtepeji: World View and Society in a Zapotec Town* (1986 [1972]), is a classic monograph about an indigenous community, organized around topics such as worldview, fatalism, diet, land use, ritual drinking and religious celebrations, etc. His later works, particularly *Reconceptualizing the Peasantry: Anthropology in Global Perspective* (1996), illustrate how anthropol-

ogy has altered existing frameworks to consider the multiple, fluid subjectivities of its subjects.

23. Most organized tours visited this or another large workshop in town, both of which featured the work of multiple artisans; guides typically received a commission from the workshop owners in return.

FAMILY PHOTO

1. I have used real names in this vignette.

2. *Milpa* may refer to a cornfield or a mixed-usage agricultural field, which commonly combines corn, bean, and squash crops.

CHAPTER THREE

1. Tomb 7 was constructed during the Classic period but was later reused in the Late Postclassic period, when nine individuals were interred (Caso 1969).

2. According to its website, INAH presently oversees 29,000 registered archaeology zones in Mexico, only 180 of which are open to the public (http://www.inah.gob.mx/index.php/iquienes-somos).

3. Subsequent interviews conducted in the spring of 2003 with the director of Monte Albán, Nelly Robles García, and the director of the INAH-Oaxaca Regional Center, Eduardo López Calzada, corroborated this information.

4. The vendors are frequently referred to as "*moneros*" by INAH employees and archaeologists, as well as some of the guides working at the site. Castañeda (2004a; 2009b) discusses the similarly disparaging term "*chac mooleros*," applied to the artisans who made and sold pre-Hispanic inspired carvings at Chichén Itzá ("Chac Mool" referring to a type of statue depicting a human figure in a reclining position with its head turned to one side). Both terms trivialize and render generic what is in reality a wider set of aesthetic forms and practices. Notably, in my conversations with Monte Albán replica artisans and sellers, they did not refer to themselves or other members in their group as "*moneros*." They instead preferred the Spanish terms "*artesano*" (artisan) and "*vendedor*" (vendor). As such, I employ the English equivalents of these terms through the text.

5. From the beginning, Arrazola women have generally not worked as vendors at Monte Albán. Exceptions include a woman in her sixties who began selling jewelry to tourists in the outside parking lot in 1992. She started selling at the urging of her husband, one of the senior vendors who worked inside the main structure of the ruins. In my conversations with her, she stated that while she initially felt strange about taking up vending, she now is comfortable with her occupation. She also said that she did not feel that there was

any social stigma attached to vending now, since other woman in the village worked selling a variety of goods, such as cosmetics (notably Avon and Jafra products), shoes, clothing, and jewelry—albeit often to others in Arrazola. Another elderly woman from the community accompanied her visually disabled husband up to the site on a semi-regular basis.

6. This is the 1972 Federal Law on Monuments and Archaeological, Artistic, and Historic Zones. Litvak King et al. (1980) provide a detailed discussion of the national and international legislation governing the protection of archaeological heritage in Mexico. See also von Droste et al. (1995) for a general outline of UNESCO policies on the protection of world cultural heritage sites.

7. These documents are part of the previously mentioned file archived in the Archaeology Division of the INAH-Oaxaca Regional Center.

8. I never spoke with Carmona, as he had died prior to the initiation of this project. The information presented here was supplied by informants who originally worked with him to legally organize the vendors. I also spoke with another lawyer in Oaxaca who had since advised the vendors and who was familiar with their history with Carmona.

9. The group's name translates as the Union of Retailers and Makers of Monte Albán Crafts. Technically a civil association, members refer to their organization as a *unión* (union).

10. Here I refer to the part of the site where a fee is charged upon entering. The largest and most visually impressive structures are contained within this area.

11. All but one of the original female vendors, none of whom were from Arrazola, have died or are no longer working at Monte Albán. Females who have since joined the group, including the one woman from Arrazola, opined that the current arrangement was fine, and noted that they did not feel discriminated against as women within the group. In separate interviews, two of them stated that the male vendors respected and frequently solicited their opinions on important matters within the union.

12. Author's translation of a letter from the personal archive of Antonio Aragón Hernández, who, at the time of the letter, served as the president of the Monte Albán vendor association.

13. As the number of vendors began to creep up from the initial forty-nine, the previous Monte Albán administration put a limit on how many new members could be added to the group. To comply with this regulation, the vendors' association regulates itself so that membership does not exceed sixty at any given time.

14. "*Dani Di'paa*" is the Zapotec name for Monte Albán, meaning "*cerro fortificado*," or protected hill (Janen 1998).

15. The entire document may be found on the Society for American Archaeology's website: http://saa.org/AbouttheSociety/Publications/TheManagementofArchaeologicalResourcesinMexi/tabid/1047/Default.aspx

16. During her tenure as director, Robles García oversaw an on-site administrator and support staff, who were responsible for much of the day-to-day operation of the site.

TO THE TOP OF MONTE ALBÁN

1. To get to the hotel where they caught the Monte Albán bus, Arrazola vendors first had to take a collective taxi from the village to the second-class bus station, located on the south side of Oaxaca. The hotel was several blocks from there.

CHAPTER FOUR

1. A copy of this manuscript is located in the library of the Welte Institute for Oaxacan Studies in Oaxaca, Mexico.

2. In the past, the son sold his figurines in the interior portion of the monument zone along with the Arrazola vendors. However, due to personal conflicts with other vendors, he moved his business outside the site entrance.

3. I was not able to find any documentation showing a historical connection between the replica makers described by Batres and the present-day replica makers discussed here.

4. No one I interviewed could recall the exact year in which the first replica crafts were sold at the site, but most placed it around 1960.

5. This was due to the fact that the vendors did not have official authorization from INAH to sell within the site. INAH employees, as well as tourist guides and Mexican students with identification, were not required to pay admission fees. Toward the end of my fieldwork, the price of admission was raised without advance notice to 37 pesos. (The regular admission price in 2011 was 51 pesos.) Admission was free for Mexican nationals on Sundays.

6. The actual number of vendors present on-site may vary slightly from the reported membership list. For instance, two men who had been removed from the vendor association in the wake of the incident with a local television crew (see previous chapter) continued to turn up at the site in order sell.

7. Vendors also sold a variety of stone masks and figures. These pieces were purchased from outside distributors, and the Arrazola men applied their own finishing treatments to enhance their appearances, as I discuss later in this chapter.

8. I knew of two other cases in which male artisans made replicas that they gave to other family members to sell for them at Monte Albán. In one, a sixteen-year-old male made replicas that his uncle sold at the site as a favor to him. He considered replica making to be more of a hobby than a full-time profession and put the extra money toward his schooling or used it to buy clothing. In the other case, a wood-carver who was experiencing diminished sales

had turned in his spare time to making replicas, which his father-in-law sold for him at Monte Albán.

9. Contemporary ceramic production in central Oaxaca is carried out by both men and women, and oftentimes the entire household will participate in the process. However, some of the biggest names in Oaxacan ceramics are women, including the Aguilar sisters of Ocotlán, and Angélica Vásquez and Dolores Porras, both of Atzompa. See Wasserspring 2000 for a chronicle of these women's histories as ceramicists.

10. Chibnik briefly speculates on the gendered division of labor that characterizes contemporary wood-carving production, noting that—with a few exceptions, such as María Jiménez of San Martín Tilcajete—women have not gained the notoriety enjoyed by their male counterparts (Chibnik 2003:166). He suggests that women's roles as primary caregivers for young children, among other domestic responsibilities, may limit the time that they are able to devote to artisan activities and/or interacting with clients.

11. Vendors reported only slightly higher average earnings in 2003 (100–180 pesos per day). The rate of exchange during the period of my fieldwork was around ten Mexican pesos to one U.S. dollar.

12. INAH does have an internal department whose duties include overseeing the production and promotion of officially licensed pre-Hispanic replicas made in its own workshops. Based in Mexico City, the reproductions department produces replicas that are sold in state museum gift shops throughout the country. I have seen these products for sale in Oaxaca at the gift shop in the Santo Domingo cultural center and museum. An article in the popular magazine *Arqueología Mexicana*, "Brígido Lara: Inventor del nuevo arte prehispánico," chronicles the life of one former replica maker from the state of Veracruz who went from making black-market copies (resulting in his arrest by Mexican authorities) to becoming an official replica artisan for INAH (Vacio 1996). To my knowledge, there has been no collaboration between INAH and the Oaxacan replica artisans discussed here.

13. Stoneware is fired at 1200–1300° Celsius and porcelain at 1250° Celsius or higher.

14. Wood (2008) describes how the use of natural dyes, particularly the red coloring obtained from cochineal, the small insects that live on maguey plants, is an important marker of authenticity in the Oaxacan textiles market. In my experience, *tapete* sellers overwhelming claim that their textiles are colored with natural dyes such as cochineal and indigo even when the low selling price indicates the use of synthetic aniline dyes.

VIEWS FROM THE PYRAMID

1. "*Güero*" refers to a person perceived to have white or light-colored skin. The term is often applied to foreigners but is also used in reference to other Mexicans.

CHAPTER FIVE

1. Gagnier made this statement prior to the civil unrest and violent government crackdown in 2006 that garnered international attention. Tourist perceptions of Oaxaca have changed in the wake of these events, particularly among U.S. travelers.

2. *Retablos* (two-dimensional religious paintings) and *ex-votos* (votive offerings to a saint) are examples of popular, religious material culture that are widely collected and displayed as folk art.

3. Gagnier also noted that her Mexican clients tend to come from Mexico City and other wealthy urban areas such as Puebla and Monterrey.

4. When I asked her what constituted a "typical" Mexican craft, she gave the example of the various types of pottery produced in Oaxaca. Because many of the archaeological artifacts on public display are ceramics, visitors often draw direct historical connections between pre-Hispanic and contemporary ceramic production, whether such links exist or not.

5. *Pelota mixteca* is played with a special rubber ball and a glove embedded with nails. Thought to be a modern derivative of pre-Hispanic ball games, it is played in Arrazola and throughout Oaxaca.

DISCRIMINATING TASTES

1. For a summary of the debates around the Oaxaca McDonald's see Richard Boudreaux's 2002 article in the *Los Angeles Times*, "A Heated Mc-Culture Clash: In a City That Holds Fast to Tradition, McDonald's Wants a Spot in the Historic Main Square."

2. Another much-publicized battle over Oaxaca's *zócalo* took place in 2005, when Ulises Ruiz's government began a massive renovation of the public space. The plan called for the replacement of much of the stonework as well as replacing "foreign" India laurel trees (planted in the 1870s) with a native species. Ironically, several of the architects and artists who designed the unpopular plan, which generated large-scale protests, were also the same people who had fought to keep McDonald's out of the *zócalo* only two years earlier (see Mark Stevenson's 2005 article in the *Los Angeles Times*, "Oaxaca Plaza's Trees Inspire Devotion, Defense").

3. Just as concho belts and velvet skirts are evocative of a broader aesthetic termed "Santa Fe style" (which was, and to some degree still is, popular among Southwest art/culture aficionados), indigenous women's clothing, particularly *huipiles* from the Amuzgo and Isthmus Zapotec groups, form part of what might be called a "Oaxaca style." This type of clothing, sometimes paired with jewelry such as a "Yalálag cross," is frequently worn by foreigners and middle- and upper-class Mexican women in Oaxaca City and may serve to communicate an appreciation or awareness of local culture.

4. I heard Oaxaca described as a "craft mecca" repeatedly during my fieldwork. Not coincidentally, the same individuals, usually tourists or folk art store owners, often described Oaxaca as a "spiritual place" and likened visiting it to making a "pilgrimage." This metaphorical use of religious terminology echoes MacCannell's (1999) idea of site sacralization and tourism as a modern form of pilgrimage.

5. The similarities between Southwestern wool textiles and the weavings produced in Oaxaca, specifically the communities of Teotitlán del Valle and Santa Ana del Valle, have not been lost on Santa Fe gallery retailers either. Many offer Oaxacan "Zapotec rugs" as an economical alternative to the much more expensive works by Native American, Hispanic, and, more recently, Anglo artists from the region. Connoisseurs of Southwestern art, as well as local weavers themselves, often comment that the textiles from Oaxaca are of an inferior quality and pose a serious threat to local weaving traditions. For a thorough discussion of the interconnections between the Southwest and Oaxaca rug markets, see *Made in Mexico* by W. Warner Wood (2008).

CHAPTER SIX

1. While English speakers often employ the term "Indian," the equivalent Spanish word "*indio*" has negative connotations in Mexico and is generally avoided in current anthropological work in both the U.S. and Mexico. The preferred term for native or indigenous peoples in Mexico is "*indígena*." I use the English term "indigenous," and "Indian" where I believe it captures the prevailing discourse, throughout this chapter. I also use "*indio*" as quoted by informants. "Mestizo" notionally refers to a person of mixed indigenous and European ancestry. Mexico is ideologically construed as a mestizo nation, a blending of pre-Conquest and European biological "races" and culture. I employ Ana Alonso's (2004) usage of "ethno-racial" in describing the terms of identity in Oaxaca, where communities are both racialized as indigenous (or mestizo) and frequently identified with an ethnic group based on native-language use.

2. Replica vendors often referred to the "*tres culturas*" (three cultures) of Monte Albán when discussing the different groups that had occupied the site; they would then proceed to list the Olmecs, Zapotecs, and Mixtecs. This seems to be a popular interpretation of certain archaeological findings that point to the appearance of Olmec iconographic elements in the Valley of Oaxaca during a period referred to as the Olmec horizon, roughly 1200–850 B.C. (Winter 2002 [1989]:28). While archaeologists generally agree that Monte Albán was utilized by two successive groups of people, today designated as Zapotecs and Mixtecs, their work does not specifically argue for an Olmec presence at Monte Albán beyond the stylistic influences mentioned here.

3. For example, see Saldívar's (2011) discussion of the National Commis-

sion for the Development of Indigenous Communities, formerly the National Indigenist Institute.

4. Examples include the *Instituto Nacional de Estadística, Geografía e Informática* (INEGI), which is responsible for collecting and compiling Mexican census data, and the *Comisión Nacional para el Desarollo de los Pueblos Indígenas* (National Commission for the Development of Indigenous Communities), which replaced the National Indigenist Institute.

5. *Tequio* (communal labor), *usos y costumbres* (system of governance), *guelaguetza* (reciprocal exchange), and *mayordomía* (religious fiesta sponsorship) are local institutions that govern, to varying degrees, the socioeconomic life in many rural Oaxacan communities. Lynn Stephen (1991) provides an excellent account of these institutions and women's changing roles within them in the community of Teotitlán del Valle.

6. Overall, Arrazola may be characterized as a monolingual Spanish-speaking town. Yet there are people living there who speak indigenous languages. Most of them have married into the community from elsewhere. I know one woman, however, who in her youth married a man from a Zapotec-speaking settlement near the town of Tlacochahuaya. She learned to speak Zapotec after decades of living there, and her children were bilingual Spanish-Zapotec speakers. She returned to live in Arrazola after the death of her husband.

7. While vendors did not have access to official jobs at the site, they did practice their own form of job inheritance within the structure of their association. I was told that vendors may pass on their membership rights to their children, or even a close relative, should they choose to retire from the group.

8. López Calzada vacated his twelve-year post as the head of the INAH-Oaxaca Regional Center in 2005 and was promoted to another position within INAH in another state. There was speculation in the press that his reassignment was tied to what many considered INAH's poor handling of the remodeling of the city's central plaza, which occurred under his direction (see Martínez 2005).

9. "*Coño*" is a Spanish idiomatic expression that generally refers to female genitalia, but may also convey other meanings, including those expressed by "damn" or "fuck" in English. The term is commonly used in Spain and the Hispanic Caribbean, but is generally avoided by Mexican speakers.

10. The Guelaguetza is a large, state-sponsored festival that culminates in two separate folkloric dance performances at a city auditorium. The dances are meant to showcase the folkloric dances from the various geographic and ethnic regions of Oaxaca as identified by the state. The performances draw thousands of tourists from all over the world.

11. These towns are known, respectively, for their green-glazed ceramics, black ceramics, and woven textiles.

12. The term "*pinche*" is a modifier commonly used in colloquial Mexican Spanish, translating variously to "fucking," "damned," or "lousy."

13. The Guatemalan term "ladino" may refer broadly to nonindigenous Guatemalans, mestizos, and so-called Westernized Indians. Of course, these categorizations are fraught, as they are in Mexico. Importantly, Hale makes clear that not all "new mestizos" desire to be accepted as ladinos, which he sees as a significant breakdown in the previously dominant racial ideology (Hale 2006:183).

Bibliography

ABRAHAMS, ROGER D.

1993 Phantoms of Romantic nationalism in folkloristics. *Journal of American Folklore* 106 (419): 3–37.

ABU EL-HAJ, NADIA

2002 *Facts on the Ground: Archaeological Practice and Territorial Self-Fashioning in Israeli Society*. Chicago: University of Chicago Press.

ADAMS, KATHLEEN M.

2006 *Art as Politics: Re-Crafting Identities, Tourism, and Power in Tana Toraja, Indonesia*. Honolulu: University of Hawai'i Press.

AHLQUIST, TASHA

2005 Beneath the paint: Changing productive roles and family importance of women in Arrazola, Mexico. MA thesis, Western Washington University.

ALONSO, ANA M.

2004 Conforming disconformity: "Mestizaje," hybridity, and the aesthetics of ethnicity. *Cultural Anthropology* 19(4): 459–490.

ANDERSON, BENEDICT

1983 *Imagined Communities: Reflections on the Origin and Spread of Nationalism*. London: Verso.

APPADURAI, ARJUN, ED.

1986 *The Social Life of Things: Commodities in Cultural Perspective*. Cambridge: Cambridge University Press.

ARDREN, TRACI

2004 Where are the Maya in ancient Maya archaeological tourism? Advertising and the appropriation of culture. In *Marketing Heritage: Archaeology and the Consumption of the Past*, ed. York Rowan and Uzi Baram, 103–113. Walnut Creek, CA: AltaMira Press.

ARNOLD, LEE

2002 Dreaming of Oaxaca. http://www.bootsnall.com/articles/02-05/dreaming-of-oaxaca-oaxaca-mexico.html (accessed Feb. 16, 2005).

BAKHTIN, M. M.

1981 *The Dialogic Imagination*. Austin: University of Texas Press.

BARBASH, SHEPARD

1991 These magicians carve dreams with their own machetes. *Smithsonian* (May): 119–129.

1993 *Oaxacan Woodcarving: The Magic in the Trees*. San Francisco: Chronicle Books.

2007 *Changing Dreams: A Generation of Oaxaca's Woodcarvers*. Santa Fe: Museum of New Mexico Press.

BARNET-SANCHEZ, HOLLY

1993 The necessity of pre-Columbian art in the United States: Appropriations and transformations of heritage, 1933–1945. In *Collecting the Pre-Columbian Past*, ed. Elizabeth Hill Boone, 177–207. Washington, DC: Dumbarton Oaks Research and Library Collection.

BARTRA, ELI

2000 Of alebrijes and ocumichos: Some myths about folk art and Mexican identity. In *Primitivism and Identity in Latin America: Essays on Art, Literature, and Culture*, ed. Erik Camayd-Freixas and José Eduardo González, 53–73. Tucson: University of Arizona Press.

BARTRA, ROGER

1987 *La jaula de la melancolía: Identidad y metamorfosis del mexicano*. Mexico: Grijalbo.

BATRES, LEOPOLDO

1902 *Exploraciones en Monte Albán*. Mexico City: Casa Editorial Gante.

1909 *Antigüedades mejicanas falsificadas: Falsificación y falsificadores*. Mexico: Imprenta de Fidencio S. Soria.

1910 *Guía para visitar los monumentos arqueológicos situados entre Puebla y Mitla, Oaxaca*. Mexico: Imprenta de Fidencio S. Soria.

BAUDRILLARD, JEAN

1988 Simulacra and simulations. In *Selected Writings*, ed. Mark Poster, 166–184. Stanford: Stanford University Press.

BENJAMIN, WALTER

1968 The work of art in the age of mechanical reproduction. In *Illuminations: Essays and Reflections*, ed. Hannah Arendt, trans. Harry Zohn, 217–251. New York: Schocken.

BERGER, DINA

2006 *The Development of Mexico's Tourism Industry: Pyramids by Day, Martinis by Night*. New York: Palgrave Macmillan.

BLANTON, RICHARD E.

1978 *Monte Albán: Settlement Patterns at the Ancient Zapotec Capital*. New York: Academic Press.

BONFIL BATALLA, GUILLERMO

1996 *México Profundo: Reclaiming a Civilization*. Trans. Phillip A. Dennis. Austin: University of Texas Press.

BOOS, FRANK H.

1966 *The Ceramic Sculptures of Ancient Oaxaca*. New York: A. S. Barnes and Company.

BOUDREAUX, RICHARD

2002 A heated Mc-culture clash: In a city that holds fast to tradition, McDonald's wants a spot in the historic main square. *Los Angeles Times*, Oct. 28.

BOURDIEU, PIERRE

1984 *Distinction: A Social Critique of the Judgment of Taste*. Trans. Richard Nice. Cambridge, MA: Harvard University Press.

1993 *The Field of Cultural Production*. New York: Columbia University Press.

BREGLIA, LISA

2006 *Monumental Ambivalence: The Politics of Heritage*. Austin: University of Texas Press.

BRODIE, NEIL, JENNIFER DOOLE, AND COLIN RENFREW, EDS.

2001 *Trade in Illicit Antiquities: The Destruction of the World's Archaeological Heritage*. Cambridge: McDonald Institute for Archaeological Research.

BROOKS, DAVID

2001 *Bobos in Paradise: The New Upper Class and How They Got There*. New York: Simon and Schuster.

BROWN, MICHAEL F.

2003 *Who Owns Native Culture?* Cambridge, MA: Harvard University Press.

BRULOTTE, RONDA L.

1999 www.alebrijes.com: The commodification of Oaxacan woodcarving in cyberspace. MA thesis, University of Texas at Austin.

BRUNER, EDWARD M.

2004 *Culture on Tour: Ethnographies of Travel*. Chicago: University of Chicago Press.

1996 Tourism in the Balinese borderzone. In *Displacement, Diaspora, and Geographies of Identity*, ed. Smadar Lavie and Ted Swedenburg, 157–170. Durham: Duke University Press.

BUENO, CHRISTINA

2010 Teotihuacán: Showcase for the Centennial. In *Holiday in Mexico: Critical Reflections on Tourism and Tourist Encounters*, ed. Dina Berger and Andrew Grant Wood, 54–76. Durham: Duke University Press.

CAMPBELL, HOWARD

1996 Isthmus Zapotec intellectuals: Cultural production and politics in Juchitán, Oaxaca. In *The Politics of Ethnicity in Southern Mexico*, ed. Howard Campbell, 77–98. Nashville: Vanderbilt University Publications in Anthropology.

CAMPBELL, HOWARD, LEIGH BINFORD, MIGUEL BARTOLOMÉ, AND ALICIA BARABAS, EDS.

1993 *Zapotec Struggles: Histories, Politics, and Representations from Juchitán, Oaxaca*. Washington, DC: Smithsonian Institution Press.

CASO, ALFONSO

1932 Monte Albán: Richest archaeological find in America. *National Geographic* 62 (4): 487–512.

1969 El tesoro de Monte Albán. *Memorias del Instituto Nacional de Antropología e Historia* 3.

CASO, ALFONSO, AND IGNACIO BERNAL

1962 *Culturas zapoteca y mixteca*. Mexico: INAH-SEP.

CASTAÑEDA, QUETZIL E.

1996 *In the Museum of Maya Culture: Touring Chichén Itzá*. Minneapolis: University of Minnesota Press.

2001 The aura of ruins. In *Fragments of a Golden Age: The Politics of Culture in Mexico since 1940*, ed. Gilbert Joseph, Anne Ruberstein, and Eric Zolov, 452–467. Durham: Duke University Press.

2004a Art-writing in the modern Maya art world of Chichén Itzá: Transcultural ethnography and experimental fieldwork. *American Ethnologist* 31(1): 21–42.

2004b "We are not indigenous!": An introduction to the Maya identity of Yucatan. *Journal of Latin American Anthropology* 9(1): 36–63.

2009a Heritage and indigeneity: Transformations in the politics of tourism. In *Cultural Tourism in Latin America: The Politics of Space and Imagery*, ed. Michiel Baud and Annelou Ypeij, 263–295. Leiden: Brill.

2009b Aesthetics and ambivalence of Maya modernity: The ethnography of Maya art. In *Crafting Maya Identity: Contemporary Wood Sculptures from the Puuc Region of Yucatán, Mexico*, ed. Jeff Karl Kowalski and Jeff Karl, 133–152. DeKalb: Northern Illinois University Press.

CASTAÑEDA, QUETZIL E., AND CHRISTOPHER MATTHEWS, EDS.

2008 *Ethnographic Archaeologies: Reflections on Stakeholders and Archaeological Practices*. Lanham, MD: AltaMira Press.

CAUSEY, ANDREW

2003 *Hard Bargaining in Sumatra: Western Travelers and Toba Bataks in the Marketplace of Souvenirs*. Honolulu: University of Hawai'i Press.

CHANCE, JOHN K.

1978 *Race and Class in Colonial Oaxaca*. Stanford: Stanford University Press.

CHIBNIK, MICHAEL

2003 *Crafting Tradition: The Making and Marketing of Oaxacan Wood Carvings*. Austin: University of Texas Press.

CLIFFORD, JAMES

1988 *The Predicament of Culture: Twentieth-Century Ethnography, Literature, and Art*. Cambridge, MA: Harvard University Press.

COE, MICHAEL D.

1962 *Mexico.* New York: Praeger.

COFFEY, MARY K.

2010 Marketing Mexico's great masters: Folk art tourism and the neoliberal politics of exhibition. In *Holiday in Mexico: Critical Reflections on Tourism and Tourist Encounters*, ed. Dina Berger and Andrew Grant Wood, 365–294. Durham: Duke University Press.

COHEN, JEFFREY H.

1999 *Cooperation and Community: Economy and Society in Oaxaca.* Austin: University of Texas Press.

COHN, DIANA, AND AMY CÓRDOVA

2002 *Dream Carver.* San Francisco: Chronicle Books.

COLLOREDO-MANSFELD, RUDI

1999 *The Native Leisure Class: Consumption and Cultural Change in the Andes.* Chicago: University of Chicago Press.

COOK, SCOTT

1993 Craft commodity production, market diversity, and differential rewards in Mexican capitalism today. In *Crafts in the World Market: The Impact of Global Exchange on American Artisans*, ed. June Nash, 59–83. Albany: State University of New York.

COOK, SCOTT, AND MARTIN DISKIN, EDS.

1976 *Markets in Oaxaca.* Austin: University of Texas Press.

COOK, SCOTT, AND JONG-TAICK JOO

1995 Ethnicity and economy in rural Mexico: A critique of the indigenista approach. *Latin American Research Review* 30(2): 33–59.

DAVIS, SUSAN G.

1997 *Spectacular Nature: Corporate Culture and the Sea World Experience.* Berkeley: University of California Press.

DE LA CADENA, MARISOL

2000 *Indigenous Mestizos: The Politics of Race and Culture in Cuzco, Peru, 1919–1991.* Durham: Duke University Press.

DE LA CADENA, MARISOL, AND ORIN STARN

2007 Introduction. In *Indigenous Experience Today*, ed. Marisol de la Cadena and Orin Starn, 1–30. New York: Berg.

DELEUZE, GILLES

1983 Plato and the simulacrum. *October* 27:45–56.

DELEUZE, GILLES, AND FÉLIX GUATTARI

2009 [1972] *Anti-Oedipus: Capitalism and Schizophrenia.* New York: Penguin.

DELPAR, HELEN

1992 *The Enormous Vogue of Things Mexican: Cultural Relations between the United States and Mexico, 1920–1935.* Tuscaloosa: University of Alabama Press.

DEL VILLAR K., MÓNICA

1996 El coleccionismo arqueológico mexicano: Otro punto de vista. *Arqueología Mexicana* 4 (21): 40–47.

DENNIS, PHILLIP A.

1987 *Intervillage Conflict in Oaxaca.* New Brunswick: Rutgers University Press.

DERRIDA, JACQUES

1974 *Of Grammatology.* Trans. Gayatri Spivak. Baltimore: Johns Hopkins University Press.

DÍAZ-ANDREU, MARGARITA

2008 *A World History of Nineteenth-Century Archaeology: Nationalism, Colonialism, and the Past.* Oxford: Oxford University Press.

DÍAZ-ANDREU, MARGARITA, AND TIMOTHY C. CHAMPION, EDS.

1996 *Nationalism and Archaeology in Europe.* London: UCL Press.

DI GIOVINE, MICHAEL A.

2009 *The Heritage-scape: UNESCO, World Heritage, and Tourism.* Lanham, MD: Lexington Books.

EDGEWORTH, MATT

2006 *Ethnographies of Archaeological Practice: Cultural Encounters, Material Transformations.* Lanham, MD: AltaMira Press.

EL GUINDI, FADWA, AND HENRY A. SELBY

1976 Dialectics in Zapotec thinking. In *Meaning in Anthropology,* ed. Keith H. Basso and Henry A. Selby, 181–196. Albuquerque: University of New Mexico Press.

ERRINGTON, SHELLY

1998 *The Death of Authentic Primitive Art and Other Tales of Progress.* Berkeley: University of California Press.

FEINBERG, BENJAMIN

2003 *The Devil's Book of Culture: History, Mushrooms, and Caves in Southern Mexico.* Austin: University of Texas Press.

FERRISS, SUSAN

1998 Mushrooming business: Popular wood carver finds mystical inspiration in hallucinogenic native plant. *Austin American-Statesman,* Oct. 4, D6.

FIELD, LES W.

1999 *The Grimace of Macho Ratón: Artisans, Identity, and Nation in Late-Twentieth-Century Western Nicaragua.* Durham: Duke University Press.

2009 Four kinds of authenticity?: Regarding Nicaraguan pottery in Scandinavian museums, 2006–08. *American Ethnologist* 36(3): 507–520.

FISCHGRUND STANTON, ANDRA

1999 *Zapotec Weavers of Teotitlán.* Santa Fe: Museum of New Mexico Press.

FJELLMAN, STEPHEN M.

1992 *Vinyl Leaves: Walt Disney World and America.* Boulder: Westview Press.

FLANNERY, KENT V., AND JOYCE MARCUS

1983 *The Cloud People: Divergent Evolution of the Zapotec and Mixtec Civilizations.* New York: Academic Press.

FLECHSIG, KATRIN S.

2004 *Miniature Crafts and Their Makers: Palm Weaving in a Mexican Town.* Tucson: University of Arizona Press.

FOUCAULT, MICHEL

1972 *The Archaeology of Knowledge.* New York: Tavistock.

1977 *Discipline and Punish: The Birth of the Prison.* New York: Pantheon.

FRIEDLANDER, JUDITH

1975 *Being Indian in Hueyapan: A Study of Forced Identity in Contemporary Mexico.* New York: St. Martin's.

GAMIO, MANUEL

1925 The utilitarian aspect of folklore. *Mexican Folkways* 1:6–8.

1948 *Consideraciones sobre el problema indígena.* Mexico: Instituto Indigenista Interamericano.

1982 [1916] *Forjando patria.* Mexico: Porrúa Hermanos.

GARCÍA CANCLINI, NÉSTOR

1993 *Transforming Modernity: Popular Culture in Mexico.* Trans. Lidia Lozano. Austin: University of Texas Press.

1995 *Hybrid Culture: Strategies for Entering and Leaving Modernity.* Trans. Chrisopher L. Chiappari and Silvia L. López. Minneapolis: University of Minnesota Press.

1997 El patrimonio cultural de México y la construcción imaginaria de lo nacional. In *El patrimonio nacional de México,* vol. 1, ed. Enrique Florescano, 57–86. Mexico: CONACULTA/Fondo Cultural Económica.

GARCÍA MORENO, GABRIELA ZEPEDA

2000 Guardianes y moneros: Patrimonio arqueológico y supervivencia campesina en el sur de Nayarit. MA thesis, Centro de Investigaciones y Estudios Superiores en Antropología Social de Occidente (Jalisco, Mexico).

GORDON, EDMUND T.

1998 *Disparate Diasporas: Identity and Politics in an African Nicaraguan Community.* Austin: University of Texas Press.

GOTTDIENER, MARK

2001 *The Theming of America: American Dreams, Media Fantasies, and Themed Environments.* 2nd ed. Boulder: Westview Press.

GRABURN, NELSON H. H.

1976 Introduction: Arts of the Fourth World. In *Ethnic and Tourist Arts: Cultural Expressions from the Fourth World,* ed. Nelson H. H. Graburn, 1–32. Berkeley: University of California Press.

GREENBERG, JAMES

1989 *Blood Ties: Life and Violence in Rural Mexico.* Tucson: University of Arizona Press.

GUSS, DAVID M.

2000 *The Festive State: Race, Ethnicity, and Nationalism as Cultural Performance.* Berkeley: University of California Press.

HADEN, JUDITH COOPER, AND MATTHEW JAFFE

2002 *Oaxaca: The Spirit of Mexico.* New York: Artisan Books.

HALE, CHARLES R.

1997 Cultural politics of identity in Latin America. *Annual Review of Anthropology* 26:567–590.

2006 *Más Que un Indio (More Than an Indian): Racial Ambivalence and Neoliberal Multiculturalism in Guatemala.* Santa Fe: School of American Research Press.

HALL, STUART

1996 The question of cultural identity. In *Modernity: An Introduction to Modern Societies,* ed. Stuart Hall, David Held, Don Hubert, and Kenneth Thompson, 595–634. Cambridge: Wiley-Blackwell.

HAMILAKIS, YANNIS, AND PHILIP DUKE, EDS.

2007 *Archaeology and Capitalism: From Ethics to Politics.* Walnut Creek, CA: Left Coast Press.

HANCOCK SANDOVAL, JUDITH

1998 *Shopping in Oaxaca.* Oaxaca: Gobierno del Estado de Oaxaca/ SEDETUR.

HANDLER, RICHARD

1988 *Nationalism and the Politics of Culture in Quebec.* Madison: University of Wisconsin Press.

HERNÁNDEZ DÍAZ, JORGE

1998 La construcción de la categoría "indio" en el discurso antropológico. In *Las imágenes del indio en Oaxaca,* ed. Jorge Díaz Hernández, 11–30. Oaxaca: Universidad Autónoma Benito Juárez de Oaxaca.

HERVIK, PETER

2003 *Mayan People within and beyond Boundaries: Social Categories and Lived Identity in Yucatán.* New York: Routledge.

HERZFELD, MICHAEL

1982 *Ours Once More: Folklore, Ideology, and the Making of Modern Greece.* Austin: University of Texas Press.

HILL BOONE, ELIZABETH

1993 Collecting the pre-Columbian past: Historical trends and the process of reception and use. In *Collecting the Pre-Columbian Past,* ed. Elizabeth Hill Boone, 315–350. Washington, DC: Dumbarton Oaks Research and Library Collection.

HOLO, SELMA

2004 *Oaxaca at the Crossroads: Managing Memory, Negotiating Change.* Washington, DC: Smithsonian Institution Press.

INEGI (INSTITUTO NACIONAL DE ESTADÍSTICA, GEOGRAFÍA E INFORMÁTICA)

2000 Resultados por localidad Estados Unidos Mexicanos. XII Censo general de población y vivienda. Aguascalientes: Instituto Nacional de Estadística, Geografía e Informática.

JAMESON, FREDRIC

1981 *The Political Unconscious: Narrative as a Socially Symbolic Act*. Ithaca: Cornell University.

JANSEN, MAARTEN

1998 *The Shadow of Monte Albán*. Leiden: CNWS.

JONES, SIÂN

1997 *The Archaeology of Ethnicity: Constructing Identities in the Past and Present*. New York: Routledge.

JOSEPH, GILBERT M., AND DANIEL NUGENT

1994 Popular culture and state formation in revolutionary Mexico. In *Everyday Forms of State Formation: Revolution and the Negotiation of Rules in Modern Mexico*, ed. Gilbert M. Joseph and Daniel Nugent, 3–23. Durham: Duke University Press.

KAPLAN, FLORA S.

1993 Mexican museums in the creation of a national image in world tourism. In *Crafts in the World Market: The Impact of Global Exchange on Middle American Artisans*, ed. June Nash, 103–125. Albany: State University of New York Press.

KASTELEIN, BARBARA

2010 The Beach and beyond: Observations from a travel writer on dreams, decadence, and defense. In *Holiday in Mexico: Critical Reflections on Tourism and Tourist Encounters*, ed. Dina Berger and Andrew Grant Wood, 320–370. Durham: Duke University Press.

KEARNEY, MICHAEL

1986 [1972] *The Winds of Ixtepeji: World View and Society in a Zapotec Town*. Prospect Heights: Waveland Press.

1995 The effects of transnational culture, economy, and migration on Mixtec identity in Oaxacalifornia. In *The Bubbling Cauldron: Race, Ethnicity, and the Urban Crisis*, ed. Michael Peter Smith and Joe R. Feagin, 226–243. Minneapolis: University of Minnesota Press.

1996 *Reconceptualizing the Peasantry: Anthropology in Global Perspective*. Boulder: Westview Press.

KELKER, NANCY L., AND KAREN O. BRUHNS

2010 *Faking Ancient Mesoamerica*. Walnut Creek, CA: Left Coast Press.

KIRSHENBLATT-GIMBLETT, BARBARA

1998 *Destination Culture: Tourism, Museums, and Heritage*. Berkeley: University of California Press.

KNIGHT, ALAN

1990 Racism, revolution, and *indigenismo*: Mexico, 1910–1940. In *The Idea of Race in Latin America, 1870–1940*, ed. Richard Graham, 71–113. Austin: University of Texas Press.

KOWALSKI, JEFF KARL, ED.

2009 *Crafting Maya Identity: Contemporary Wood Sculptures from the Puuc Region of Yucatán, Mexico.* DeKalb: Northern Illinois University Press.

LAWRENCE, D. H.

1926 *The Plumed Serpent.* London: W. Heinemann.

LEIGH, HOWARD

1979 Stories of a collector. Unpublished memoir as told to Linnea and David Wren. Welte Institute for Oaxacan Studies, Oaxaca, Mexico.

LITTLE, WALTER

2004a *Mayas in the Marketplace: Tourism, Globalization, and Cultural Identity.* Austin: University of Texas Press.

2004b Outside of social movements: Dilemmas of indigenous handicrafts vendors in Guatemala. *American Ethnologist* 31 (1): 42–59.

2009 Contesting heritage in Antigua, Guatemala. In *Cultural Tourism in Latin America: The Politics of Space and Imagery,* ed. Michiel Baud and Annelou Ypeij, 217–244. Leiden: Brill.

LITVAK KING, JAIME, LUIS GONZÁLEZ R., AND MARÍA DEL REFUGIO GONZÁLEZ, EDS.

1980 *Arqueología y derecho en México.* Mexico: UNAM.

LOEWE, RONALD

2010 *Maya or Mestizo?: Nationalism, Modernity, and Its Discontents.* Toronto: University of Toronto Press.

LOMNITZ, CLAUDIO

2001 *Deep Mexico, Silent Mexico: An Anthropology of Nationalism.* Minneapolis: University of Minnesota Press.

LOMNITZ-ADLER, CLAUDIO

1992 *Exits from the Labyrinth: Culture and Ideology in the Mexican National Space.* Berkeley: University of California Press.

LÓPEZ, RICK A.

2010 *Crafting Mexico: Intellectuals, Artisans, and the State after the Revolution.* Durham: Duke University Press.

LOWENTHAL, DAVID

1992 Authenticity? The dogma of self-delusion. In *Why Fakes Matter: Essays on Problems of Authenticity,* ed. Mark Jones, 184–192. London: British Museum Press.

LUTZ, CATHERINE A., AND JANE COLLINS

1993 *Reading National Geographic.* Chicago: University of Chicago Press.

MACCANNELL, DEAN

1992 *Empty Meeting Grounds: The Tourist Papers.* New York: Routledge.

1999 [1976] *The Tourist: A New Theory of the Leisure Class.* Berkeley: University of California Press.

MARTÍNEZ, RACIEL

2005 Relevo en el INAH. *Noticias de Oaxaca,* May 22.

MARTÍNEZ GRACIDA, MANUEL, ED.

1883 *Colección de cuadros sinópticos de los pueblos, haciendas y ranchos del estado libre y soberano de Oaxaca.* N.p.

MARTÍNEZ VÁSQUEZ, VÍCTOR RAÚL

1994 *Historia de la educación en Oaxaca, 1825–1940.* Oaxaca: Instituto de Investigaciones Sociológicos, UABJO.

MASSUMI, BRIAN

1997 Realer than real: The simulacrum according to Deleuze and Guattari. http://www.anu.edu.au/HRC/first_and_last/works/realer.htm.

MASUOKA, SUSAN N.

1994 *En Calavera: The Papier-Mâché Art of the Linares Family.* Los Angeles: UCLA Fowler Museum of Cultural History.

MATHER, CHRISTINE, AND SHARON WOODS

1986 *Santa Fe Style.* New York: Rizzoli.

MATHER, CHRISTINE, SHARON WOODS, AND JACK PARSONS

2002 *Santa Fe Houses.* New York: Clarkson Potter.

MEISCH, LYNN A.

2002 *Andean Entrepreneurs: Otavalo Merchants and Musicians in the Global Arena.* Austin: University of Texas Press.

2009 Tourism, the state, and the marketing of traditional Andean artesanías: Problematic encounters, pitfalls, and competing interests. In *Cultural Tourism in Latin America: The Politics of Space and Imagery,* ed. Michiel Baud and Annelou Ypeij, 141–160. Leiden: Brill.

MESKELL, LYNN, ED.

1998 *Archaeology under Fire: Nationalism, Politics, and Heritage in the Eastern Mediterranean and the Middle East.* New York: Routledge.

2009 *Cosmopolitan Archaeologies.* Durham: Duke University Press.

MESSENGER, PHYLLIS MAUCH, ED.

1989 *The Ethics of Collecting Cultural Property: Whose Culture? Whose Heritage?* Albuquerque: University of New Mexico Press.

MEYER, KARL E.

1973 *The Plundered Past.* New York: Atheneum.

MEYER, MICHAEL C., AND WILLIAM L. SHERMAN

1995 *The Course of Mexican History.* New York: Oxford University Press.

MONGE, PASCAL

1987 Les "urnes funéraires" zápoteques: "Collectionnisme" et contrefaçon. *Journal de la Société des Américanistes* 73:7–50.

2000 Le faux zapoteque et la collection Gustave Bellon: Iconographie, thermoluminescence et nouvelle considerations. *Techne: La science au service de l'histoire de l'art et des civilizations* 11:53–64.

MONTES GARCÍA, OLGA

1998 El indio visto por una oligarquía regional: El caso de Oaxaca. In *Las imágenes del indio en Oaxaca,* ed. Jorge Díaz Hernández, 31–51. Oaxaca: Universidad Autónoma Benito Juárez de Oaxaca.

MORTENSEN, LENA, AND JULIE HOLLOWELL

2009 Introduction: Ethnographies and archaeologies. In *Ethnographies and Archaeologies: Iterations of the Past*, ed. Lena Mortensen and Julie Hollowell, 1–17. Gainesville: University of Florida Press.

MURPHY, ARTHUR D., AND ALEX STEPICK

1991 *Social Inequality in Oaxaca: A History of Resistance and Change*. Philadelphia: Temple University Press.

MYERS, FRED R.

2001 Introduction: The empire of things. In *The Empire of Things: Regimes of Value and Material Culture*, ed. Fred R. Myers, 3–61. Santa Fe: School of American Research Press.

NAGENGAST, CAROLE, AND MICHAEL KEARNEY

1990 Mixtec ethnicity: Social identity, political consciousness, and cultural relativity. *Latin American Research Review* 25(2): 61–91.

NASH, JUNE C.

1993 Introduction: Traditional arts and changing markets in Middle America. In *Crafts in the World Market: The Impact of Global Exchange on Middle American Artisans*, ed. June Nash, 1–22. Albany: State University of New York Press.

NORGET, KRISTIN

2006 *Days of Death, Days of Life: Ritual in the Popular Culture of Oaxaca*. New York: Columbia University Press.

NOVELO, VICTORIA

1976 *Artesanías y capitalismo en México*. Mexico: SEP/INAH.

PADDOCK, JOHN

1966 *Ancient Oaxaca*. Stanford: Stanford University Press.

PAZ, OCTAVIO

1985 *The Labyrinth of Solitude and Other Writings*. Trans. Lysander Kemp, Yara Milos, Rachel Phillips Belash. New York: Grove Press.

PIKE, FREDRICK B.

1992 *The United States and Latin America: Myths and Stereotypes of Civilization and Nature*. Austin: University of Texas Press.

POOLE, DEBORAH

2004 An image of "Our Indian": Type photographs and racial sentiments in Oaxaca, 1920–1940. *Hispanic American Historical Review* 84(1): 37–82.

PRICE, SALLY

1989 *Primitive Art in Civilized Places*. Chicago: University of Chicago Press.

2007 *Paris Primitive: Jacques Chirac's Museum on the Quai Branly*. Chicago: University of Chicago Press.

RADNÓTI, SÁNDOR

1999 *The Fake: Forgery and Its Place in Art*. Trans. Ervin Dunai. Lanham, MD: Rowman and Littlefield.

RICOUER, PAUL

1981 Narrative time. In *On Narrative*, ed. W. J. T. Mitchell, 165–186. Chicago: University of Chicago Press.

1984 *Time and Narrative*. Vol. 1. Chicago: University of Chicago Press.

ROBLES GARCÍA, NELLY M.

1993 *Monte Albán: Libro guía*. Mexico City: Codex Editores.

1996 El manejo de los recursos arqueológicos en México: El caso de Oaxaca. PhD diss., University of Georgia, Athens.

2000 *The Management of Archaeological Resources in Mexico: Oaxaca as a Case Study*. Trans. Jack Corbett. Society for American Archaeology and the U.S. National Park Service. 1 April 2004. http://saa.org/AbouttheSociety/Publications/TheManagementofArchaeologicalResourcesinMexi/tabid/1047/Default.aspx.

ROSEBERRY, WILLIAM

1989 *Anthropologies and Histories: Essays in Culture, History, and Political Economy*. New Brunswick: Rutgers University Press.

ROTHSTEIN, ARDEN AIBEL, AND ANYA LEAH ROTHSTEIN

2007 *Mexican Folk Art from Oaxacan Artist Families*. Atglen, PA: Schiffer.

RUBIN, JEFFREY W.

1997 *Decentering the Regime: Ethnicity, Radicalism, and Democracy in Juchitán, Mexico*. Durham: Duke University Press.

SALDÍVAR, EMIKO

2011 Everyday practices of *indigenismo*: An ethnography of anthropology and the state. *Journal of Latin American and Caribbean Anthropology* 16(1): 67–89.

SANSONE, LIVIO

2003 *Blackness without Ethnicity: Constructing Race in Brazil*. New York: Palgrave Macmillan.

SARAGOZA, ALEX

2001 The selling of Mexico: Tourism and the state, 1929–1952. In *Fragments of a Golden Age: The Politics of Culture in Mexico since 1940*, ed. Gilbert Joseph, Anne Rubenstein, and Eric Zolov, 91–115. Durham: Duke University Press.

SEDETUR (SECRETARÍA DE DESAROLLO TURÍSTICA DEL ESTADO DE OAXACA)

2001 *Informe encuesta perfil del visitante a la Ciudad de Oaxaca*. Oaxaca: SEDETUR.

SELLEN, ADAM

2002 The face that launched a thousand fakes. *Archaeological Newsletter* 3(14): 1–4. Royal Ontario Museum, Toronto.

2004 Is this the face that launched a thousand fakes? *Rotunda* 6(3): 32–39.

SERRIE, HENDRICK

1964 The emerging artist in a society of craftsmen: Three case studies. MA thesis, Cornell University.

SMILES, SAM

1994 *The Image of Antiquity: Ancient Britain and the Romantic Imagination.* New Haven: Yale University Press.

SMITH, ANTHONY D.

2001 Authenticity, antiquity, and archaeology. *Nations and Nationalism* 7(4): 441–449.

SMITH, SANDRA S.

1998 *Portraits of Clay: Potters of Mata Ortíz.* Tucson: University of Arizona Press.

SMITH, VALENE L., ED.

1989 [1977] *Hosts and Guests: The Anthropology of Tourism.* Philadelphia: University of Pennsylvania Press.

STEEL, GRIET

2009 Dishing up the city: Tourism and street vendors in Cuzco. In *Cultural Tourism in Latin America: The Politics of Space and Imagery*, ed. Michiel Baud and Annelou Ypeij, 161–176. Leiden: Brill.

STEINER, CHRISTOPHER B.

1999 Authenticity, repetition, and the aesthetics of seriality: The work of tourist art in the age of mechanical reproduction. In *Unpacking Culture: Art and Commodity in Colonial and Postcolonial Worlds*, ed. Ruth B. Phillips and Christopher B. Steiner, 87–103. Berkeley: University of California Press.

STEPHEN, LYNN

1991 *Zapotec Women.* Austin: University of Texas Press.

1993 Weaving in the fast lane: Class, ethnicity, and gender in Zapotec craft commercialization. In *Crafts in the World Market: The Impact of Global Exchange on Middle American Artisans*, ed. June Nash, 25–57. Albany: State University of New York Press.

2002 *Zapata Lives! Histories and Cultural Politics in Southern Mexico.* Berkeley: University of California Press.

STEVENSON, MARK

2005 Oaxaca's plaza trees inspire devotion, defense. *Los Angeles Times*, May 22.

STEWART, KATHLEEN

1996 *A Space on the Side of the Road: Cultural Poesis in an "Other" America.* Princeton: Princeton University Press.

TAYLOR, WILLIAM B.

1972 *Landlord and Peasant in Colonial Oaxaca.* Stanford: Stanford University Press.

TENORIO-TRILLO, MAURICIO

1995 *Mexico at the World's Fairs: Crafting a Modern Nation.* Berkeley: University of California Press.

THIEME, MARY S.

2007 Changes in the style, production, and distribution of pottery in Santa

María Atzompa, Oaxaca, Mexico, during the 1990s. *Museum Anthropology* 30(2): 125–140.

TORRES, REBECCA M., AND JANET D. MOMSEN

2004 Gringolandia: The construction of a new tourist space in Mexico. *Annals of the Association of American Geographers* 95(2): 314–335.

TURNER, JOHN KENNETH

1911 *Barbarous Mexico.* Chicago: C. H. Kerr and Company.

URRY, JOHN

1990 *The Tourist Gaze: Leisure and Travel in Contemporary Societies.* London: Sage.

1995 *Consuming Places.* New York: Routledge.

VACIO, MINERVA

1996 Brígido Lara: Inventor del nuevo arte prehispánico. *Arqueología Mexicana* (4)21: 56–61.

VAN DEN BERGHE, PIERRE L.

1994 *The Quest for the Other: Ethnic Tourism in San Cristóbal, Mexico.* Seattle: University of Washington Press.

VAN DER SPEK, KEES

2008 Faked antikas and "modern antiques": The production and marketing of tourist art in the Theban Necropolis. *Journal of Social Archaeology* 8(2): 163–189.

VASCONCELOS, JOSÉ

1997 *The Cosmic Race: A Bilingual Edition.* Trans. Didier T. Jaen. Baltimore: Johns Hopkins University Press.

VAUGHN, MARY KAY, AND STEPHEN E. LEWIS, EDS.

2006 *The Eagle and the Virgin: Nation and Cultural Revolution in Mexico, 1920–1940.* Durham: Duke University Press.

VÁZQUEZ LEÓN, LUIS

1996 *El leviatán arqueológico: Antropología de una tradición científica en México.* Leiden: Research School CNWS.

VELASCO RODRÍGUEZ, GRISELLE J., AND HORTENCIA AGUILAR SÁNCHEZ

2000 *Monografía del Municipio de Santa Cruz Xoxocotlán, Centro Oaxaca.* Oaxaca: Instituto Politécnico Nacional/CIIDIR.

VON DROSTE, BERND, HARALD PLACHTER, AND MECHTILD RÖSSLER, EDS.

1995 *Cultural Landscapes of Universal Value: Components of a Global Strategy.* New York: Gustav Fischer.

WADE, PETER

1997 *Race and Ethnicity in Latin America.* London: Pluto Press.

WARREN, KAY B.

1998 *Indigenous Movements and Their Critics: Pan-Maya Activism in Guatemala.* Princeton: Princeton University Press.

WASSERSPRING, LOIS

2000 *Oaxacan Ceramics: Traditional Folk Art by Oaxacan Women.* San Francisco: Chronicle Books.

WEILL, CYNTHIA

2007 *ABeCedarios: Mexican Folk ABCs in English and Spanish.* El Paso: Cinco Puntos Press.

WEISMANTEL, MARY

2001 *Cholas and Pishtacos: Stories of Race and Sex in the Andes.* Chicago: University of Chicago Press.

WHIPPERMAN, BRUCE

2000 *Oaxaca Handbook.* Emeryville, CA: Avalon Travel Publishing.

WHITECOTTON, JOSEPH

1977 *The Zapotecs: Princes, Priests, and Peasants.* Norman: University of Oklahoma Press.

1996 Ethnic groups and ethnicity in southern Mexico and northern New Mexico: A historical comparison of the valley of Oaxaca and the Española Valley. In *The Politics of Ethnicity in Southern Mexico*, ed. Howard Campbell, 1–32. Nashville: Vanderbilt University Publications in Anthropology.

WILLIAMS, RAYMOND

1973 *The Country and the City.* New York: Oxford University Press.

1977 *Marxism and Literature.* New York: Oxford University Press.

WINTER, MARCUS C.

1986 Another fake on genuine. *Codex Filatélica: Mesoamerican Archaeology Study Unit* 12(2): 9–11.

2002 [1989] *Oaxaca: The Archaeological Record.* Mexico City: Editorial Minutiae Mexicana.

WOLF, ERIC

1957 Closed corporate peasant communities in Mesoamerica and central Java. *Southwestern Journal of Anthropology* 13:1–18.

WOOD, W. WARNER

2000 Stories from the field: Handicraft production and Mexican national patrimony: A lesson from B. Traven. *Ethnology* 39(3): 183–203.

2008 *Made in Mexico: Zapotec Weavers and the Global Ethnic Art Market.* Bloomington: Indiana University Press.

ZÁRATE AQUINO, MANUEL

1995 *Pequeño diccionario enciclopédico de Oaxaca.* Oaxaca: Universidad José Vasconcelos de Oaxaca.

ZORN, ELAYNE

2004 *Weaving a Future: Tourism, Cloth, and Culture on an Andean Island.* Iowa City: University of Iowa Press.

Index

Italic page numbers refer to figures.

www.ingramcontent.com/pod-product-compliance
Lightning Source LLC
LaVergne TN
LVHW091132080826
845145LV00008B/2126
9780292754263